Postcolonialism, Feminism, and Religious Discourse

Postcolonialism, Feminism, and Religious Discourse

Edited by

Laura E. Donaldson and Kwok Pui-lan

ROUTLEDGE • New York • London

BL
458
.P67
2002

Published in 2002 by
Routledge
29 West 35th Street
New York, NY 10001

Published in Great Britain by
Routledge
11 New Fetter Lane
London EC4P 4EE

Routledge is an imprint of the Taylor & Francis Group.

Copyright © 2002 by Routledge

Printed in the United States of America on acid-free paper.

All rights reserved. No part of this book may be reprinted or reproduced or utilized in any form or by any electronic, mechanical or other means, now known or hereafter invented, including photocopying and recording or in any information storage or retrieval system, without permission in writing from the publishers.

"Multiple Critique: Islamic Feminist Rhetorical Strategies" by Miriam Cooke originally published in *Nepantla*, 1:1 (2000), pp. 91–110. Copyright 2000, Duke University Press. All rights reserved. Reprinted with permission.

A version of "Body, Representation, and Black Religious Discourse" by M. Shawn Copeland appears as "The Wounds of Jesus, the Wounds of My People" in *Telling the Truth: Preaching against Sexual and Domestic Violence*, ed. John S. McClure and Nancy J. Ramsey (Cleveland: United Church Press, 1998). Used by permission.

Portions of "Sartorial Fabric-ations: Enlightenment and Western Feminism" adapted from *Colonial Fantasies: Towards a Feminist Reading of Orientalism* by Meyda Yeğenoğlu (Cambridge: Cambridge University Press, 1998). Reprinted with the permission of Cambridge University Press.

"Captivity" in *Jacklight* by Louise Erdrich, © 1984 by Louise Erdrich. Reprinted by permission of Henry Holt and Company.

LIBRARY OF CONGRESS CATALOGING-IN-PUBLICATION DATA

Postcolonialism, feminism and religious discourse / edited by Laura E. Donaldson and Kwok Pui-lan.
    p. cm
Includes bibliographical references and index.
ISBN 0-415-92887-7 —ISBN 0-415-92888-5 (pbk.)
1. Women and religion. 2. Feminism—Religious aspects. 3. Postcolonialism.
I. Donaldson, Laura E. II. Kwok Pui-lan.
BL458 .P67 2001
200'.82—dc21   00-062815

JKM Library
1100 East 55th Street
Chicago, IL 60615

Contents

v

In loving memory of our fathers,

James Carmichael Donaldson

and

Kwok Kut

Acknowledgments

Any book represents the combined effort of many people: the authors, the editors, the production staff, and all those whose scholarly work have informed our perspectives. In this vein, we would like to thank the Women and Religion Section and the Feminist Theory and Religious Reflection Group of the American Academy of Religion for sponsoring the panel from which the idea for this anthology was engendered, as well as the many colleagues who have encouraged us along the way. Special appreciation goes to the Episcopal Divinity School for support from the Theological Writing Fund. Our research assistants, Anna Greenwood, Thomas Eoyang, and Wesley Kisting, provided critical help in preparing the manuscripts.

We are grateful to the editors and staff at Routledge, William P. Germano, Mathew Byrnie, Damian Treffs, and Henry Bashwiner, for their helpful comments and for shepherding the manuscripts at various stages of production. We thank Gretchen Grimshaw for her help in proofreading.

We would also like to thank our families for their patient cooperation in this effort. Laura thanks Mike, whose humor, capacity for loving and flyfishing acumen proved such an irrepressible combination. Pui-lan wants to thank her family for their steadfast support for her scholarly pursuit, giving her time and peace of mind to think and work.

Introduction

The interactions among colonialism, gender, and religion constitute some of the most significant and contradictory forces influencing our world today. Although some scholars have addressed "race, gender and sexuality in the colonial contest"[1] and others "the postcolonial Bible,"[2] few have seriously engaged *all* the members of this critical trilogy. These intellectual projects establish crucial connections between religion and colonialism, or gender and colonialism; however, each would greatly benefit from a more expansive critical perspective incorporating all the threads in this intricate web. The importance of the trio informing this anthology is amply demonstrated in the arena of global politics. For example, the rise of religious fundamentalisms in the United States and in formerly colonized countries has negatively impacted the ability of women to use family planning and control their own reproduction, exercise their right to travel, and receive an education. Ironically, women themselves are often key players in the fundamentalist game. According to postcolonial theorist Ania Loomba, in India "women like Sadhvi Rithambara and Uma Bharati have stridently mobilised for Hindu nationalism by invoking fears of Muslim violence. In other words, women are objects as well as subjects of fundamentalist discourses, targets as well as speakers of its most virulent rhetoric."[3] This example also highlights how, in the larger historical arena, women's intellectual, psychological, and political positions under the regimes of colonialism, gender, and religion have often been contradictory, since women exist both as colonized patriarchal objects and colonizing race-privileged subjects.[4]

The widespread use of sexual violence as a strategy of conquest and the role of religion in facilitating such violence provides another compelling argument for the importance of colonialism, gender, and religious discourse. Sexual violence as a strategy of North American conquest has been well-documented, and the legitimation of rape continues in contemporary video games of conquest such as *Custer's Revenge*. Here, players assume the persona of Lt. Col. George Armstrong Custer (killed with his men at the battle of Little Big Horn) and receive points each time they rape an Indian woman.[5] The widespread use of rape by Serbian (Christian) forces against Bosnian (Muslim) women also emerged from the historical crucible of colonialism, gender, and religious discourse. While the media representation of the conflict often reduced it to a simplistic form of "ethnic cleansing," the current conflicts in Bosnia in fact represent a much more complicated reality. The area now known as Bosnia-Herzegovina has suffered multiple conquests over the centuries, including those by the Roman Empire, Austria-Hungary, and, in the throes of World War II, the Axis powers, who invaded and dismantled it. However, one of the most important episodes of colonization involved the fifteenth-century conquest by the Ottoman Empire, since it was during this era that many Slavs converted to Islam. The conflicts in Bosnia consequently embody much more than race hatred; they also manifest overtones of the Crusades, in which triumphalist Christians declared war upon Muslims to ensure the dominance of their theological beliefs. As the editors of *Remembering Conquest: Feminist/Womanist Perspectives on Religion, Colonization, and Sexual Violence* note, "It is critical that we understand the roots of colonialism, the ways in which sexual violence was and is used to promote and sustain it, and the intersection with religious doctrine, teaching and practice."[6]

Since the introduction of gender as a category critical to the study of religion, the feminist study of religion in the United States—done mostly by Euro-American women—has been preoccupied with the relationship between cultural-religious traditions and the sex/gender system. Feminist scholars interested in postcolonial studies might address race, gender, and sexuality in the context of colonialism, but ignore the critical importance of religion to these dimensions. And, although a number of books have been published on postcolonial studies of the Bible and religion, they have not included gender as an integral part of their analysis.[7] Without critical attention to colonial representation and epistemic violence, feminist scholarship in religion has the danger of replicating the colonial gaze in the name of serving a feminist agenda. Likewise, any discussion of colonialism and religion must recognize that gender asymmetry was (and still is) a dominant metaphor for describing the colonizers and the colonized, domination and submission.

The contributors of this multicultural and multireligious anthology explore how postcolonialism and feminism might challenge and transform the fields of religion, ethics, and liberation theologies. They write from different academic backgrounds and cultural heritages: Native American (Cherokee), Chinese, Batswana, Turkish, Jewish, African-American, and Euro-American. In the religious academy, where there are few opportunities for scholars to work across religious traditions, the inclusion of such a diversity of scholars in one volume is a cause for celebration. The coeditors are deeply grateful for the commitment of the contributors, some of whom they did not know before this project, as well as for their solidarity and their early encouragement of this project. Readers will notice that the authors write in different styles and engage a wide range of materials: religious texts, women's literature, field interviews, historical archives, critical theories, and even rap music. Together, they form a mosaic with varying colors and different textures as well as geometrical shapes. Perhaps the strength of the anthology is the fluid manner in which the pieces move throughout a broad range of historical inquiries, anecdotes, and close readings of literature and theory.

We the coeditors of this volume—Laura Donaldson and Kwok Pui-lan—come from very different social locations and educational backgrounds. We have known one another for several years, collaborating together in professional gatherings and working on projects concerning the implications of postcolonialism for religious and gender studies. Laura is Cherokee and Scotch-Irish and was trained in the fields of American Indian and English literatures, religion, and women's studies. She comes not only from a long line of Cherokee Methodist women whose Christian faith testifies to their acculturation, but is also descended from the Chickamauga band of Cherokee—so named for their ancestral territory just north of present-day Atlanta, Georgia—who fiercely resisted both the white "civilizers" and their Holy Book. Such contradictory intersections of colonialism, gender, and religion run very deep in Laura's family as well as in Cherokee history. Indeed, Native women often became the special target of missionaries, especially in matrilineal cultures like the Cherokee where family and clan identities are passed from mothers to their children. Isaac Baird, who served at the Odanah, Wisconsin mission of the Presbyterian Church, articulates this strategy in an 1883 letter: "The girls will need the training more than the boys & they will wield a greater influence in the future. If we get the girls, we get the race."[8] Many Cherokee (and other Native) women did respond positively to the message of Christian workers, but this seldom promoted "getting the race." Some used the power of their new positions as Christians to redress the imbalances caused by white contact, while others adapted Christianity to their traditional roles as intermediaries.[9] At the very least, then, Native women's appropriation of the Christian faith must be seen as attempts to forge a new postcolonial identity out of the "cultural bricolage" available to them in a postcontact world.[10] However, this colonial context and its material legacies are very different than those experienced by Kwok Pui-lan.

Pui-lan prefers to put her family name, Kwok, in front of her given name to honor her Chinese heritage. She was educated in the areas of theology, Chinese studies, gender, culture, and society. Unlike the settler colonialism that Laura experienced, Pui-lan grew up in Hong Kong where the Chinese, who made up 97 percent of the population, were ruled by the small minority of British colonial officials and their collaborators for 155 years. In 1800 the British Empire consisted of 1.5 million square miles and 20 million people. By 1900 the Victorian Empire was made up of 11 million square miles and about 390 million people. In the 1920s the West controlled almost half of the world's territories and total population.[11] English was the only official language in Hong Kong until 1971, which meant that many people who arrived as refugees after World War II could not even read government notices or file official forms. The majority of high school students attended schools in which they had to communicate with their Chinese teachers in English. Pui-lan experienced firsthand the missionaries' and colonial officials' deployment of Christianity to justify their superiority and facilitate colonial rule. A pioneer in Asian feminist theology, she has critiqued Western imperialism, lifted up the subjugated voices of Asian women, and challenged the complicity of white women in colluding with the colonial stance. With Laura and other feminist scholars from the Third and Fourth Worlds, she has introduced postcolonial theories to the study of the Bible and religion.

Coediting this volume has allowed us to share our different experiences with colonialism and to learn from our colleagues how postcolonial theory may be applied to their experiences or fields of studies. Because we believe that it is important not to elide such differences, the rest of the introduction will retain our two distinct voices and present our related perspectives on the uneasy intersections of postcolonialism, feminism, and religious discourse. The separation of our voices illustrates that these topics can be broached from vastly different entry points. Our two readings will also benefit readers trained in different fields who are familiar with different texts and reading strategies. Laura will use several case studies to outline how ideologies of gender and religion were integral to the Anglo-European colonialist enterprise; Pui-lan will revisit some of the foundational moments pertaining to Asian religions in the discipline. Her aim is to illustrate how ideologies of gender and colonialism form the metanarrative driving the comparative, psychological, and (white) feminist study of religion. Readers are encouraged to examine the intersection of postcolonialism, feminism, and religious discourse from their own disciplines and to develop different sets of reading registers. The introduction will conclude with Laura's discussion of the sections and chapters of the anthology.

"God, Gold, and Gender"

Laura E. Donaldson

The establishment of the so-called new world order calls for a new kind of analysis as well as a new world slogan: rather than "God, gold, and glory," which asserts the motivations usually ascribed to the Anglo-European colonial system, the motto of this transformed thinking should instead foreground the alliance of "God, gold, and gender."[12] Although the processes underlying "God, gold, and gender" have assumed a heightened significance in the arena of contemporary politics, they also possess a long, often unrecognized, symbolic and hegemonic history. Any introduction to the questions posed by postcolonialism, feminism, and religious discourse must therefore acknowledge this history and detail its most consequential moments. Given the particular contexts of my own colonial history, I would include such moments as Martin Waldseemüller's (re)naming of "America," Mary Rowlandson's captivity narrative, and Charlotte Brontë's novel *Jane Eyre*. Excavating the cultural archaeologies of these texts reveals a continuity of preoccupations with the present as well as insights about how colonialism, gender, and religion shaped, and continue to shape, individuals and societies.

I have chosen these sites for several reasons. First, each foregrounds issues largely ignored in current configurations of postcolonial studies: the centrality of religion, the importance of the Fourth World (that of indigenous peoples), and the persistence of "the woman question." Second, each highlights the crucial role of Christianity in promoting the Anglo-European imperialist project. Although this anthology does focus on other religious traditions—Islam, Judaism, and Hinduism—one cannot overestimate the historical influence of the Christian tradition in disseminating imperialist ideologies. While many countries occupied and dominated foreign territories, only the group of nations claiming Christian identity implemented a global colonial system upon which the sun never set. As Michael Prior notes in *The Bible and Colonialism*, the social transformation resulting from the decision to encroach on a foreign terrain reflects the determination of the colonizers to alter radically a region's politics in favor of the colonists—and the introduction of Christianity functioned as a powerful tool of such transformation. An all-too-common paradigm for this process excluded the land's indigenous inhabitants from these new arrangements: "Several motivations combined to exclude the indigenes, and for those influenced by religious considerations, the biblical paradigm provided a ready justification for it. The exclusivist tendencies in North America and South Africa have been ascribed to the influence of the Old Testament in the Puritan faith in the case of the former, and in the Dutch Reformed Church in the latter."[13] Although some might criticize our emphasis on Christian narratives of colonialism, I believe that this stress constitutes an essential component of decolonizing the myths and ideologies still undergirding the entire colonialist enterprise. Until all peoples grasp the intricate relationships binding colonialism, gender, and religion together, the dream of a genuinely new world order will remain only the shadow of an ideal.

From Amerigo to "America"

Early in the sixteenth century, a group of humanists assembled in the tiny French village of Saint Dié to form the "Gymnasium Vosgianum"—a kind of intellectual advocacy group whose goal was to disseminate certain important books. Among their numbers was a young clergyman named Martin Waldseemüller, whose interest in cartography subsequently altered the course of history. Stefan Zweig notes that no one would have heard the conversations of either Waldseemüller or this "miniature academy" if a printer named Walter Ludd had not decided to set up a press in Saint Dié.[14] For his first publishing venture, Ludd—a chaplain and secretary to the duke of Lorraine—responded to the public's interest in travel narratives by combining Ptolemy's *Cosmographia* with Amerigo Vespucci's memoir of his exploratory sea voyages. Ptolemy's *Cosmographia* had been regarded as Europe's ultimate geographical authority for more than a millennium, but the latter part of the fifteenth century had challenged its authority through the "discovery" of hitherto unknown lands. Consequently, any reprinting of the *Cosmographia* had to incorporate these new lands into the old maps in order to revise and complete them.[15] It was Martin Waldseemüller who not only drew these newly revised cartographic charts but also, in the view of many, authored the entire text. His fateful decision to name the *quarta orbis pars*, or "fourth part of the world," after Amerigo Vespucci occurs in chapter 9 of the *Cosmographia Introductio*, which appeared in print on April 25, 1507. According to Waldseemüller:

> Now, these parts of the earth have been more extensively explored and a fourth part has been discovered by Amerigo Vespucci (as will be set forth in what follows). Inasmuch as both Europe and Asia received their names from women, I see no reason why any one should justly object to calling this Amerige, i.e., the land of Amerigo, or America, after Amerigo, its discoverer, a man of great ability.[16]

In Latin, "o" represents the masculine ending for words, so by changing "Amerigo" to the feminized "Ameriga," or "America," Waldseemüller metaphorically transforms "him" into a "her." Mary Louise Pratt observes that the process of cartographic naming joined together [Eurocentric] religious and geographical projects in the quest for European expansion. Its agents claimed the world by christening landmarks and topographic formations with Euro-Christian names.[17] Other scholars have noted the performative character of mapping as well as its exemplary role in demonstrating the discursive practices of colonialism. Graham Huggan, for example, argues that mapping's reinscription and enclosure of space parallel historical colonialism's acquisition, management, and reinforcement of military and political power.[18] Waldseemüller's (re)naming of Turtle Island joins the discourses of religion and geography in a similar ideological enterprise; it also, however, precipitates a gendered crisis in colonial representation.[19]

The havoc that "America" wreaks among the globe's feminine names (which I will address shortly) actually displaces another, perhaps more urgent, conflict: "her" disruption of the patriarchal assignment of the world to the sons of Noah. According to biblical tradition, the descendants of Japheth (Noah's oldest son) populated what is now called Europe; the descendants of Shem, Asia; and the descendants of Ham, Africa. This particular (re)naming seems tragically prophetic, since "Japheth" most likely derives from the Hebrew cognate, *phatah*: "to spread" or "enlarge." Since the Japhetic origin of Europe was virtually uncontested until the nineteenth century,[20] these connotations of latitude, width, and expansion ominously prefigure the regimes of Anglo-European imperialism. Yet, the insertion of a feminized "America" into this previously masculine field engenders a profound anxiety, which Jan van der Straet's 1575 painting of "her" originary encounter with Vespucci symptomatically manifests. Since I discuss both this anxiety and the painting more fully in my essay "The Breasts of Columbus," I will say here only that the discovery and subsequent conquest of "America"—whether material or symbolic—destabilizes the myth of European self-sufficiency and confronts "him" with the prospect of engulfment by "her."

Of course, Waldseemüller presents "America" as an affirmation of women, or at least of women's names. Subsequent mapmakers suppressed the potential of this new member to introduce discord by confining her to an iconographic continuum operating between what one can only describe as the naked and the dressed. In Mercator's 1636 *Atlas*, for instance, Europe appears as an elaborately clothed woman who also wears a crown and holds a book in her hands. Also clothed (but without a crown), Asia extends her bejeweled arms toward Europe. Africa forms a dramatic contrast, since she is both dark-skinned and unclothed. Unlike the formal sovereignty displayed by Europe, Mercator portrayed "America" as an Indian Queen who wore a crown of upright feathers, but who was also naked and supplicating.[21] In *Inventing A-M-E-R-I-C-A*, José Rabasa succinctly demystifies the colonialist imaginary structuring this sartorial difference: "Dressed and learned in the sciences, Europe rules and supersedes Asia, the origin of science, art, and religion. In contrast, Africa and America in their nudity testify to the dominance of the feminine and typify the barbarous states that are, nonetheless, full of treasures for Europe. . . .The work process of a colonialist machinery disappears under the facade of the world offering its riches to Europe."[22] If mapping uniquely connects historical imperialism's textual and material vectors,[23] then Mercator's feminine spectacle figures the textual and material vectors of colonialism's women. The relations among them affirm not only that religion and gender exerted important influences in colonialism's founding moments, but also that any postcolonial analysis must similarly attend to their effects.

Mercator's *Atlas* possesses an "American" analogue in the captivity tale of Mary Rowlandson, and a brief revisiting of its story will illuminate much more intensively the volatile conjunctures of postcolonialism, feminism, and religious discourse.

On Bibles in Babylon

The Twelfth Remove. It was upon a Sabbath-day morning that they prepared for their Travel. This morning, I asked my Master, whether he would sell me to my Husband? He answered, Nux, which did much rejoyce my spirit. My Mistress, before we went, was gone to the burial of a Papoos; and returning, she found me sitting and reading in my Bible; she snatched it hastily out of my hand, and threw it out of doors; I ran out and catcht it up, and put it into my pocket, and never let her see it afterward.

Mary Rowlandson, on her captivity among the Narragansett

On February 10, 1676, Mary Rowlandson and her three children were taken captive by Narragansett Indians engaged in what Euro-American historians call "King Philip's War." Rowlandson was subsequently given to the household of Weetamoo, a *sunksquaw* of the Pocasset and a crucial member of Metacomet's (King Philip) Wampanoag Confederacy. On the morning of the incident just described, Weetamoo had just returned from the burial of a young Narragansett child. When she came across Rowlandson reading her Bible, she grabbed the book and angrily hurled it outside her wigwam. For Rowlandson, this episode constituted just another link in the chain of her unrelieved oppression as a captive among these "Barbarous Creatures"; for Weetamoo, however, it signified something very different, since her people were fleeing the wrath of the Massachusetts militia, and conditions were extremely harsh. As Rowlandson herself noted: "There were hundreds, old and young, some sick and some lame; many had papooses at their backs, the greatest number at this time with us were Squaws; and they travelled with all they had, bag and baggage."[24] Food was scarce, and the people faced starvation. Rowlandson described how a member of Weetamoo's household journeyed through dangerous territory for more than three weeks just to retrieve some corn that was hidden in storage. Not surprisingly, this hardship and lack of food exacted a severe toll on the Narragansett—a toll that included the death of Weetamoo's own baby. Given the association of this tragedy with the book of God so ardently proclaimed by the invaders, Weetamoo's anger at its presence in her home is understandable. After all, it was the alleged working of divine providence that led the Puritans to claim Turtle Island and to demonize the sacred beings of the Algonquin: Kautantowitt (the Creator of the human world), Maushop (who created Narragansett Bay), and Maushop's wife, Squant (the protector of women). Despite their profound dissimilarities, however, these two women were also remarkably alike: both fought to survive in the most desperate conditions, both grieved the loss of their children, and both showed amazing resourcefulness under extreme duress. It is precisely this uneasy balance between difference and sameness that renders "A True History of the Captivity and Restoration of Mrs. Mary Rowlandson" such a rich nexus of colonialism, gender, and religious discourse.

"A True History" was the first printed account of a New Englander captured by Native North Americans; it was also, according to feminist scholar Annette Kolodny, the first published account of a white woman's journey through what she perceived as a vast and desolate wilderness.[25] I would add that Rowlandson's narrative also exists as one of the earliest documents to chronicle the relationships between colonizing and colonized women as well as Christian and Native ways of knowing. Although many historical and literary scholars have focused on the complex layers of religious symbolism embedded within Rowlandson's narrative,[26] few have recognized the importance of gender and colonialism to its construction. And, although feminist scholars have touted the "True History" as emblematic of women's estate in early New England, they have consistently neglected the Native women populating its pages and the regions its heroine travels. Like Waldseemüller's (re)naming of America, Mary Rowlandson's captivity reveals why the discourses of gender *and* religion are so integral to any analysis of colonial history.

While Rowlandson certainly occupied the position of colonizer (and invader) in relation to the Narragansett people who kidnapped her, a much more fractured colonial subjectivity actually emerged from her travails. Her abundant appeals to the Jewish exile in Babylon as a biblical paradigm for her situation reinforced her separation from the "Barbarous Creatures" who snatched Rowlandson from her life as a settler; her experience of suffering, however, also created a cognitive dissonance that allowed her partially to recognize the mutual humanity of her Native captors.[27] For example, when Weetamoo's baby died after two weeks on the forced march, Rowlandson's response was notable for its dehumanization of, and calloused response to, this tragedy: "That night they bade me go out of the Wigwam again; my Mistress's *Papoos* was sick, and it died that night; and there was one benefit in it, that there was more room" (30). On the other hand, the solicitude of Metacomet's followers for Rowlandson when she wept tears of grief elicited a much different response:

> But now I may say, as *Psal. CXXXVII.* I, *By the rivers* of Babylon, *there we sate down, yea we wept when we remembered Zion.* There one of them asked me, why I wept? I could hardly tell what to say; yet I answered, they would kill me: No, said he, none will hurt you. Then came one of them and gave me two spoonfuls of Meal to comfort me, and another gave me half a pint of Pease, which was more worth than many Bushels at another time. (22)

The specter of a Babylonian (American Indian) comforting, and even sacrificing for, the Jew (Christian) confronts Rowlandson with irrevocable evidence that the (Native) Other inhabiting her colonialist framework acted in many ways like the (Euro-American) Self. After an Indian woman not only gave her a piece of fresh pork and salt, but also the frying pan to cook it in, Rowlandson expressed a "delightful relish" for this kindness and even mused that humans often take such common mercies for granted.

Interestingly, or perhaps symptomatically, Rowlandson's epiphanies about the human nature of Indians did not extend to her mistress, Weetamoo, whom she consistently portrayed in a negative light: "A severe and proud

Dame she was; bestowing every day in dressing herself near as much time as any of the Gentry of the land; powdering her hair and painting her face, going with her Neck-laces, with Jewels in her ears, and bracelets upon her hands: When she had dressed herself, her Work was to make Girdles of Wampom and Beads" (34). In this passage, Rowlandson interprets Weetamoo's care with her appearance as an expression both of vanity and of class arrogance. If one did not know better, the reader of Rowlandson might think that a sartorially splendid Weetamoo ventured out every night to aristocratic balls and otherwise lived a life of self-indulgent ease. However, a hallmark of colonialist ideology is its erasure of indigenous history and, in this case, "A True History" is actually false inasmuch as it distorts the meaning of Weetamoo's behavior.

In precontact Algonquin societies, women often became *sunksquaws*, which Roger Williams mistranslated as "queens," but which more accurately connotes female leaders who held authoritative positions on the basis of respect rather than coercion. These women conducted diplomatic relations, negotiated treaties, actively participated in all major tribal decisions, and even led men into battle.[28] While such offices were usually hereditary (and often passed from mother to daughter), the Pocasset Nation passed the office to the child or younger relative who seemed best fitted for it.[29] That the Pocasset chose Weetamoo, the daughter of their leader, Corbitant, demonstrates their confidence in her guidance and ability to make decisions in the best interests of the people. Rowlandson's description of Weetamoo as severe and proud most likely reflects her discomfort with the kind of power *sunksquaws* possessed as part of their office. The sexually differentiated nature of this discomfort seems clear, since Rowlandson developed a significant respect for male leaders such as Metacomet and Quinnapin (Weetamoo's Narragansett husband). In fact, Rowlandson's comment that her mistress's work "was to make Girdles of Wampom and Beads" unwittingly betrays Weetamoo's stature since *mampampeag*—the Pequot word badly transliterated as "wampum"—possessed economic, political, and spiritual significance for many Northeastern Native peoples.

Mampampeag consisted of purple and white beads made from clam shells, which were then threaded into strings and belts. While it originally encoded sacred texts and later certified the validity of treaties, "wampum" also became the transnational exchange currency of seventeenth-century New England.[30] William Apess (Pequot) illustrates the importance of *mampampeag* in a story about how Metacomet fed his people with the coat off his back. During the throes of "King Philip's War," some of Metacomet's men experienced severe shortages of food and lacked materials to make the necessary weapons for battle. Apess recounts that, upon hearing this, the leader ordered that his *sachem*'s coat, "neatly wrought with mampampeag (i.e., Indian money) . . . be cut into pieces and distributed . . . among all his chiefs and warriors."[31] Meta-comet's act consequently involved literally carving his *mampampeag*—those markers of wealth and tribal authority—into individual portions that could be exchanged as "wampum." This so cheered the hearts of the Wampanoag that they were motivated "still to persevere to maintain their rights and expel their enemies."[32]

Historian John Strong relates the story of how an unnamed seventeenth-century *sunksquaw* from Long Island distributed thirty fathom of "wampum" equally among the English and the powerful leaders of the Narragansett Nation. She clearly intended the "wampum" to function as a diplomatic gesture sealing this newly formed alliance among her own people, the English and the Narragansett. That the gesture was ultimately unsuccessful does not detract from its importance as a political currency or from the power of the women who wielded it on behalf of their people.[33] Given such interpretive and material contexts, Weetamoo's girdles of *mampampeag* take on a radically different meaning than the negative one offered by Rowlandson.

If the term *postcolonial* connotes the process of disengagement from the whole colonial syndrome,[34] then writer Louise Erdrich (Chippewa/German-American) offers a postcolonial interpretation of the "True History" in her poem "Captivity." In this poem, Erdrich creatively visualizes a woman returned to the bosom of the Euro-American, patriarchal family and plagued with doubts about her place in the colonizers' society:

> *Rescued, I see no truth in things.*
> *My husband drives a thick wedge*
> *through the earth, still it shuts*
> *to him year after year.*
> *My child is fed of the first wheat.*
> *I lay myself to sleep*
> *on a Holland-laced pillowbeer.*
> *I lay to sleep.*
> *And in the dark I see myself*
> *as I was outside their circle.*[35]

While such subversive speculations are provocative, the "True History" of Mary Rowlandson nonetheless exists as a cautionary tale about the spiritual and epistemological barriers erected by colonialism, patriarchalism, and religion, and their capacity to obscure the development of understanding among different communities of women. One discovers a somewhat different cautionary tale in the final site that I will discuss—Charlotte Brontë's nineteenth-century novel *Jane Eyre*.

Plain Jane's Religion

One contemporary attempt to engage the intertwining of colonialism, gender, and religious discourse originates in the work of Gayatri Chakravorty Spivak, one of the most provocative and celebrated voices in the field known as "postcolonial studies." In 1985, Spivak published an essay titled "Three Women's Texts and a Critique of Imperialism," which examines "the unexamined and covert axiomatics of imperialism" manifested by one of feminism's most influential texts: Charlotte Brontë's novel *Jane Eyre*.[36] "Three Women's Texts" exposed the vexed history of the "feminist-as-imperialist" in the trajectories of Western critical theory and literature,[37] and subsequently initiated numerous conversations about the relations between colonialism and feminism. In the essay Spivak briefly turns her keen eye on the character of St. John (Eyre) Rivers, Jane's newly discovered cousin, who saves her from certain death after she flees the matrimonial deceptions of Mr. Rochester. St. John Rivers, described by Jane as "inexorable as death," yearns for the "wild field of mission warfare"[38] and desires nothing more than to leave Europe for the East—and the sooner the better. His most fervent hope is to be "numbered in the band who have merged all ambition in the glorious one of bettering their race—of carrying knowledge into the realms of ignorance—of substituting peace for war—freedom for bondage—religion for superstition—the hope of heaven for the fear of hell" (329). According to Spivak, the parenthetic narrative of St. John, to whom Brontë grants the important task of concluding the novel, embodies the imperialist project of transforming the heathen into a human so that he can then be treated as an end in himself (267). She also argues that such desire, which is left unquestioned by both Jane Eyre and Charlotte Brontë, plays a crucial part in the failure of many First World scholars to recognize how imperialism's territorial projects undergird feminism's commitment to the individualist emancipation of the female subject.

Of course, another consideration of the novel's problematic might yield somewhat more complicated negotiations among the discourses of postcolonialism, feminism, and religion. Just as Waldseemüller's (re)naming of "America" precipitates a gendered crisis in colonial representation, the issue of religion in *Jane Eyre* precipitates what one can only describe as a crisis of feminist Orientalism. In other words, Orientalism—broadly construed as the strategies through which the West produced and codified knowledge about nonmetropolitan areas[39]—and feminism, or advocacy on behalf of women, bring each other to crisis. St. John's proposal to Jane functions as the catalyst for this state of emergency. When he finally receives his charge as a missionary to India, St. John asks Jane to marry him so that she can become a "conductress of Indian schools and a helper amongst Indian women" (355). Jane refuses because her often-stated horror of being "grilled alive in Calcutta" only equals her horror at the patriarchal submission that St. John evokes in her:[40] "I was tempted to cease struggling with him—to rush down the torrent of his will into the gulf of his existence, and there lose my own" (368). This exists as perhaps the novel's clearest expression of Jane's feminist individualism. The litany of terrors that she associates with India (and with St. John) exhibits an intricate Orientalist design, however: the fear of Calcutta as a certain instrument of death not only produces "India" as the distorted object of Western knowledge but also indirectly conjures the specter of *sati*, or the burning of wives on the funeral pyres of their dead husbands. Historically, the British used the practice of *sati* as a legitimating condition for Indian occupation; in Brontë's text, Jane's implied fear of it displaces sexual onto colonial anxiety under the (dis)guise of religious discourse. It would be difficult to find a more telling example of the complications engendered by the relationships among colonialism, gender, and religion.

My intention in revisiting Waldseemüller, Rowlandson, and Brontë is to suggest that issues of gender and religion are integral to colonialism's foundational moments and that the imbrication of these discourses possesses a significance crossing geographical, cultural, and national boundaries. In her section, my coeditor will highlight the interaction of postcolonialism, feminism, and religious discourse in three texts that originate more specifically from the discipline of religion.

Gender, Colonialism, and the Study of Religion

Kwok Pui-lan

The academic study of religion, which emerged in the European universities in the mid-nineteenth century, was thoroughly embedded in the colonial ethos and political configurations of its time. Fredrich Max Müller (1823–1900), who coined the term *Religionswissenschaft* in 1867, has often been designated as the founder of the comparative study of religion. Claiming to be objective, *Religionswissenschaft* was a supposedly impartial and scientific comparison of the religions of humankind. But in practice, the study of religion in the nineteenth century relied on colonial power for support and provided justification for the "civilizing" mission of the West. The study of myths and rituals of the so-called "primitives" and "savages" reinforced the cultural hegemony of Europe and undergirded the evolutionary view of the development of humankind. The study of Buddhist and Hindu classical texts created the myth that the East was static, unchanging, and that its glory was long gone, surpassed by the vitality and progress of the Christian West. Furthermore, the acquisition of ancient manuscripts by missionaries and colonial officials in Asia greatly assisted the study of these ancient texts. Early ethnographic studies and field research in religion would not be possible without the disparate power differentials between the white men and their native informants.

The foundational moments in the study of religion have often been discussed in the context of intellectual ferment in Europe and the institutionalization of comparative religion in European and American universities.[41] Such a liberal and Eurocentric account has been challenged by critics who raise fundamental questions regarding the constitution of religion as a field of study, the frameworks of its analysis, and the complicity of religious scholars with the cultural and political hegemony of Europe. They have described the numerous ways that the study of religion has participated in and contributed to the epistemic violence maintained by Western studies and narrations of the Other. Some of these critics examine the multifaceted relations between the study of religion and colonialism by deploying the Foucauldian analysis of power/ knowledge and responding to Edward Said's pioneering work on Orientalism.[42] These criticisms, though laudable, fail to consider gender and to elucidate how gender was used to construct colonial asymmetries, create images of domination and submission, and reify differences among human races.

For some time, feminist scholars in religion have pointed to the obliteration of women's religious experiences as a result of androcentric biases in male scholarship. They have exposed deep-seated patriarchal religious norms and practices, presented new knowledge about women's religious roles and leadership, and reclaimed women's subjectivity and consciousness. In the debate of whether feminism is scholarship or advocacy (which I shall discuss later), some feminists subscribe to the liberal ideals that scholarship must be value neutral and assume that an "objective" and "descriptive" account of religion is possible.[43] The discussion of the collusion of the study of religion with colonialism and empire building is therefore foreclosed. Without this critical and methodological self-reflexivity, feminist scholarship, even with good intentions, might nevertheless reinscribe colonialist paradigms.

In unraveling the dense web of significations created by the intersection of gender, colonialism, and religious discourse, I would follow Laura Donaldson's example by selecting three critical moments in the study of religion. These include Max Müller's founding or "fathering" the science of religion, Carl Jung's romance with the East, and Rita Gross's introduction to feminism and religion. Each of these authors has shown considerable fascination with Asian cultures and explicitly discussed the relation between the East and the West.[44] In excavating these sites, I want to trace how gender was deployed to signify racial and psychological differences, to gauge the development of cultures and religion, and to inscribe Western hegemony in the "scientific" study of religion.

Müller and the Quest for Mother India

Since the beginning of the twentieth century, Max Müller has been widely regarded as the founding figure of the science of comparative religion. Louis Henry Jordan's first comprehensive study of the discipline, *Comparative Religion: Its Genesis and Growth* (1905), included Müller as one of the "Prophets and Pioneers." Joachim Wach, Mircea Eliade, Eric Sharpe, and more recently, Rita Gross have all bestowed upon Müller that honor.[45] His *Comparative Mythology*, published in 1856, was hailed as a foundational text for the discipline. The designation of Max Müller as the prophet-pioneer places the nascent discipline of comparative religion in the dense and thick discussions of comparative philology, the origin of human history, the creation of the Aryan myth, and the racialized anthropology of nineteenth-century Europe.

Born in 1823 at Dessau in Germany, Müller was trained in classical languages at Leipzig University before he decided to concentrate on the study of Sanskrit. As a professor of comparative philology at Oxford, he edited and published the first Sanskrit edition of the *Rig Veda* in Europe, with support from the French government, the Prussian government, and finally, from the East India Company.[46] His voluminous output included books on language, myth, and religion, the translation of Kant's *Critique of Pure Reason*, and the fifty-volume *Sacred Books of the East* (1879–1910), which he edited and partially translated. Although his philological studies were highly technical and remained foreign to his English audience, Müller managed to publish periodically *Chips from a German Workshop*, dispensing wisdom gathered from his philological library for the general public. Even though he lived in Britain for more than half a century, he wrote to his friends that he missed spending "the evening of life in German air" and remained German at heart.[47]

Before examining Müller's *Comparative Mythology* in more detail, it is important to grasp the significance of philology in the search for "German" cultural identity and self-representation. Unlike the words *English* and

French, which can be traced to a country or a people, the words *deutsch* and *Deutsche* have their origins in a common language that existed before the German nation was consolidated in the latter part of the nineteenth century. The lack of clear national boundaries and a unified people living in a particular geographical locale created anxieties and necessitated the search for a German antiquity and origin. The word *comparative* must be understood in this cultural matrix, as Spivak notes in her book *A Critique of Postcolonial Reason*:

> Cultural and intellectual "Germany," the place of self-styled difference from the rest of what is still understood as "continental" Europe and Britain, was the main source of the meticulous scholarship that established the vocabulary of proto-archetypical ("comparative" in the disciplinary sense) identity, kinship, without direct involvement in the utilization of that other difference, between the colonizer and the colonized; in the nascent discourses of comparative philology, comparative religion, even comparative literature.[48]

Even before Müller's time, the search for the origins of history and culture preoccupied some of the greatest minds in Europe. Müller—émigré, philologist, and Orientalist—added a new foundation by providing a "scientific" basis for the study of comparative religion through his skills in philology, since he was widely regarded as the leading European Sanskrit scholar.

In the eighteenth century, some European thinkers sought to free themselves from the confines of Christian thought and looked outside of Europe for inspiration. Following the biblical account, conventional wisdom dictated that human beings had their common origin in Adam and they were dispersed after the flood in Noah's time. Hebrew was considered the most ancient language, the tongue that Adam spoke. But the Enlightenment challenged the biblical story and the common Jewish genealogy, calling for the need to create a new narrative. French and German thinkers at the time toyed with the idea that the first human beings came from the mountains of Asia and that Sanskrit might be the most ancient language. In Germany Johann-Gottfried Herder was responsible for introducing the passion for India into Germanic lands and stimulating the Romantics to seek affiliation with Mother India.[49] Jacob Grimm, whose works Müller cited and who collaborated with his father, believed that all peoples in Europe emigrated from Asia in the remote past.[50]

This quest for India as the birthplace of all human cultures and religions—indeed, the "womb of the world"[51]—formed an important backdrop for Müller's *Comparative Religion*. It justified the importance of his studies of the Veda, and allowed him to plot a genealogy of human languages and trace the origin of Indo-Europeans distinct from the Semites. Müller devoted a substantial part of *Comparative Mythology* to a discussion of the affinities among the words of the Sanskrit, Greek, Latin, Gothic, Slavic, and Irish languages. His aim was to show that though we know nothing about the Aryan race before it was dispersed into different nations, traces of that ancient history can still be found in these languages. Müller was eager to find the "proto-archetypical" identity of humanity and the early period in the history of the human mind, which he called the *mythpoetic* stage.[52] The latter part of the book is devoted to the discussion of his famous solar myth theory, in which he argues that mythology is an ancient form of language, arising out of early human beings' experience of nature, especially the majesty and power of the sun. His "comparative" study of different mythologies around the sun and the dawn again shows the primacy of the study of Sanskrit and the Veda for understanding the earlier stratum of these myths. Believed to be the oldest existing book, the Veda supposedly contains the depository of the primitive ideas and language. Müller has said: "This shows the value of the *Veda* for the purpose of comparative mythology, a science which, without the *Veda*, would have remained mere guesswork, without fixed principles and without a safe basis" (120).

Like many intellectuals in this period, Müller believed that the origin of the Aryan race was in Asia. From the linguistic evidence he had gathered, he postulated that there was a period in human history before the beginning of the most ancient known dialects of the Aryan world and prior to the origin of Sanskrit and Greek. This era was also previous to the time when the Greeks arrived on Asia Minor and called the vast land and sea to the west and north *Europa* (60). For him, the homeland of the "Aryans," a term that derives from Sanskrit, was to be found in the middle of Asia, and the Aryan race once spoke a common real language: "During this early period, the ancestors of the Aryan race must have occupied a more central position in Asia, whence the southern branches extended toward India, the northern to Asia Minor and Europe" (60–61). The obsession of Müller and his contemporaries with India was influenced by the Romantics who dreamed of breaking from the yoke of European law and culture and reconnecting with an earlier time when human beings lived freely, following the laws of "Mother Nature." They projected such a dreamland onto the snow-covered and mysterious mountains of the Himalayas. While they rejected the Christian-spiritual and "masculine" genealogy of religion, the material and maternal India had great appeal. The maternal images projected onto India facilitated the dream of a golden age when the entire human race was unified and integrated with a peaceful and innocent universe.[53]

Müller's hypothesis that Europeans and (Asian) Indians belonged to one Aryan race did not sit well with his English audience, who found it hard to believe that they had sprung from the same stock as the Indians they had colonized. Nevertheless, in India, the myth of the common origin of the Aryan race was deployed by missionaries and colonial officials to justify the "Aryan reunion" of Britain and India. The Western Aryans, with their social and technological innovations, were seen as superior and destined to rule over the Eastern Aryans, whose culture was decadent and had made no progress. Acceptance of Christianity was seen as the evolutionary imperative for Indians in order to save their nation from moral and spiritual decline.[54]

Though Müller spent most of his life studying the ancient language and classics of India, he never landed on the soil of India, choosing to gaze at it from the confines of his German workshop. He was fascinated by India's golden past, which he reconstructed from the *Sacred Books of the East*, but was not concerned with India in the present, and its population of living Indians. His voluminous output helped to construct a "textual India" to be studied, dissected, and compared by scholars in their European libraries. While most Indians encountered the Veda through the oral medium, Müller's publication of the Veda created a reified product, decontextualized from its audience, and popularized the idea that the study of Hinduism meant the study of a body of texts. Richard King notes: "Müller in fact was instrumental in fetishizing the Vedas, representing them as the authentic embodiment of Hindu religiosity that had been 'misunderstood and perverted' by the 'theological twaddle' of the later Brahmanas."[55] In *Comparative Mythology*, Müller clearly assumed that he possessed a knowledge of the Veda which was superior to that of Indian religious gurus and pundits. For example, he showed that the Indians misunderstood the ancient practice of *sati* in their sacred texts. He noted that when the English government prohibited this custom, the Brahmans appealed to the Veda as the ultimate authority on the ancient rite. But according to Müller, these Brahmans hardly knew their own texts since they "mangled, mistranslated, and misapplied" the passage concerned (46). While the politics of *sati* will be discussed in my own chapter in this anthology, suffice it to say that Müller believed he could understand and represent the Indian past better than the Indians. The Indians could not be trusted to represent themselves; they had to be represented.

Jung and Western Man's Search for Anima

In many ways Carl Jung (1875–1961) is different from Müller. Müller was trained in philology, and Jung in medicine. Müller spent most of his life at

Oxford discovering the Indian past, while Jung could not read any Asian languages and lived his later life on the banks of Lake Zürich, speculating about the structure of the unconscious. Müller did not bother to visit India, but Jung went in 1938 for the twenty-fifth anniversary of the founding of the University of Calcutta, at the invitation of the British government. However, if we look deeper into their lives, we will discern similarities in their backgrounds and their personal and scholarly quests. Both came from families with strong literary backgrounds, well versed in German culture and thought. Müller's father, Wilhelm, was a poet and librarian who died when Müller was very young. His passion for German Romanticism was shared, however, by his offspring. Jung identified deeply with the Germanic ancestors on his father's side, and his paternal grandfather was a famous physician, playwright, and scientist, alleged to be the illegitimate son of Goethe.[56] Both Müller and Jung were interested in regressing to a prehistoric, prediscursive "dreamtime," when human beings were one family. For Müller, the archeology of human languages would retrace the process of cultural evolution, yielding clues about the common origin of the Aryans. For Jung, the archeology of human consciousness through dreams, free association, mythology, and drawings would provide access to the deeper layers of the psyche, reaching back to the collective unconscious. If Müller was interested in the proto-archetype of human genealogy and racial theory, Jung was preoccupied with the universal archetypes in his depth psychology. Müller needed Mother India for his hypothesis of the origin of Aryan race, and Jung needed the East (India and China) for Western man's soul searching and for his claim that the archetypes were indeed "universal."

Although many of Jung's followers tend to deemphasize Jung's rendezvous with the East, his interest in Taoism, yoga, Buddhism, and Eastern meditation was long-lived. J. J. Clark has noted: "Right from the early days when he was distancing from Freud and fashioning his own distinctive approach to psychology, up to the 1930s when his ideas were reaching their full expression and maturity, Eastern ideas and concepts wove their ways in and out of his writings, and were used in various ways to clarify and substantiate his own controversial views."[57] His interest in Eastern philosophy and religion was stimulated by his explorations of the occult and mythology, his dissatisfaction with Christianity, and his search for symbols of transformation. Toward the end of his life, he studied Buddhism and saw Buddhism's concern for human suffering as resonating with his own passion for psychic healing. He befriended scholars studying Eastern philosophies, most notably Richard Wilhelm, and invited some of them to lecture at the Zürich Psychological Club.

Jung's commentary on *The Secret of the Golden Flower* (1929) was his first major work on Eastern thought. He was delighted to find that Wilhelm's translated text opened up to him a new world which, in the wake of his split with Freud and his retreat from the psychoanalytical movement, confirmed his insights about the human psyche.[58] He discussed in the commentary his major ideas such as the inner world of the psyche, the process of integration of the consciousness and the unconsciousness, anima and animus, and images of mandalas. He spoke highly of the importance of Wilhelm's work on *The Secret of the Golden Flower* and the *I Ching*:

> Wilhelm's life-work is of such importance to me because it clarified and confirmed so much that I had been seeking, striving for, thinking and doing in my efforts to alleviate the psychic suffering of Europeans. It was a tremendous experience for me to hear through him, in clear language, things that I had dimly divined in the confusion of our European consciousness.[59]

Why were these difficult and abstruse texts important for Jung? Jung saw in these texts a rich depository of a human mind that was not so dominated by consciousness, reason, and technical proficiency. Jung popularized the idea that there were basic differences between Western and Eastern mind-sets because of the different developments in their respective cultures and histories. He used expressions such as "primitive mentality," "dreamlike," and "childlike" to describe people of the East and showed both fascination and estrangement from that world. According to Jung, the East was indispensable for helping Western man to rediscover the vast territory of the "unconscious" that he had forgotten or suppressed. In "What India Can Teach Us," written after his trip in 1938, he summarized what the white man could learn about himself in India: "India seems so dreamlike: one gets pushed back into the unconscious, into the unredeemed, uncivilized, aboriginal world, of which we only dream, since our conscious denies it. India represents the other way of civilizing man, the way without suppression, without violence, without rationalism."[60] The East could be an excellent mirror for the West, Jung noted, because the East "came to the knowledge of the inner things in childlike ignorance of the external world,"[61] whereas the West was obstructed by its knowledge of science and history. But even though Jung spoke longingly of "partaking of the spirit of the East,"[62] he also recognized the strangeness of the Eastern world and warned against indiscriminate imitation of Eastern meditative techniques and yoga, because Westerners could not fully understand that world.[63]

Jung often describes the East and the West through the deployment of polar opposites: The East is unchanging and circumspect; the West is progressive and extrovert. The West thinks in terms of causality, while the East in terms of synchronicity. Eastern consciousness is characterized by the apperception of totality and wholeness, while the West focuses on differentiation and the parts. The East represents the unconscious, while the West the conscious:

> Long experience with the products of the unconscious has taught me that there is a very remarkable parallelism between the specific character of the Western unconscious psyche and the "manifest" psyche of the East. . . . One can venture the hypothesis that the mind of the Far East is related to our Western consciousness as the unconscious is, that is, as the left hand to the right.[64]

If the West and the East were conceived in such complementary opposite terms, how would this divergence affect the individuation process of people in the East and the West? Individuation was considered by Jung as the personality's highest stage of fulfillment, when a person could integrate all the parts of the psyche, the conscious with the unconscious. If Jung's analyses above were correct, then Westerners would have to search for the unconscious in the deep stratum of their soul, while Easterners would have to complement their "dreamlike" innocence with logic, reason, and thinking. This, however, would disrupt Jung's characterization of his important anima and animus archetypes.

He used *anima* and *animus* to designate the unconscious contrasexual element (the anima as the feminine component of the male psyche, and the animus as the masculine component of the female psyche). Based on his observation of the psychical structure of Western men, he defined *anima* as a personification of the unconscious, the feminine, and the maternal Eros, whereas *animus* represented the conscious, the masculine, and the paternal Logos. But what would be the characterizations of the anima for Eastern men? Jung noticed this discrepancy when he included a brief but fascinating cross-cultural exploration of anima in his commentary on *The Secret of the Golden Flower*. He discussed Wilhelm's translation of Chinese words *p'o* and *hun* into "anima" and "animus" and noted that the East "sees consciousness as an effect of the anima" (108). If anima could be constructed so differently in diverse cultural worlds, Jung would have been forced to reconsider or modify the transcendental nature of his "universal" archetypes. But Jung did not follow this route, for he believed Western men represented the norm of masculinity, and considered Eastern men as not quite masculine enough. The childlike Eastern man, following his primitive instincts (111) and living close to yellow earth (113), was seen as more feminine than masculine. Although

Jung never visited China or treated a Chinese patient, he nevertheless offered the following observation in his essay "Woman in Europe":

> No one can get around the fact that by taking up a masculine profession, studying and working like a man, woman is doing something not wholly in accord with, if not directly injurious to, her feminine nature. She is doing something that would scarcely be possible for a man to do, unless he were a Chinese. Could he, for instance, be a nursemaid or run a kindergarten?[65]

Jung's comment on the Chinese was not a "slip," but based on his construction of the Chinese world through painstaking engagement with translated ancient texts.

His commentary on *The Secret of the Golden Flower* was written to offer a psychological interpretation of the Chinese mind, and to build a bridge between the East and the West. His writings on Eastern thought have often been credited with introducing Eastern thinking in a language that Western people can understand. Jung's portrayal of Eastern people as feminine, childish, and their cultures as unchanging and their mentality primitive reinforces the prevalent stereotypes in colonial discourse. Throughout the twentieth century, many have come to discover the East through Jung's psychological lenses. Though not a Sinologist or Indologist, Jung functions as the authority, who not only represents the East to the West, but the East to itself as well. Ironically, some Asians have consequently found their traditions validated by a Western, and presumably scientific, authority.[66]

It is unfortunate that scholars who are interested in Jung's thought on the East seldom bring to the forefront the dimension of gender.[67] They have assumed, and perhaps rightly so, that when Jung refers to the Eastern mind and the Western mind, he is talking about the minds of men. When feminist scholars debate whether Jungian psychology is compatible with feminism, they rarely bring in Jung's discussion on the East and tend to universalize "women."[68] In both cases the discussion on "Eastern women" is foreclosed. But if we connect the feminist axis with the East-West axis, we will begin to generate new questions, to explore how the interstices disrupt Jung's artificially constructed "universal" archetypes, and what and who is at stake in Western man's drive to find his anima.

Gross and the Possibility of Postpatriarchal Religion
If Müller and Jung are concerned with the past, Rita Gross dreams about the future—a time when sexist religious traditions will be transformed and postpatriarchal religion will flourish. As a graduate student at the University of Chicago in the 1960s, Gross wrote the first dissertation on feminism and

religious studies, focusing on aboriginal Australia. As a Jew, she has written on female God language and Judaism; as a Buddhist, she has written about women's roles in Buddhism and proposed a feminist reconstruction of the Buddhist tradition.[69] After teaching courses in women and religion in a large state university for many years, Gross surveys "the issues that have been central to feminism and religion over the past twenty-five years" in her book *Feminism and Religion: An Introduction.*[70]

What is feminism and how does it relate to the discipline of religious studies? Gross defines feminism as the following:

> The most basic definition of *feminism* is the conviction that women really do inhabit the human realm and are not "other," not a separate species. Sometimes I wear a T-shirt that proclaims: "Feminism is the radical proposition that women are human beings." This proclamation seems so simple and obvious, but its implications are profound and radical because neither conventional scholarship nor lifestyles really take the humanity of women seriously. (16–17)

This definition, simple and clear enough, places Gross solidly in the tradition of liberalism and the modernist discourse on humanism. For her, what is wrong with sexism and androcentric scholarship is that women are not treated on an equal footing with men, as full human beings. Like feminist scholars of her generation, Gross names patriarchy as the chief enemy of women and does not take into serious consideration the fact that women are also oppressed because of their class, race, colonialism, and sexual orientation. Her proposal of androgyny as a two-sex model of humanity (20) is, therefore, limited in its scope and insufficient as a guiding principle.

In the first chapter, Gross carefully separates feminism as an academic method from feminism as a social vision. As an academic method, it demands that women's experiences be made visible in scholarship, but it should abide by the academic requirements of neutrality and objectivity. As a social vision, feminism is a critical stance, demanding transformation of patriarchal culture, religious traditions, and society (16–17). The need for separating the two is important for both women's studies and religious studies if they want to claim they are academic disciplines without political implications and agenda. Gross is conscious of the tension between descriptive scholarship and normative judgment, especially when one needs to make judgments about a culture or a religion that is not one's own (100–104).

However, even Gross's somewhat mild feminist approach earns the ire of Katherine Young, a scholar in Hinduism. Young faults Gross for forsaking neutrality and objectivity in scholarship and for leaving men out because of her feminist stance. She criticizes the double standard in Gross's book and alleges that Gross challenges the bias of "sexist" authors, but not the bias of feminists. In particular, Young wishes to remind Gross of the training she has received under eminent mentors, including Eliade, in the academic study of religion: "She [Gross] fails to acknowledge, moreover, that bias can be reduced considerably by adopting well-known methods such as epoché and empathy, even though she herself pays homage to these while establishing her credentials as a historian of religions at the beginning of her book."[71] In her response, Gross retorts that it is better to acknowledge openly the ambiguity and difficulty of "neutrality" and "objectivity":

> We need to practice neutrality and objectivity in so far as they are possible, while at the same time recognizing their ambiguity and limitations, their ultimate impossibility. They would be possible only in a world in which all players agree to the same standpoint from which to be "objective" and "neutral," or worse, a world in which one standpoint claims hegemony over all others and ignores them. We do not live in such a world any more. Cultural and religious pluralism forces us to acknowledge that all knowledge is *ultimately* situated and contextualized, relative and limited.[72]

The exchange between Young and Gross is significant because it illustrates two different points of views in the academic study of religion. Working with a modernist paradigm, Young has ignored the radical challenge of abundant scholarship in postcolonial studies, cultural studies, self-criticisms in anthropology, and critical reflections on Eliade's legacy and comparative studies of myths. She refuses to see that under the disguises of "neutrality" and "objectivity," the study of religion has furthered the cause of imperialism. What the colonized need is not "empathy," but justice in terms of both political liberation and cultural representation. Gross is certainly more honest and self-critical in her methodology, yet she has taken a culturally and religiously pluralistic approach without seriously interrogating the power differentials undergirding the West's fascination, re-presentation, assimilation, and alienation of the religious and cultural Other since the beginning of the comparative study in religion. Nowhere in her book does she reflect on the epistemological assumptions of feminist scholars, the commonalities and divergences between malestream and feminist scholarship beyond the gender axis, and the ways feminist scholars may unconsciously continue the colonialist paradigm. To her credit, she does call attention to the need to avoid cultural imperialism, ethnocentrism, and colonialism (100–101). What is missing is her reflections on how these processes might have influenced the very construction of the discipline, defining the questions asked, the data gathered, and the conclusions made.

A telling example of this problematic is the way different world religions are evaluated in terms of how "user friendly" they are to women. Given the diverse methodological standpoints of Gross and Young, it is amazing to find that they can agree that religions can be weighed on a scale according to how male dominant they are. Young ranks the world's religions along a continuum, from those manifesting a pronounced male dominance to those that show more acceptance and inclusion of female power: Judaism, Hinduism, Confucianism, Islam, Christianity, Buddhism, Tantra, and Taoism. Gross modifies this order and suggests instead the following ranking: Judaism, Confucianism, Islam, Hinduism, Christianity, Buddhism, and Taoism (91). The ability of these two scholars to speak authoritatively on so many complex and constantly changing religions is breathtaking. Several questions immediately come to mind, however. First, who is speaking for feminism, and who is consulted? In short, who can adequately represent women's participation and experiences in these different religions? Second, although Gross discusses separately women in the indigenous traditions (90), who stands to gain or lose when she and others perpetuate the distinction between the "world religions" and "tribal" or "indigenous" traditions? Third, why is there a need to present some kind of schema, ordering, hierarchy, or scoring for the "world religions?" Since the nineteenth century, religions have been constantly on parade, along the polytheism-monotheism axis, the general and special revelation scheme, the historical and cosmological hypothesis, the inner-worldly and outer-worldly order. What is added or diminished when religions are scrutinized according to the gender axis? What has one gained or lost to "know" that Judaism is most patriarchal and Taoism the least?

After discussing whether religions are inherently sexist, Gross follows a grand narrative in her interpretation of the religious history of humankind, which she divides into prepatriarchal, patriarchal, and postpatriarchal stages. She presents the arguments for and against the existence of a "feminist utopia" dominated by goddesses in prehistorical time (151–62). Then she discusses the scholarly debates about the creation of patriarchy (162–65), before moving on to a discussion of the triumph of monotheism in Judaism, Christianity, and Hinduism (69–90). Although Gross does not support the hypotheses that there was a feminist golden past based on the findings in Chatal Huyuk, Old Europe, and Crete (157–58), and rightly criticizes the Eurocentric bias of the prepatriarchal hypothesis (165–66), she reinscribes the power of this position when she organizes her chapter in this way, even though she includes a counter-narrative on Buddhism at the end. Gross may defend herself by saying that she is guided by feminist scholarship developed in the last several decades, but she does not reflect on the fact that she is basically telling a story about white women.

She began the story of feminist studies of religion by tracing (white) women's critique of patriarchal religion in the nineteenth century in the United States, then (white) women's access to graduate schools and the pioneering texts in the 1960s. She describes the emergence of voices of women of color in the field as "expanding the [white] circle" (53). The reader is left to imagine what a multicultural introduction to feminism and religion might look like and how it might be organized. Such a multicultural approach would subject (white) women's religious history and story to a much broader cultural and historical perspective than Gross has presented. For example, the quest of feminist scholars for a prehistoric golden past would be read not only as (white) women's search for usable history (168), but also as Europeans' and Euro-Americans' search for self-representation. It is interesting to note that at an earlier age, the golden past was found in India; this time it has moved closer to Europe in Chatal Huyuk in Anatolia. Furthermore, the rise of the goddess movement and the neopagan movement must not be interpreted within the confines of women's religious history and spirituality. The larger cultural, social, and political forces that facilitate the emergence of such movements would have to be examined. Why are these movements predominantly white? Do white women in the United States have more freedom to challenge and leave established religions? If we look at the broader contexts of cultural history, *völkisch* utopianism and neopaganism revived in Europe toward the end of the nineteenth century, and some of these groups were politically quite conservative.[73] What can we learn from history about the rise of the neopagan movement a hundred years later?

Gross gives herself a tall order to imagine postpatriarchal religion at the end of her book. She emphatically states that postpatriarchal religious visions can better be imagined when women avail themselves of the symbolic and spiritual resources of humankind and do not confine themselves to Western sources (245–47). While Jane Eyre expresses apprehension about going to India, Gross enters and inhabits the spiritual world of Asia, bearing the loneliness of living as a Buddhist in the North American confines of Wisconsin.[74] She faults the modern Jane Eyres, who refuse to "travel" to the East and acquire the "comparative mirror" to better understand their own religious traditions. Gross recounts her spiritual "travel narrative," describing how her journeys into Hinduism and Buddhism have deeply broadened her thinking and enriched her life. Gross considers the encounter of Buddhism with Western feminism an "auspicious coincidence" (215), with the potential to benefit Buddhism worldwide:

> These causes and conditions for the demise of patriarchy are more apparent in Western societies than in the Asian homeland of Buddhism. . . . The Buddhist feminist concerns are especially dependent on Western feminism and are taken more seriously by Western Buddhists. The most powerful agent promoting post-patriarchal Buddhism is the auspicious coincidence of feminism and Buddhism in the West.[75]

Gross's discussion completely overlooks the feminist movements that are developing in many parts of Asia, and does not envisage that Asian Buddhist women can be change agents within Buddhism. Resonating with Müller's Aryan theory, Gross thinks Western Buddhists have the manifest destiny of rejuvenating Buddhism and bringing it to its fulfillment: "After the magical meeting, the tasks and assignments are transmitted. Western Buddhists are in the position to model and to theorize sane gender arrangements that would finally manifest, in everyday reality, what the Buddhist *dharma* has said explicitly and implicitly for so long."[76] Gross, with good intentions, encourages women to learn from other religious traditions and cautions against cultural borrowing and misappropriation (246). But she does not seem to be aware of the danger of constructing travel narratives (physical or spiritual) that replicate the colonial relationships that have shaped so much of the cross-cultural encounter in the modern period.

If we juxtapose Laura Donaldson's three foundational moments with the three I have selected, we see how gender, religion, and colonialism are intricately linked in physical acts of conquering and dominating others, in cultural imaginations, and in religious discourses. This anthology represents a multicultural and multireligious attempt to examine the intersections of the three, exploring new feminist spaces, plotting new histories, and opening possibilities to create new narratives about the past and the future.

The Anthology: Uneasy Intersections

As the reader has undoubtedly gathered from our respective introductions, this anthology explores the often uneasy intersections between postcolonialism and feminist religious discourse. Much feminist religious scholarship has emerged from Christian women of Caucasian descent and, because of its Eurocentric framework, has perpetuated colonialist structures of thought: excluding the lives and experiences of women of color and colonized women, misappropriating indigenous cultural resources, and using Orientalist paradigms. Although the chapters of this volume are written from a variety of transnational, theoretical, disciplinary, and religious perspectives, they all offer important critiques of the way religious and feminist knowledge is constructed, as well as exciting new visions for the development of anticolonialist, antiracist and antisexist discourses of liberation. For organizational purposes, we have divided this collection into two constituent parts. The first we have identified as *Challenging Feminist Religious Discourse* and the second, *Rethinking Texts and Traditions*. Each of the chapters can be read individually, but, as members of a group, they also work together to build a kind of methodological and thematic context.

The essays in *Part One, Challenging Feminist Religious Discourse*, engage the problematic paradigms of feminist religious discourse in a variety of ways. Chapter 1, Laura Donaldson's, "The Breasts of Columbus: A Political Anatomy of Postcolonialism and Feminist Religious Discourse," begins this effort by shifting the dialogue between women of color and Euro-American women from a moral paradigm emphasizing accusation and blaming (or denial and defensiveness) to one foregrounding how feminists produce knowledge about the colonized woman. As a case in point, she focuses on (white) feminist theology's production of knowledge about Native North American women. Not content to remain within the bounds of critique, Donaldson fashions a provocative counter-narrative based on the history of Cherokee women at Ft. Loudon and the challenge they pose to any simple construction of their agency as either powerless victim or triumphalist survivor. Through this example, she attempts to tease out, in the words of Gayatri Chakravorty Spivak, the "testimony of [Native] women's voice-consciousness" from the colonial archives and, in so doing, sketch the contours of a more productive relationship between postcolonialism and feminist religious discourse.

In "Unbinding Our Feet: Saving Brown Women and Feminist Religious Discourse," Kwok Pui-lan addresses the historical and theoretical deployment of colonialist feminism, which is motivated by the alleged task of saving brown women from brown men. According to Kwok, this rationale actively obscures the violence and brutality of colonialism by presenting it as social mission. Like Donaldson, Kwok chooses to probe this dynamic through the use of a case study—here, the representation of Chinese footbinding in Mary Daly's influential book *Gyn/Ecology*. Daly, one of the earliest and most prolific feminist "thealogians," has been publicly taken to task by women of color such as Audre Lorde for her misrepresentation of African tradition and African women. Kwok criticizes Daly's misappropriation of footbinding in order to prove the existence of a universal patriarchy as well as her portrait of Chinese women as only oppressed, passive victims. In a different voice, Kwok both historicizes the practice of footbinding and makes visible the ways

Chinese women articulated their own resistance to it. Finally, she offers a compelling alternative by rewriting Daly's script and creating a new postcolonial space in which gender is no longer used to justify racism, genocide, and colonization.

During the Gulf War, most of the media coverage focused on the male protagonists who were fighting the war either as soldiers or heads of state. One of the few television segments produced on women concerned the issue of driving automobiles in Saudi Arabia: the freedom of North American women to use their cars versus the inability (and failure) of Muslim women to obtain the same privileges. While this feature might seem innocuous, it microcosmically figures Euro-America's dominant relationship to Islam by portraying Saudi Arabian women—and by extension, Islam and the Middle East—only in terms of *absence*: the absence of women's freedom to drive, which stands in for the larger absence of Westernized progress and liberal democracy. In the third chapter, "Sartorial Fabric-ations: Enlightenment and Western Feminism," Meyda Yeğenoğlu unravels the complicated colonial dynamics underlying the persistent Eurocentric link between Islam and absence, and particularly examines how Muslim women function as a metonym for the entirety of "the Orient." Of course, the most notorious example of Muslim women's metonymic function arises from the historically vexed practice of veiling. The veiled woman, according to Yeğenoğlu, mistakenly becomes the concrete embodiment of the Islamic tradition's inherent oppressiveness. Indeed, she notes, criticism of how the religious customs of Oriental societies "monstrously" oppress women has often provided the ideological justification for colonization and the imposition of a colonial culture. In one of its most significant turns, this chapter reverses the transparent position of those who demand unveiling by deconstructing, and then reconstructing, the imperative "not-to-veil": if veiling can be perceived as a specific practice of marking and disciplining Muslim women's bodies in accordance with certain cultural requirements, then so can unveiling. Yeğenoğlu argues that "not-to-veil" needs to take its place as one among many practices of corporeal inscription—a status that would deprive it of any claim to naturalness or universality. While Yeğenoğlu's chapter does not specifically address the field of feminist theology, it subjects a broad range of feminist religious discourse to much-needed scrutiny.

The final chapter in this section is Musa W. Dube's "Postcoloniality, Feminist Spaces, and Religion." Dube presents an overview of feminism within the framework of postcoloniality and identifies decolonizing feminist strategies of liberation among "Two-Thirds World" women—so named because the "Third World" actually holds two-thirds of the world's population. Dube seeks to answer the following questions: What are the characteristics and practices of Two-Thirds World feminists within a postcolonial space? What are their concerns and strategies? What is the role of religion in the colonization and decolonization of postcolonialist feminist spaces and subjects? More particularly, she examines how colonization constructs and affects African women who participate in the Setswana religion as well as the role of Christianity in facilitating this process. Finally, although Dube acknowledges the diversity of the postcolonial spaces belonging to "Two-Thirds World" women, she also articulates the strategies and concerns that they share in the quest to decolonize and "depatriarchalize" their respective societies.

One of the most important processes of decolonization is the act of writing back to the center of empire and the rewriting of canonical stories.[77] *Part Two* of our anthology, *Rethinking Texts and Traditions,* rewrites and recontextualizes the canonical stories of various religious traditions—Hindu, Muslim, Jewish, African-American—in a variety of ways. Laurie Patton's piece, "The Prostitute's Gold: Women, Religion, and Sanskrit in one Corner of India," elaborates on the ways in which women are reconfiguring the intellectual division of labor within Hinduism and, more particularly, within Sanskrit as a scholarly field. In a radical paradigm shift, traditionally male-dominated institutions of Sanskrit have become feminized in some regions of India—a state of affairs raising many questions for the intersection of postcolonialism, gender, and religious discourse. Patton weaves these issues through a series of interviews she conducted with women Sanskrit scholars in the Indian state of Maharashtra, the cumulative results of which inform her essay. These interviews reveal a number of unexpected insights: that caste consciousness rather than gender informed the choice of many women to become Sanskritists; that their study of Sanskrit has motivated them to adopt definitions of women's place which often echo the conservative maternalism of Euro-American cultural feminists; and finally (at least from one reader's perspective) that women's participation in Sanskrit leaves many unanswered questions about their complicity in troubling forms of Hindu nationalism. Patton subsequently makes several suggestions for developing a transformative practice of textual reading – suggestions initially concerning the content field of Sanskrit, but which also carry implications for the more general practice of sacred reading under the gendered sign of postcolonialism.

Miriam Cooke's contribution, "Multiple Critique: Islamic Feminist Rhetorical Strategies," intersects with the work of Meyda Yeğenoğlu insofar as it also considers the practice of veiling. Yet, Cooke examines veiling from the perspective of how Muslim women, and particularly the group whom Cooke identifies as "Islamic feminists," deploy this controversial custom for their own purposes and theorize it on their own terms. The attitudes of Muslim women on veiling illustrate how, according to Cooke, they are claiming the right to freedom and equality with men at a time when they seem, to outsiders, far from both. The complex negotiations of Islamic feminists in constructing new and multiple identities for themselves within Islam and in relation to the larger global arena is represented by the rhetorical strategy of "multiple critique." Cooke creates this complex neologism from the already existing notions of "double critique" and "multiple consciousness," and uses it to illuminate the lives and experiences of women who refuse to accept "Islamic feminism" as an oxymoron. In a dramatic and moving way, this chapter illustrates how contemporary Muslim women are attempting to rewrite their own religious and cultural traditions and to create a space for themselves in which their multiple identities as Muslims and as feminists can coexist safely and with dignity.

Chapter 7, "Letting Go of Liberalism: Feminism and the Emancipation of the Jews," by Laura Levitt, rewrites Jewish tradition by interrogating the historical and ideological grounds of the Jewish emancipation in France. Many colonial contexts were marked by what one might call the politics of defective assimilation, in which the colonized were encouraged—and in many cases, forced—to speak the colonizer's language and assume the trappings of the occupying culture. At the same time, however, they were not allowed to attain equality with colonial settlers. The federal boarding school system for American Indians provides a vivid example of this dynamic. The system was designed to acculturate Indians into white society as industrious farmers, individualist property owners, and docile citizens (or, in the phrase coined by General Philip Sheridan, "kill the Indian but save the man"). Yet what Native students learned in these boarding schools ensured that they would remain subordinate to their Euro-American counterparts, since the schools taught inadequate and antiquated technologies and curricula. Such institutions worked hand in hand with more explicit colonial ideologies to subjugate American Indians while seeming to emancipate them. Levitt's essay deals with a similar contradiction: the deceptive premises of emancipation for French Jews. While the social context of European Jews is not at all similar to that of American Indians, the limits of emancipation, or the admission of Jews to the full rights and responsibilities of French citizenship, provides a link between these diverse histories. Like the attempts to detribalize Native North Americans, one of the most pernicious effects of emancipation was its imposition of an individualist ideology upon Jews; as Levitt notes, all aspects of collective Jewish life subsequently came under the aegis of the liberal state. This chapter's trenchant examination of the "liberal/colonial project" has ramifications beyond its particular referent and raises many issues not only for Jews, but for women and colonized peoples.

Issues of epistemic violence are threaded through this anthology, and chapter 8, Shawn Copeland's "Body, Representation, and Black Religious Discourse," is no exception. It foregrounds this concern in critiquing how African-American women have been symbolically dismembered in a diverse array of cultural and historical forums: the institution of slavery, gangsta rap and hip-hop music, as well as the black sermon. In each of these, black women are reduced to body parts and subjected to a kind of racist pornographic gaze, or a racist and sexist lens that reduces them to a deformed and distorted sexuality. Copeland also focuses on the ideological and rhetorical dimensions of the black sermon, which she argues is a privileged site not only of black women's oppression within the black Christian church, but also of their potential liberation from this oppression. How, she asks, can the black sermon manifest the signs of a decolonizing discourse? Through its capacity to mobilize the imagery of the human person—including women—as dynamic moral agents, the black sermon jettisons an "aesthetics of submission" that works to subjugate black women and instead, fosters the creative visualization of a transformed world.

By including work from a number of different academic, social, and personal locations, this anthology cuts a wide swath across the intersecting fields of postcolonialism, feminism, and religious discourse. We acknowledge that there are many questions left unanswered, but hope that the body of work contained here will make it easier for others to continue and extend this project.

Notes

1. Anne McClintock, *Imperial Leather: Race, Gender and Sexuality in the Colonial Contest* (New York: Routledge, 1995).

2. R. S. Sugirtharajah, ed., *The Postcolonial Bible* (Sheffield, U.K.: Sheffield Academic Press, 1998).

3. Ania Loomba, *Colonialism/Postcolonialism: The New Cultural Idiom* (London: Routledge, 1998), 227.

4. Laura E. Donaldson, *Decolonizing Feminisms* (Chapel Hill and London: University of North Carolina Press, 1992), 6.

5. I take this example from Andrea Smith's essay "Sexual Violence and American Indian Genocide," in *Remembering Conquest:Feminist/Womanist Perspectives on Religion, Colonization, and Sexual Violence*, ed. Nantawan Boonprasat Lewis and Marie M. Fortune (New York: Haworth Pastoral Press, 1999), 31–52.

6. Nantawan Boonprasat Lewis and Marie M. Fortune, introduction to *Remembering Conquest*, 3.

7. See Donald S. Lopez, Jr., ed., *Curators of the Buddha: The Study of Buddhism under Colonialism* (Chicago: University of Chicago Press, 1995); Richard King, *Orientalism and Religion: Postcolonial Theory, India, and the "Mythic East"* (London: Routledge, 1997).

8. He made this comment in a letter to John Lowrie dated July 14, 1883; as quoted in Carol Devens, "Missionary Education of Native American Girls," in *Journal of World History* 3 (1992): 225.

9. Michael Harkin and Sergei Kan, introduction to the special issue "Native American Women's Responses to Christianity," *Ethnohistory* 43 (1996): 566.

10. Ibid.

11. Samuel P. Huntington, *The Clash of Civilization and the Remaking of World Order* (New York: Simon and Schuster, 1996), 51, 91.

12. Ali A. Mazrui, *Cultural Forces in World Politics* (London: James Currey, 1990), 61.

13. Michael Prior, *The Bible and Colonialism: A Moral Critique* (Sheffield: Sheffield Academic Press, 1997), 175.

14. Stefan Zweig, *Amerigo: A Comedy of Errors in History*, trans. Andrew St. James (New York: Viking, 1942), 51.

15. Ibid., 52.

16. Martin Waldseemüller, *The Cosmographia Introductio in Facsimile*, United States Catholic Historical Society, Vol. 4, ed. Charles George Herbermann, trans. Joseph Fischer and Franz von Wieser (New York: United States Catholic Historical Society, 1907), 70. Of course, historians now know that Amerigo Vespucci was not the original explorer of the so-called New World, and even Waldseemüller himself became convinced of his mistake after the publication of the *Cosmographia*.

17. Mary Louise Pratt, *Imperial Eyes: Travel Writing and Transculturation* (London: Routledge, 1992), 32.

18. Graham Huggan, "Decolonizing the Map: Post-Colonialism, Post-Structuralism and the Cartographic Connection," in *Past the Last Post: Theorizing Post-Colonialism and Post-Modernism*, ed. Ian Adam and Helen Tiffin (Calgary: University of Calgary Press, 1990), 25.

19. "Turtle Island" is the name that the Haudenosaunee (Iroquois) gave to the land now called "North America." It comes from a creation story, which tells how the turtle volunteered to use his shell as an anchor for the earth.

20. Denis De Rougement, *The Idea of Europe*, trans. Norbert Guterman (New York: Macmillan, 1966), 21.

21. See Rayna Green, *Women in American Indian Society*, ed. Frank W. Porter III (New York: Chelsea House, 1992).

22. José Rabasa, *Inventing A-M-E-R-I-C-A: Spanish Historiography and the Formation of Eurocentrism* (Norman: University of Oklahoma Press, 1993), 204.

23. Simon Ryan, "Inscribing the Emptiness: Cartography, Exploration and the Construction of Australia," in *De-Scribing Empire: Post-Colonialism and Textuality*, ed. Chris Tiffin and Alan Lawson (London: Routledge, 1994), 128.

24. Mary Rowlandson, "A True History of the Captivity and Restoration of Mrs. Mary Rowlandson," in *Colonial American Travel Narratives*, ed. Wendy Martin (New York: Penguin Books, 1994), 19. Hereafter page references will be cited in the text.

25. Annette Kolodny, *The Land before Her: Fantasy and Experience of the American Frontier, 1630–1860* (Chapel Hill: University of North Carolina Press, 1984), 18.

26. Ibid.

27. Wendy Martin, *Colonial American Travel Narratives*, xi.

28. John A. Strong, "Algonquian Women as Sunksquaws and Caretakers of the Soil: The Documentary Evidence in the Seventeenth Century Records," in *Native American Women in Literature and Culture*, ed. Susan Castillo and Victor M. P. Da Rosa (Porto, Portugal: Fernando Pessoa University Press, 1997), 196.

29. Paula Gunn Allen and Patricia Clark Smith, *As Long as the River Flows: The Stories of Nine Native Americans* (New York: Scholastic Press, 1996), 9.

30. In 1622, a Dutch trader named Jacques Elekens seized the Pequot *sachem* named Tatobem and threatened to behead him if he did not pay a hefty ransom. Tatobem swiftly paid the equivalent of an enormous sum in *mampampeag* and, as a result of this incident, the West India Company discovered the value of these strings of small beads. Wampum became the currency of choice in payments for furs and mercantile goods. Ironically, it was Philip's refusal to pay England's demand for tributary wampum that, among other factors, precipitated "King Philip's War." For a discussion of the origins of wampum, see Lynn Ceci, "Native Wampum as a Peripheral Resource in the Seventeenth-Century World-System," in *The Pequots in Southern New England: The Fall and Rise of an American Indian Nation*, ed. M. Hauptman and James D. Wherry (Norman: University of Oklahoma Press, 1990), 48–63.

31. William Apess, *On Our Own Ground: The Complete Writings of William Apess: A Pequot*, ed. Barry O. Connell (Amherst: University of Massachusetts Press, 1992), 297.

32. Ibid.

33. See Strong, "Algonquian Women," 195–96.

34. Loomba, *Colonialism/Postcolonialism*, 19.

35 Louise Erdrich, *Jacklight* (New York: Henry Holt and Company, 1984), 27.

36. Gayatri Chakravorty Spivak, "Three Women's Texts and a Critique of Imperialism," in *"Race," Writing, and Difference*, ed. Henry Louis Gates, Jr. (Chicago: University of Chicago Press, 1986), 263.

37. Leela Gandhi, *Postcolonial Theory: A Critical Introduction* (New York: Columbia University Press, 1998), 83.

38. Charlotte Brontë, *Jane Eyre*, Second Norton Critical Edition, ed. Richard J. Dunn (New York: W. W. Norton, 1987), 324. Hereafter page references will be cited in the text.

39. Patrick Williams and Laura Chrisman, eds., *Colonial Discourse and Post-Colonial Theory: A Reader* (New York: Columbia University Press, 1994), 5.

40. It is actually Diana Rivers who speaks this phrase. However, Jane has expressed many similar sentiments and in this case, the subject positions of the speakers are interchangeable.

41. Joachim Wach, *The Comparative Study of Religions* (New York: Columbia University Press, 1958), 3–26; Joseph M. Kitagawa, "The History of Religions in America," in *The History of Religions: Essays in Methodology*, ed. Mircea Eliade and Joseph M. Kitagawa (Chicago: University of Chicago Press, 1959), 1–30.

42. See Lopez, Jr. ed., *Curators of the Buddha*. King, *Orientalism and Religion*.

43. See the exchange between Katherine K. Young and Rita M. Gross. Young, "Having Your Cake and Eating It Too: Feminism and Religion," *Journal of the American Academy of Religion* 67 (1999): 167–84, and Gross's "A Rose by Any Other Name . . .: A Response to Katherine K. Young," in the same issue, pp. 185–94.

44. I fully understand the false generalizations of using the terms such as "the East" and "the West" or "Western mind" and "Eastern mind." Nineteenth-century scholars used these terms all the time and it will be too troublesome to put these terms in quotation marks at every single mention.

45. See the discussion in Tomoko Masuzawa, *In Search of Dreamtime: The Quest for the Origin of Religion* (Chicago: University of Chicago Press, 1993), 58–59; Rita M. Gross, *Feminism and Religion: An Introduction* (Boston: Beacon Press, 1996), 8.

46. Masuzawa, *In Search of Dreamtime*, 62.

47. See his letter to Jacob Bernays as cited in Masuzawa, *In Search of Dreamtime*, 65.

48. Gayatri Chakravorty Spivak, *A Critique of Postcolonial Reason: Toward a History of the Vanishing Present* (Cambridge, Mass.: Harvard University Press, 1999), 8.

49. Léon Poliakov, *The Aryan Myth: A History of Racist and Nationalist Ideas in Europe*, trans. Edmund Howard (New York: Meridian, 1971), 186–87.

50. Ibid., 198.

51. This expression was used by Jules Michelet, see ibid., 199.

52. Max Müller, *Comparative Mythology* (New York: Arno Press, 1977), 28. Hereafter page references will be given in parentheses in the text.

53. Poliakov, *The Aryan Myth*, 204.

54. Martin Maw, *Visions of India: Fulfilment Theology, the Aryan Race Theory, and the Work of the British Protestant Missionaries in Victorian India* (Frankfurt and Main: Verlag Peter Lang, 1990), 37–74.

55. King, *Orientalism and Religion*, 128.

56. Richard Noll, *The Jung Cult: Origins of a Charismatic Movement* (Princeton, N.J.: Princeton University Press, 1994), 20.

57. J. J. Clark, introduction to C. G. Jung, *Jung on the East*, ed. J. J. Clark (London: Routledge, 1995), 1.

58. Ibid., 13.

59. Jung, ""Richard Wilhelm: In Memoriam," in *Jung on the East*, 47–48.

60. Jung, "What India Can Teach Us," in *Jung on the East*, 59.

61. Jung, "Commentary on The Secret of the Golden Flower," in *Jung on the East*, 109. Hereafter page references will be given in parentheses in the text.

62. Jung, "Richard Wilhelm," 42.

63. Jung, "Yoga and the West, " in *Jung on the East*, 159–65.

64. Jung, "Forward to Lily Abegg, The Mind of East Asia," in *Jung on the East*, 61.

65. C. G. Jung, "Woman in Europe," in *The Collected Works*, ed. G. Adler et al., trans. R. F. C. Hull, 2d ed. (Princeton, N.J.: Princeton University Press, 1964), 10: 117–18. Naomi R. Goldenberg has noted the racism of Jung in his portrayal of the Chinese, see "A Feminist Critique of Jung," in *Jung and Christianity in Dialogue: Faith, Feminism, and Hermeneutics*, ed. Robert L. Moore and Daniel J. Meckel (New York: Paulist Press, 1990), 106.

66. See discussion on Jung and India in Luis O. Gómez, "Oriental Wisdom and the Cure of Souls: Jung and the Indian East," in *Curators of the Buddha*, 226.

67. J. J. Clark, *Jung and Eastern Thought: A Dialogue with the East* (London: Routledge, 1994); Howard Coward, *Jung and Eastern Thought* (Albany: State University of New York Press, 1985).

68. Demaris S. Wehr, *Jung and Feminism: Liberating Archetypes* (Boston: Beacon Press, 1987), and essays by Naomi R. Goldenberg, Demaris S. Wehr, and Ann Belford Ulanov in the anthology *Jung and Christianity in Dialogue*. Goldenberg lifts up Jung's biases against women, Jews, and blacks in "A Critical View of Archetypal Thinking," in her *Returning Words to Flesh: Feminism, Psychoanalysis, and the Resurrection of the Body* (Boston: Beacon Press, 1990), 98–100.

69. Rita M. Gross, *Buddhism after Patriarchy: A Feminist History, Analysis, and Reconstruction of Buddhism* (Albany: State University of New York Press, 1993).

70. Rita M. Gross, *Feminism and Religion*, 1. Hereafter page references will be given in parentheses in the text.

71. Young, "Having Your Cake," 175.

72. Gross, "A Rose by Any Other Name," 191.

73. Noll, *The Jung Cult*, 103–8.

74. Rita M. Gross, "Buddhism after Patriarchy," in *After Patriarchy: Feminist Transformations of the World Religions*, ed. Paula M. Cooey, William R. Eakin, and Jay B. McDaniel (Maryknoll, N.Y.: Orbis Books, 1991), 74–75.

75. Gross, *Buddhism after Patriarchy*, 218.

76. Ibid., 220.

77. Bill Ashcroft, Gareth Griffiths and Helen Tiffin, *The Empire Writes Back: Theory and Practice in Post-colonial Literatures* (London Routledge, 1989), 97.

Part One

Challenging Feminist
Religious Discourse

1

The Breasts of Columbus

*A Political Anatomy of Postcolonialism and
Feminist Religious Discourse*

LAURA E. DONALDSON

*I do not hold that the earthly Paradise has the form
of a rugged mountain, as it is shown in pictures, but
that it lies at the summit of what I have described as
the stalk of the pear.*

—Christopher Columbus, *Log,* Third Voyage

Whether they are large and plump, small and flat, or positively undulating, women's breasts embody sexual difference in the identity discourses of the West; however, the meaning these discourses generate about breasts is radically divergent. On the one hand, the socialization of women as objects of the male gaze has induced many to spend millions of dollars enlarging, sometimes reducing, but always disciplining their breasts through the rigors of plastic surgery. In contrast, feminists such as Hélène Cixous suggest that a woman's breasts (along with her other reproductive organs) defy the centralized phallicism of men and engender an alternative libidinal organization as well as a distinctly feminine way of knowing. However, we should also remember that breasts possess a colonial history and that the female mammary glands constitute a significant part of imperialism's political anatomy.[1]

Who can forget, for example, the recent struggle of indigenous people for the hills of Welatye Therre, or "Two Breasts," where Australian aboriginal women have danced and sung for thousands of years?[2] Both the songs associated with the site and its sacred objects nurture the dissemination of women's knowledge. As one Arrernte woman declared: "Like you've got women's liberation, for hundreds of years we've had ceremonies which control our conduct, how we behave and act and how we control our sexual lives. . . . They give spiritual and emotional health to Aboriginal women."[3] Specific knowledge about the Welatye Therre is forbidden to non-Native outsiders as well as to aboriginal men, yet the Arrernte women who claim this place were forced to disclose its significance (and thus risk its sacredness) to protect it from flooding by a proposed hydroelectric dam. After an effective and vigorous opposition campaign they defeated the dam proposal, and the "Two Breasts" of Arrernte culture continue to nurture their people.

The breasts of "Sheba," which come to life in the pages of H. Rider Haggard's novel *King Solomon's Mines*, exist as perhaps the most (in)famous European counterpart to the Welatye Therre. In Haggard's nineteenth-century adventure tale, a mercenary Portuguese trader named Jose da Silvestre ironically draws a map to the chamber containing the riches of King Solomon while he is starving to death on the "nipple" of "Sheba's Breasts"—the name of an African mountain that rightly refuses to nurse such a destructive child. Described by Malek Alloula as the half-aesthetic concept of the "Moorish bosom," the specter of the colonized's dark, seductive breasts (even such topographical ones as Sheba's) both titillated and haunted the European social imaginary during the centuries of conquest. In his analysis of suberotic breast images in *The Colonial Harem*, Alloula documents their circulation through the postcards that French colonists in Algeria sent home to the mother country. These postcards function as a virtual "anthology of breasts" whose diversity ultimately reveals a pattern of sameness: "Generally topped off with a smiling or dreamy face, this Moorish bosom, which expresses an obvious invitation, will . . . be offered to view, without any envelope to ensure the intimacy of a private correspondance [sic]."[4]

Perhaps the most haunting chronicler of the postcolonial breast is the West Bengali writer and activist Mahasweta Devi, whose collection *Breast Stories*

(1998) explores in literary form many of the questions I will raise here. *Breast Stories* includes, for example, the story of Draupadi, a tribal woman who leads a resistance movement on behalf of her people, and Senanayak, the police chief who pursues her, and in whom Gayatri Chakravorty Spivak finds a cautionary tale of the expert on Third World resistance literature nourished by First World societies. Devi also introduces her readers to Jashoda, a lower-caste woman who becomes a professional wet nurse (through the practice of suckling) to her master's sons, and Gangor, another tribal woman and nursing mother who works as a migrant laborer. Gangor's breasts become objects of obsession and oppression through the circulation of an ill-advised photograph. According to Spivak, who translated and introduced Devi's collection:

> The breast is not a symbol in these stories. In "Draupadi," what is represented is an erotic object transformed into an object of torture and revenge where the line between (hetero)sexuality and gender violence begins to waver.[5] In "Breast Giver" [Jashoda's story], it is a survival object transformed into a commodity, making visible the indeterminacy between filial piety and gender violence, between house and temple, between domination and exploitation. . . . In "Behind the Bodice" [Gangor's story], [Devi] bitterly decries the supposed "normality" of sexuality as male violence.[6]

This confluence of colonialism and patriarchy so brilliantly explored by Devi also conjures the colonial breasts of most immediate concern to this essay: those fantasized by Columbus, whose voyages in search of the East convinced him that the world was not round, but rather, pear-shaped and topped by a protuberance much like a woman's nipple.

The "nipple" envisioned by Columbus was none other than Guanahaní, the land of the Taino, which the Spanish renamed San Salvador. Feminist critic Anne McClintock identifies Columbus' breast fantasies as a genre of "pornotropics" that draws on "a long tradition of male travel as an erotics of ravishment" for its content.[7] For example, earlier travelers' tales had regaled their European readers with stories of men's breasts flowing with milk and militarized Amazonian women lopping theirs off.[8] To readers satiated with such exoticized sexualities, the mammillary imaginings of Rider Haggard and Columbus must have seemed quite tame. In her essay, "The Breast, the Apocalypse, and the Colonial Journey" (later revised as the chapter "De/colon/izing Spaces" in *Apocalypse Now and Then)*, Catherine Keller offers her own engagement with the breasts of Columbus as well as the only explicit engagement by a Euro-American feminist theologian with the 1992 quincentennial.

Keller describes this essay as contributing "a Euroamerican feminist fragment to the postcolonial project" and articulates its goal as decolonizing the "androcentric" minds whose visions of imperialism were so heavily influenced by the "mammillary trope."[9] To this end, she examines the "gender codes" structuring the colonial enterprise and, more particularly, the gender codes that coalesced not only in Christopher Columbus' apocalyptic discourse but in all speculations about the end of the world.[10] For Keller, androcentric myths of the holy warrior, an appeal to male-on-male violence, and a rejection of the feminized and sexualized body link both Revelation's New Jerusalem and the New World's Terra Incognita.[11] While Columbus' attempts to formulate an individual politics were ultimately negligible, Keller asserts that his personal apocalyptic beliefs nevertheless transformed "the collective mythic structures of the Western world."[12] This claim tends to exaggerate the sociopolitical importance of apocalypse in fourteenth and fifteenth-century Europe, however, since one could argue that a 1366 amendment by the Priors of Florence to the laws governing the import and sale of "infidel" slaves had an even greater impact on the agendas of conquest.

In this decision, the Holy Roman Church defined the word *infidel* so that it encompassed anyone born a non-Christian, regardless of any subsequent conversion they might have experienced. From this moment forward, racial and ethnic origin rather than religious difference became the foundation of slavery—an evolving context of discrimination that nurtured the notion of non-Europeans as separate, distinct, and inferior "races."[13] This semantic and theological redefinition of the infidel also influenced the belief that God created American Indians for the specific purpose of becoming slaves to European Christians. Overestimating the influence of apocalyptic thought consequently deflects our attention away from equally important attitudes and policies, along with the complicity of the institutional Church in facilitating the emergence of both colonialism and white supremacy. Despite this tenuous interpretation of Columbian apocalypticism, projects with Keller's twin foci are long overdue: contemporary postcolonial theory consistently subsumes the particularity of women's estates under its appeals to an homogenous category called "the colonized,"[14] and it has largely overlooked the collusion of colonialist as well as indigenous patriarchies. Gayatri Chakravorty Spivak cautions us about correcting this neglect with an uncritical flight into the realm of the postcolonial, however: "Much so-called cross-cultural disciplinary practice, even when 'feminist,' reproduces and forecloses colonialist structures: sanctioned ignorance, and a refusal of subject-status and therefore human-ness [for the subaltern]."[15] In other words, despite the cognitive commitments to antiracism and decolonization of many Euro-American feminists, the structures of thought and research methods organizing their scholarship continue to thwart the progressive goals they espouse. Spivak's emphasis upon the reproduction of two particular "colonialist structures"—sanctioned ignorance and the refusal of subject status to the oppressed—constitutes a starting point for examining this question, since both foreground questions of how scholars produce knowledge rather than personal culpability. My hope is that this exploration of postcolonialism and feminist religious discourse will shift the dialogue among women of the Third and Fourth Worlds and those of the First from a moral to an epistemological paradigm. As Keller herself has noted, blaming or denouncing each other may correct a situation by achieving a "behavior-modifying shame" and an institution-shifting conscience," but it will never heal the "systemic complex which provoked it."[16] The epistemological shift I am suggesting begins, but certainly does not end, this process of healing.

On Not Sanctioning Ignorance

The whites told only one side. Told it to please themselves. Told much that is not true.
—Yellow Wolf, Nez Percé, c. 1877

Although apocalypse functions as the hinge upon which issues of knowledge turn in this essay, I want to begin my discussion not with a state of knowing, but rather, with the exigencies of "sanctioned ignorance," or the way in which certain forms of not-knowing are both legitimated and rewarded in the Euro-American academy. Spivak, who coined the notion of sanctioned ignorance, has a specific definition in mind: the ways in which intellectual practices of "Third Worldism" mask urgent problems such as the globalization of transnational monopoly capitalism and the renewed vigor of neocolonialism. She notes, for example, that "our own mania for 'third world literature' anthologies, when the teacher or critic often has no sense of the original languages, of the subject-constitution of the social and gendered agents in question (and when therefore the student cannot sense this as a loss), participates more in the logic of translation-as-violation" than in any emancipatory enterprise.[17] Sanctioned ignorance is obviously more complex than any individual's moral intention, as this illustration demonstrates. In the case of scholarship on Native peoples or feminist responses to the quincentennial of Columbus' voyage to America, sanctioned ignorance most often emerges through an intertextual chain of information retrieval: those who have no firsthand knowledge cite highly touted sources—virtually all of them non-Native—to produce authoritative, but often highly inaccurate, accounts of indigenous experience. Since those citing do not necessarily "know" the violations their sources effect, they certainly cannot convey to their readers/students any sense of loss (or outrage, perhaps a more appropriate response). And Keller's production of knowledge about the relation between American Indians and apocalypticism provides a model of how, even with an explicit commitment to decolonization, one can become caught in this conundrum.

In *Apocalypse Now and Then*, Keller rightly insists that no one should construct a counter-apocalyptic conception of community solely on the basis of white European sources. This statement occurs in her use of the Muscogee (Creek) "Red Stick War" as a illustrative example of certain characteristics exhibited by apocalyptic millennial movements. Indeed, Keller articulates her argument by constructing a homology between the Red Stick War and its alleged European ancestors: "The analogies of the Red Stick revolt to the European precedents [Thomas Münzer, the Münster Anabaptists, and Gerald Winstanley's Diggers] expose a pattern of community desperately attempting to redeem an original identity—whether of the first church or of tribal tradition—by a purifying violence that willy-nilly results in group martyrdom."[18] She thus presents Muscogee millenarianism as exhibiting the same violent propensity for revolutionary purification and homogenization manifested by many European movements. In addition, she notes, this apocalyptic pattern "does not seem to occur apart from Christian influence."[19] There are several problems with Keller's conjectures, however, not the least of which is that Keller—contradicting her own statement about the limitations of white European sources—draws solely on the work of two Euro-American scholars for her understanding of the Muscogee people and their history: Joel W. Martin's *Sacred Revolt: The Muskogees' Struggle for a New World* (1991) and Bryan R. Wilson's *Magic and the Millennium: A Sociological Study of the Religious Movements of Protest among Tribal and Third World Peoples* (1973). This sets into motion an intertextual chain of sanctioned ignorance whose ultimate result is the reduction of the Red Stick War to a symptom of Christian millennialism.[20]

In *Sacred Revolt*, Joel Martin characterizes the Red Stick War as an anticolonial religious movement dedicated to relieving the beleaguered Muscogees from the afflictions of white invasion. Its conflict pitted the "Redsticks"—Muscogee traditionalists opposed to acculturation—against their mixed-blood and more assimilationist brothers and sisters. Interestingly, *Sacred Revolt* actually disputes Keller's claim that the war possessed predominantly Christian roots, although Martin does characterize it in Eurocentric terms. According to Martin, whenever participants in such movements appropriated Christian notions, they tended to borrow only those that meshed well with already existing indigenous religious practices.[21] As Dave

Edmunds (Cherokee) and other Native scholars have persuasively argued, the Red Sticks were much more influenced by the teachings of Tenskwatawa, the brother of the Shawnee leader Tecumseh, than they were by Christianity. Indeed, the war began with the execution of some Red Sticks who were accused of murdering white settlers on their return journey from Prophetstown, the village founded by Tenskwatawa and Tecumseh. It was Tecumseh who taught his Muscogee allies the Dance of the Lake and demonstrated to them the potent Red Stick (the medicine bundle for which the war was named) that located his enemies and then overwhelmed them.[22] Since both the Dance of the Lake and the Red Stick resonate with traditional Muscogee beliefs about the efficacy of words and rituals, there is no need to suggest a preponderance of Christian origins, although it certainly possessed some Christian overtones. Cherokee religious historian Alan Kilpatrick notes that belief in the powerful, concretizing dimension of ritualistic language was (and is) shared by many American Indian groups.[23] More particularly, Muscogee practitioners of magical songs and formulae articulated similar beliefs about the ability of their invocations to evoke miraculous states: "By a word," a man could stand aside in the warpath and render himself invisible to enemies.[24] The adoption of Shawnee prophetic beliefs and practices thus complemented already existing Muscogee beliefs and practices.

Both Keller's misidentification of this movement as "millenarian" and her mistaken insistence upon its Christian genesis illustrate the process of citationality so crucial to the structures of sanctioned ignorance. Some have even argued that the entire colonial episteme is maintained by precisely such reiteration or circulation of certain statements and representations.[25] The most well-known example of this process is the form of othering known as "Orientalism," which, according to Edward Said, is "less a place than . . . a set of references that seems to have its origin in a quotation . . . or a citation from someone's work on the Orient, or some bit of previous imagining, or an amalgam of all these."[26] It is this process that guarantees the "factual" status of certain representations, while simultaneously concealing the conventions upon which it is based:[27] Keller quotes Martin, who in turn references the work of Arnold Van Gennep as well as Victor Turner, and future scholars will cite both in a legitimating circuit of misinformation. The end result is a serious distortion of Muscogee culture and history.

A case in point is Keller's contention that the Red Sticks were attempting to "redeem an original identity by a purifying violence." This representation occludes the fact that this sort of homogeneity is not, and never has been, a sociopolitical goal of the Muscogee (or indeed, of most American Indian peoples). On the contrary, like many southeastern tribes, they cherished the values of decentralization and individual as well as communal autonomy. Even the Red Stick War chiefs could not force men to join their military campaigns, but instead had to rely upon their rhetorical ability and moral credibility for successful recruitment. Further, the Red Sticks did not fight to redeem some original identity, but rather, to defend their families and towns against physical and cultural imperialism—even if that meant killing assimilationist members of their own communities. They assumed that "these traitors could be vanquished by the active intervention of a new kind of anticolonial warrior, a dancer guided by fresh contact with the sacred."[28] While that sacred included Christian elements, it first and foremost expressed a Muscogee reality adapted to the catastrophic colonial context of their era. If, in its most general sense, the postcolonial refers to a "*process* of disengagement from the whole colonial syndrome, which takes many forms,"[29] then despite its benign moral purpose, the sanctioned ignorance of *Apocalypse Now and Then* obstructs such a disengagement by its production of knowledge about Native peoples. We gain a fuller picture of the epistemological decolonization necessary to interrupt this process by examining the second colonialist structure mentioned by Spivak: the refusal of subject status to the oppressed.

The Cherokee Women of Fort Loudon

Colonial situations invite one to rethink the hermeneutical legacy.
—Walter D. Mignolo, *The Darker Side of the Renaissance*

In *Dislocating Cultures: Identities, Traditions, and Third-World Feminism*, Uma Narayan identifies the refusal of subject status to the colonized, that is, the failure to recognize them as creative, innovative subjects of their own history, as one of the most insidious aspects of colonialist representation.[30] Keller creates this effect by dematerializing indigenous women's colonial history, and particularly by explaining Anglo-European colonialism through yet another problematic homology: man is to woman as colonizer is to colonized. She not only accepts this comparison; she even extends it with connotations of sexual violence: man is to woman as colonizer is to colonized metamorphoses into male batterer is to female battered as European conqueror is to the conquered Taino. Keller's account begins with the "honeymoon," during which Spanish (husbands) depict "the natives" as good, loving, and generous (wives); however, she notes, "as in all abuse relationships, this honeymoon phase carries within it the seeds of its own demise . . . and could only consummate itself in rape."[31] Ultimately, the Taino become subordinated to "a kind collective male abjection of the female" and subsumed under the universalizing sign of the battered woman. By the end of the essay, the Taino have disappeared completely, and all we glimpse are the "bits of feather and beadwork" littering Keller's "post-colon-ial" map.[32] It would be hard to find a more graphic illustration of what Spivak diagnoses as a symptom of much U.S. Third Worldism: the benevolent First World appropriation and reinscription of the Third World—or here, the Fourth—as a dehumanized Other.[33]

I have elsewhere criticized the use of the man/woman = colonizer/colonized homology because it lacks any awareness of gender or colonialism as a contested and contradictory field.[34] The use of it to construct Taino identity in terms of a victimization-extinction complex not only erases their much more complex history, but obscures the fact that a Taino nation still survives in the Caribbean. Where on Keller's map is Anacaona, a woman whose story evokes a very different narrative of conquest? Anacaona was a principal leader of the Taino who, for more than a decade, evaded Spanish demands for labor and eventually summoned more than eighty of her subchiefs to her statehouse in order to conduct diplomatic negotiations with the intruders. Although the Spanish burned the statehouse and eventually hung Anacaona, her heritage is not one of tragic disappearance. Or where is Enrique, the son of a leader killed in the massacre of Anacaona's subchiefs, who waged a successful guerrilla war on the Spanish, forcing them to sign a truce guaranteeing the remaining Taino their freedom? Clearly, figures such as Anacaona and Enrique challenge the positioning of indigenous peoples as always already the beaten and raped colonial bride. Although the genocidal legacy of conquest remains, these figures leave another, equally important, witness. In the words of Cherokee poet Victoria Lena Manyarrows: "Behind me stands a long line of warriors/ women so many, and men/ fighters who defied relocation, extermination/ seeking mountains, their safety and solitude/ calling to me on the wind/ that they have given to me for breath/ *carry us forward into the future/ do not forget us/ we have saved this day for you.*"[35]

Both the original and revised version of "The Breast, the Apocalypse, and the Colonial Journey" suppress the memory and subject status of indigenous peoples because, like Keller's discussion of apocalypse, they rely upon an intertextual genealogy of sanctioned ignorance. Rather than Martin's views of apocalypse, however, Kirkpatrick Sale's *The Conquest of Paradise: Christopher Columbus and the Columbian Legacy* (1990) now serves as Keller's source. In both the original and revised essay, she states, "I rely upon his [Sale's] rereading of Columbus."[36] The dangers of such dependence are revealed early in *The Conquest of Paradise*, which consistently privileges ecological interests in constructing its narrative of colonialism. For example, Sale's "comprehensive list" of the "Columbian achievement" includes the expansion of the European subcontinent, Europe's accumulation of wealth and power, the vast, purposeful and accidental redistribution of life-forms and an unprecedented transformation of nature.[37] It lacks any mention of Native peoples or the genocide effected by conquest. This fact should not surprise one, however, since Sale's rereading of colonialism not only relegates the question of indigenous cultures to the textual and historical margins, but also implies that Europe's "record of deforestation, erosion, siltation, exhaustion, pollution, extermination, cruelty, destruction, and despoliation" far outweighs any suffering of Native South and North Americans (note that extermination and cruelty are only listed *after* the litany of ecological ills inflicted by Europeans). Of course, Sale does briefly address the victimization of indigenous women by the *conquistadors* and very late in the book acknowledges the authoritative position that many women held in their precontact societies.

Indeed, the first substantive appearance of Native women in *The Conquest of Paradise* tellingly occurs in a rape scene described by an Italian nobleman named Cuneo. In this account, Cuneo describes how, while he was aboard Columbus's ship, he captured a "very beautiful Carib woman" and "conceived desire to take pleasure." When he attempted to "execute" his desire, the woman resisted by severely lacerating him with her fingernails. After he whipped her with a rope, Cuneo said, "we came to an agreement in such manner that I can tell you that she seemed to have been brought up in a school of harlots."[38] Sale immediately laments that "it is every rape fantasy ever penned, dripping with ugly macho triumph. One longs to know the young woman's version."[39] His observation that Taino women seemed "naturally resistant" to the advances of European men is proved false by this example: while we do not have direct access to the young woman's story, her behavior suggests a much more vigorous and self-conscious resistance than that of some "natural" immunity to the pathogens of masculinist colonialism. The ecological rhetoric Sale uses here cannot help conjuring implicit analogies between Native women and prairie dogs who have developed a natural resistance to the plague, or plants that fend off enemies through biological strategies evolved over thousands of years. Such language ironically grants Cuneo a human status that it denies to his victim. In important ways, then, Sale's investment in theories of European domination—whether of nature or one Taino woman—leads him to extinguish indigenous people's subject status, and their capacity to act, improvise, innovate, and dissent within histories of their own making. When a scholar receives her vision of colonialism solely from such problematic "rereadings" (I would describe them more accurately as misrepresentations), disseminating oppressive practices and attitudes of Western scholarship becomes almost inevitable. But the question of responsible interpretation remains, especially in terms of producing knowledge about indigenous women.

Cherokee scholar Rayna Green remarks that "the written record is of course an important source of information when reconstructing any history. But for a long time it was provided by outsiders who were male and non-Indian, such as missionaries, diplomats, traders, and explorers; thus, much of it was biased. Therefore, historians have to examine the sources of such information and ask what interests and opinions the 'informer' might have had."[40] Keller's failure to ask *why* Sale privileges the European domination of nature poses an important lesson for everyone interested in the production of knowledge, since it ultimately inflicts a kind of epistemic violence on the subjects of her study. "Epistemic violence" describes one of colonialism's most insidious yet predictable effects: violating the most fundamental way that a person or people know themselves. In her essay "Subaltern Studies: Deconstructing Historiography," Spivak foregrounds a crucial component of such transgressions in her observation that, while Western intellectuals express genuine concern about the destructiveness of neocolonialism in their own nation-states, "they are not knowledgeable in the history of imperialism, in the epistemic violence that constituted/effaced a subject that was obliged to cathect (occupy in response to a desire) the space of the imperialists' self-consolidating other."[41] The feminized and infantilized natives of Keller's counter-history occupy this self-consolidating position in relation to Euro-American women when they are forced to undertake the work of sexual difference and establish sexism's primary position. This compulsory intellectual labor appropriates indigenous peoples—and particularly Native women—as merely one more sign of a universal patriarchalism.

I wonder how Keller, or Sale for that matter, might interpret the following story, which is recounted in the 1765 memoirs of Lieutenant Henry Timberlake:

> Many of the soldiers in the garrison of Fort Loudon, having Indian wives, these brought them a daily supply of provisions, though blocked up, in order to be starved to a surrender, by their own countrymen; and they persisted in this, notwithstanding the express orders of Willinawaw, who, sensible of the retardment this occasioned, threatened death to those would assist their enemy; but they laughing at his threats, boldly told him, they

would succour their husbands every day, and were sure, that, if he killed them, their relations would make his death atone for theirs. Willinawaw was too sensible of this to put his threats into execution, so that the garrison subsisted a long time on the provisions brought to them in this manner.[42]

This provocative anecdote concerns the Cherokee women who helped British soldiers withstand a siege of Fort Loudon (in present-day South Carolina) by other Cherokees. For Lieutenant Timberlake, their actions clearly exist as a shining example of how, in contrast to those Indian women who changed partners "three or four times a-year,"[43] these wives gave a "proof of fidelity not to be equaled by politer ladies, bound by all the sacred ties of marriage."[44] Clearly, his interest is in contrasting the moral behavior of those who married Englishmen with the allegedly loose behavior of Cherokee women who took Cherokee husbands and lived according to traditional Cherokee ways. A feminist critique such as Keller's might consequently conclude that these women were subordinated by their Euro-American marriages and thus chose their British husbands over the wishes of their communities as well as Cherokee leaders. Contrary to Timberlake's triumphalist version, this version of the women's actions promotes "fatal impact" historiography, or the belief that colonialism was completely effectual in its genocidal and culturecidal intent.[45]

According to ethnographer Nicholas Thomas, however, such views often exaggerate imperial power and diminish the extent to which indigenous resistance and accommodation shape colonial histories.[46] While no one should underestimate Anglo-Europe's appetite for world domination, the dream of establishing a global empire upon which the sun never sets was only partially realized. In fact, colonizers were frequently haunted by a sense of insecurity, terrified by the obscurity of the "native mentality," and overwhelmed by indigenous societies' apparent intractability in the face of government.[47] For example, Jan van der Straet's 1575 depiction of America's "discovery" stages an encounter between a fully armored Amerigo Vespucci, for whom "America" is named, and a naked, erotically inviting woman representing the "New World." A distant scene of female cannibals roasting a human leg situates itself in between Amerigo and America. According to Anne McClintock, the familiar European trope of cannibalism projects a fear of engulfment onto colonized peoples as *their* determination to devour the intruder.[48] Van der Straet's painting of colonialism's inaugural scene consequently tells the "double story" of an imperialism suspended between rape and emasculation as well as male imperial aggression and the terror of engulfment.[49] A feminist production of knowledge ignores this double story at its own peril. In terms of the Cherokee women of Fort Loudon, an interpretation viewing them as subordinated manipulates the colonial archive so that they emerge, to paraphrase Spivak, as coerced agents/instruments/witnesses for the colonialism and patriarchalism of capital.[50]

An alternative and more optimistic reading might conjecture that the construction of Fort Loudon in 1756 afforded Cherokee women a unique opportunity to continue their pattern of economic independence by selling corn and other foodstuffs to the hungry British garrison. This contact predictably led to intermarriages between Cherokee women and British men, and when war was declared in 1760, these women continued to visit the fort bearing both provisions and information.[51] Rather than a betrayal of their people—or, in Keller's terms, a collective male abjection of the female—the women's spirited resistance might signify their traditional allegiance to family and clan as well as the Cherokee principle of autonomy. These women did not perceive themselves as citizens of some abstract nation ruled by warriors, but rather, thought of themselves as the mothers of warriors, the cultivators of corn, members of clans, and the wives of men with whom they had reciprocal responsibilities.[52] In other words, the episode narrated by Timberlake suggests that they contradict not only the edicts of Willinawaw, but also any feminist construction of them as colonialism's battered brides. My interests as a woman of Cherokee descent lie strongly with this second account. Yet, I also need to examine how such a positive—some might say "nativist"—rendering smooths out a more rough-edged reality. Indeed, this interpretation begs the (in)famous question asked a decade ago by Spivak: Can the subaltern speak?

Since her controversial contention that the subaltern woman exists in a silenced space, Spivak has constructed a more nuanced, and to many a more satisfying, response to her original question. In her 1999 book, *A Critique of Postcolonial Reason*, she admits the possibility of encountering "the testimony of women's voice consciousness" despite colonialism's repressive mechanisms. Spivak formed her original query after researching the 1926 suicide of Bhubandeswari Bhaduri, who was a member of an armed group engaged in the struggle for Indian independence and who killed herself after her failure to complete a political assassination. In order to ensure that family and friends understood that her death was not due to illicit pregnancy or unrequited love, Bhaduri turned her body into a text of woman/writing by waiting until the onset of menstruation to take her own life.[53] According to Spivak, "the immediate passion of my declaration 'the subaltern cannot speak', came from the despair that, in her own family, among women, in no more than fifty years, her attempt had failed."[54] The intervening years and conversations with other critics led her to reconsider this pessimism, however.

Women can and do "speak" within the colonial archive: the testimony of women's voice consciousness is not "ideology-transcendent or 'fully' subjective, of course, but it would constitute the ingredients for producing a countersentence."[55] In terms of the Cherokee women of Fort Loudon, such a countersentence is composed with the grammar of both their subjectivity, that is, their capacity to respond innovatively and creatively to hostile situations, and their subjection: the knowledge that they brought their traditional Cherokee values and strengths to bear upon a colonialist context that had irrevocably changed Cherokee culture.

While these women certainly thought of themselves as the mothers of warriors, the cultivators of corn, members of clans, and the wives of men with whom they had reciprocal responsibilities, they also contributed to the disintegration of the Cherokee by going to live with their British husbands. Throughout Cherokee history, women have occupied a central social and spiritual place—a centrality embodied by such practices as passing clan identities down through women's lineages and Cherokee men going to live with their wives. In the case of divorce, men left the woman's home, and any children stayed with their mother and the mother's family. Thus, in the very act of asserting their autonomy as wives, the women in Timberlake's memoir also displaced and transformed the culture that had conferred such considerable status on them. Because of this, I can only claim that my more positive account "can at best mark rupture, fadeout, colonial discontinuity"[56] with fatal impact historiography. Additionally, the "Indian wives" of Fort Loudon thwart any configuration of colonialism as a coherent masculinist imposition and instead necessitate that we attend to its complexly negotiated gender relations. My turn to sources of information outside the Euro-American academy—in this case, Cherokee history and oral tradition as well as the memoirs of Timberlake—has enabled me to construct an alternate, albeit partial, history for these Cherokee women.

Maori scholar Linda Tuhiwai Smith observes that for indigenous people, coming to know the past constitutes a crucial part of the critical pedagogy of decolonization: "To hold alternative histories is to hold alternative knowledges. The pedagogical implication of this access to alternative knowledges is that they can form the basis of alternative ways of doing things. Transforming our colonized views of our own history (as written by the West), however, requires us to revisit, site by site, our history under Western eyes."[57] Both the Red Stick War and the memoirs of Lieutenant Henry Timberlake forge very important links in this critical pedagogy of decolonization. They teach us that it demands analyses constructed along multiple perspectival and interpretive axes. Walter Mignolo has described such heterogeneity as *pluritopic* (literally, multiply placed) and argued that the meaning of (post)colonialism can be explained only through the *topoi* of many different cultural, political, and interpretive sites.[58] I present the term *pluritopic* in order to pun upon it, since I would also argue for a *pluritropic*, or multiply figured, analysis of colonialism: not only the battered and raped bride, but also the independent and resourceful Cherokee women of Fort Loudon; not only the breasts of Columbus but also the breasts of one Scranton Teodorus Roy, the youngest son of a Quaker father and a reclusive poet mother, who established a small Pennsylvania community based on intelligent conversation. Jilted at love by an alluring actress, Scranton Roy "went against the radiant ways of his father" by enlisting in the United States Army. And it is with the story of Private Roy that I would like to end my essay.

The Breasts of Columbus, Re-visioned

The breast is indeed a powerful part object, permitting the violent coming-into-being of the human, on the uncertain cusp of nature and culture.

—Gayatri Chakravorty Spivak, introduction to
Mahasweta Devi's *Breast Stories*

*Milk is the beginning of a journey
that opens into other journeys.*
—Linda Hogan, *The Book of Medicines*

The opening sequences of *The Antelope Wife*, Louise Erdrich's 1998 novel, confront the reader with the harrowing scene of a killing field: a peaceful Ojibwa village attacked by a unit of the U.S. Calvary based at Fort Sibley, Minnesota. In the midst of this slaughter, Private Scranton Roy discovers that he is most disturbed by the "feral quiet" of the children and by the pleasure he feels when he bayonets an aged woman whose only weapon is the stone she plucks from the ground. As he extracts the bayonet from her body, he spies a dog running into the woods with a child cradled on its back. Private Roy chases after them not only (as the narrator tells us) in sympathy for the orphaned baby, but also to escape his own acts of violence. He comes upon the dog and child at dawn. Removing the infant from her wrappings, he bathes and then tries to feed the girl a tiny piece of rabbit. She rejects this offering and, "after a night of deprivation, her tiny face crumpled in need.

Her cries filled a vastness that nothing else could. They resounded, took over everything, and brought his heart clean to the surface."[59] Because of its importance, Roy's response warrants a full quotation:

> Scranton Roy cradled the baby, sang lewd camp tunes, then stalwart hymns, and at last remembered his own mother's lullabies. Nothing helped. It seemed, when he held her close upon his heart as women did, that the child grew angry with longing and desperately clung, rooted with its mouth, roared in frustration, until at last, moved to near insanity, Roy opened his shirt and put her to his nipple.
>
> She seized him. Inhaled him. Her suck was fierce. His whole body was astonished, most of all the inoffensive nipple he never noticed or appreciated until, in spite of its pain, it served to gain him peace. As he sat there, the child holding part of him in its mouth, he looked around just in case there should be any witness to the act which seemed to him strange as anything that had happened in this sky-filled land. Of course, there was only the dog. Contented, it lolled appreciatively near. So the evening passed and then the night. Scranton Roy was obliged to change nipples, the first one hurt so, and he fell asleep with the baby tucked beside him on his useless teat.[60]

Just as traveler's tales once regaled readers with stories of male breasts flowing with milk, the narrative of Private Roy beguiles us with a similar spectacle. Drowsy after nursing the infant, this military refugee suddenly feels a rush and a "pleasurable burning" on one side of his chest. He "fell asleep again only to wake to a huge burp from the baby, whose lips were curled back from her dark gums in bliss, whose tiny fists were unclenched in sleep for the first time, who looked, impossibly, well fed."[61] Here, healing flows from the ravages of massacre, and, while Private Roy's breasts may not exactly flow with milk, they do provide this Ojibwa baby life-giving sustenance and reassurance.

In *Apocalypse Now and Then*, Catherine Keller also deploys a transgendered mammillary trope—one that involves a "rather intimate four-breasted milking procedure" between the Holy Spirit and God the Father.[62] The early Christian Church pronounced this commingled effluence to be the substance of Christ and even celebrated the consumption of its milk as a sacramental component of the Eucharist. For Keller, this intersubjective identity of the pre-Nicene, nonorthodox Father reveals a relationalist, "eco-social" view requiring that "we recognize ourselves in relation to each other in particular and to 'reality' in general."[63] In a surprising move, however, she suggests that Harold Bloom's "anxiety of influence" model of the Western literary tradition provides a paradigm through which this nexus of "influential feminisms" might emerge.

Bloom developed his anxiety of influence paradigm to describe the fierce struggle at the heart of Euro-American literature: a battle between "strong equals, fathers and sons as mighty opposites, Laius and Oedipus at the crossroads."[64] According to Bloom, the artist inevitably experiences a profound fear that he [*sic*] is not his own creator and that the works of his predecessors will supercede his own. More particularly, the connection between succeeding literary generations assumes the relationship of father to son as defined and elaborated by Sigmund Freud. Bloom insists that every poet must struggle as a warrior in battle for his place in the canon, and that he can attain his vocation only by slaying the literary father.

Through this genealogy of anxiety, Bloom openly acknowledged the patriarchal nature of Western literary history. According to feminist critics Sandra Gilbert and Susan Gubar, he not only identified and defined the patriarchal psychosexual context of the Western literary tradition that embed literary texts, but distinguished the anxieties and achievements of female writers from those of men.[65] In other words, the value of Bloom's model lies in its *descriptive* rather than its *prescriptive* power. Its phallocentric and Eurocentric psychology renders it extremely problematic, and its use as a liberating standard has been largely discredited in the field of feminist literary criticism. As Gilbert and Gubar remark, the battle of the female artist is not against her male precursor's reading of the world, but against his reading of her: "Her revisionary struggle, therefore, often becomes a struggle for what Adrienne Rich has called 'Re-vision—the act of looking back, of seeing with fresh eyes, of entering an old text from a new critical direction . . . an act of survival.'"[66] The image of Private Scranton Roy somatically and metaphorically embodies just such an act of re-visioning—in this case, of the complicated gender relations within the texts of colonial history. *The Antelope Wife*'s presentation of Roy—a colonizer who transforms a phallic bayonet into the milk of Mother Earth and turns killing into nurturing—articulates a more intricate narrative of (post)colonialism than that evoked by the breasts of Columbus or the anxiety of influential feminisms inspired by Keller's pre-Nicene Fathers.

This re-visioned narrative manifests both a pluritopic and pluritropic political anatomy of feminism and postcolonialism: one that emanates from many different sites and assumes the (dis)guise of many different figures. It recognizes the horrors of genocide as well as Native "survivance";[67] it documents the subjugation of Native North and South Americans as well as the resistance of indigenous men and women to colonization. It foregrounds the production of knowledge rather than the intentions of any particular person and, in so doing, should give scholars pause about their often unwitting affirmation of sanctioned ignorance, their denial of subject status to the colonize, and their reading of the colonial archives. While my efforts in this particular instance do not definitively answer the many questions that remain, I hope at least to begin the journey to that feminist and postcolonial terrain which is flowing with milk and sweet with the honey of decolonization.

Notes

The epigraph opening the chapter is from *The Four Voyages of Christopher Columbus*, ed. and trans. J. M. Cohen (New York: Penguin Books, 1969).

1. For the purposes of this chapter, I am adopting Edward Said's succinct differentiation between "imperialism" and "colonialism": *imperialism* refers to the practice, theory, and attitudes of a dominant metropolitan center ruling a distant territory, while *colonialism* is the implanting of settlements on distant territory. Edward Said, *Culture and Imperialism* (New York: Viking, 1993), 9.

2. This is from an Arrernte press release, as quoted in Jane M. Jacobs, "Earth Honoring: Western Desires and Indigenous Knowledges," in *Writing Women and Space: Colonial and Postcolonial Geographies*, ed. Allison Blunt and Gillian Rose (New York: Guilford Press, 1994), 184.

3. Ibid.,186.

4. Malek Alloula, *The Colonial Harem* (Minneapolis: University of Minnesota Press, 1986), 105.

5. After her capture, Senanayak authorizes a gang rape of Draupadi in order to extract information from her. When she is ordered to come to his quarters, she comes naked, and exposing the breasts that are now torn and bleeding becomes her ultimate act of resistance. Gangor, on the other hand, loses her breasts, which were cut off after a similar gang rape by the police.

6. Gayatri Chakravorty Spivak, introduction to Mahasweta Devi, *Breast Stories*, trans. Gayatri Chakravorty Spivak (Calcutta: Seagull Press, 1998), vii.

7. Anne McClintock, *Imperial Leather: Race, Gender, and Sexuality in the Colonial Contest* (New York: Routledge, 1995), 22.

8. Ibid.

9. Catherine Keller, *Apocalypse Now and Then: A Feminist Guide to the End of the World* (Boston: Beacon, 1996), 173.

10. A focus on messianic apocalypticism in Columbus's thought is not new. Historian David Stannard (whose work Keller does not mention) addressed this issue much earlier and much more thoroughly in *American Holocaust: The Conquest of the New World* (New York: Oxford University Press, 1992).

11. Catherine Keller, "The Breast, the Apocalypse, and the Colonial Journey," *Journal of Feminist Studies in Religion* 10:1 (spring 1994): 68.

12. Ibid., 70.

13. Stannard, *American Holocaust*, 209.

14. Bill Ashcroft, Gareth Griffiths, and Helen Tiffin, *The Empire Writes Back: Theory and Practice in Post-colonial Literatures* (London: Routledge, 1989), 103.

15. Gayatri Chakravorty Spivak, *A Critique of Postcolonial Reason: Toward a History of the Vanishing Present* (Cambridge, Mass.: Harvard University Press, 1999), 167.

16. Keller, *Apocalypse Now and Then*, 260.

17. Spivak, *A Critique of Postcolonial Reason*, 164.

18. Keller, *Apocalypse Now and Then*, 198. The Red Stick War became one of the bloodiest and most costly military campaigns in U.S. history, and ended only when Andrew Jackson's troops killed more than one thousand Red Stick warriors during the (in)famous battle of Horseshoe Bend. As a result of this defeat, the Muscogee lost more than two-thirds of their land in Alabama and Florida.

19. Ibid.

20. Cherokee historian Dave Edmunds coins a more apt phrase when he characterizes movements such as the Red Sticks in terms of their "messianic nativism."

21. Joel W. Martin, *Sacred Revolt: The Muskogees' Struggle for a New World* (Boston: Beacon, 1991), 179.

22. Angie Debo, *The Road to Disappearances* (Norman: University of Oklahoma Press, 1941), 76.

23. Alan Kilpatrick, *The Night Has a Naked Soul: Witchcraft and Sorcery among the Western Cherokee* (Syracuse, N.Y.: Syracuse University Press, 1997), 27.

24. Ibid.

25. Meyda Yeğenoğlu, *Colonial Fantasies: Towards a Feminist Reading of Orientalism* (Cambridge: Cambridge University Press, 1998), 38.

26. Edward Said, *Orientalism* (New York: Viking, 1978), 177.

27. Yeğenoğlu, *Colonial Fantasies*, 38.

28. Martin, *Sacred Revolt*, 182.

29. Ania Loomba, *Colonialism/Postcolonialism* (New York: Routledge, 1998), 19. For a fuller discussion of the limits and possibilities of this term, as well as my own definition of it, see my editor's introduction to the special issue "Postcolonialism and Scriptural Reading," *Semeia* 75 (1996).

30. Uma Narayan, *Dislocating Cultures: Identities, Traditions, and Third-World Feminism* (New York: Routledge, 1997), 47.

31. Keller, "The Breast, the Apocalypse, and the Colonial Journey," 57–58.

32. Ibid., 72.

33. Spivak, *A Critique of Postcolonial Reason*, 278.

34. Laura Donaldson, *Decolonizing Feminisms: Race, Gender, and Empire-building* (Chapel Hill: University of North Carolina Press, 1992), 6.

35. Victoria Lena Manyarrows, "Confronting and Surpassing the Legacy of Columbus: A Native Woman's View," in *With-Out Discovery: A Native Response to Columbus*, ed. Ray Gonzalez (Seattle: Broken Moon Press, 1992), 167.

36. Keller, *Apocalypse Now and Then*, 154.

37. Kirkpatrick Sale, *The Conquest Of Paradise: Christopher Columbus and the Columbian Legacy* (New York: Alfred A. Knopf, 1990), 4.

38. Ibid., 140.

39. Ibid.

40. Rayna Green, *Women in American Indian Society*, ed. Frank W. Porter III (New York: Chelsea House, 1992), 16.

41. Gayatri Chakravorty Spivak, "Subaltern Studies: Deconstructing Historiography, " in *The Spivak Reader: Selected Works of Gayatri Chakravorty Spivak*, ed. Donna Landry and Gerald MacLean (New York: Routledge, 1996), 219.

42. Henry Timberlake, *Memoirs: 1756–1765*, ed. Samuel Cole Williams (Marietta, Ga.: Continental Book Company, 1948), 89–90.

43. Cherokee women were free to divorce their partners, and serial relationships were very common. When a woman and man separated, the children traditionally stayed with their mothers while the father/husband would leave and return to his own family.

44. Timberlake, *Memoirs*, 89.

45. Nancy Shoemaker, "The Rise or Fall of Iroquois Women." *Journal of Women's History* 2: 3 (winter 1991): 39–57.

46. Nicholas Thomas, *Colonialism's Culture: Anthropology, Travel and Government* (Princeton, NJ: Princeton University Press, 1994), 15.

47. Ibid., 16.

48. McClintock, *Imperial Leather*, 27.

49. Ibid., 25–26.

50. Spivak, *A Critique of Postcolonial Reason*, 246.

51. Theda Perdue, *Cherokee Women: Gender and Cultural Change, 1700–1835* (Lincoln: University of Nebraska Press, 1998), 74.

52. Ibid., 101.

53. Spivak, *A Critique of Postcolonial Reason*, 308.

54. Ibid.

55. Ibid., 287.

56. Ibid., 241.

57. Linda Tuhiwai Smith, *Decolonizing Methodologies: Research and Indigenous Peoples* (London: Zed Books, 1999), 34.

58. Mignolo, *The Darker Side of the Renaissance*, 11.

59. Louise Erdrich, *The Antelope Wife* (New York: HarperFlamingo, 1998), 6.

60. Ibid.

61. Ibid., 7.

62. Keller bases this on the following passage from the *Odes of Solomon*: "The Holy Spirit opened Her bosom, and mixed the milk of the two breasts of the Father." Catherine Keller, "Seeking and Sucking: On Relation and Essence in Feminist Theology," in *Horizons in Feminist Theology: Identity, Tradition, and Norms*, ed. Rebecca S. Chopp and Sheila Greeve Davaney (Minneapolis: Fortress Press, 1997), 54.

63. Ibid., 78.

64. Harold Bloom, *The Anxiety of Influence* (New York: Oxford University Press, 1973), 26.

65. Sandra M. Gilbert and Susan Gubar, *The Madwoman in the Attic: The Woman Writer and the Nineteenth-Century Literary Imagination* (New Haven, Conn.: Yale University Press, 1979), 48.

66. Ibid., 49.

67. The term *survivance* is used by Gerald Vizenor (Chippewa) to describe the complicated gestures of Native survival in the contact zone of contemporary American culture. See his *Manifest Manners: Postindian Warriors of Survivance* (Hanover, N.H.: University Press of New England, 1994).

2

Unbinding Our Feet

Saving Brown Women and Feminist
Religious Discourse

KWOK PUI-LAN

The mentality of the missionaries who came to
China was not prepared to meet a culture that could
rival the one they had been used to; they only looked
for the dark and the savage, such as they had looked
for and found in dark Africa.

—Sophia H. Chen, "A Non-Christian Estimate
of Missionary Activities"

Those who claim to see racism and/or imperialism
in my indictment of these atrocities [sati, footbind-
ing, and genital mutilation] can do so only by
blinding themselves to the fact that the oppression of
women knows no ethnic, national, or religious
bounds.

—Mary Daly, *Gyn/Ecology*

Sophia H. Chen, a Chinese woman teaching in one of the Chinese universities, once attended a lecture in New York given by a missionary who had returned from China. Before the missionary began the lecture, she took a piece of white chalk and put a tiny dot on the blackboard and said: "You see this tiny white spot? This is the only light of culture and one that the missionaries have brought to the ignorant Chinese women, whose educational prospect is as completely in darkness as this big blackboard."[1] Listening to such patronizing remarks, Chen, a non-Christian who came from a family of the literati whose women have been educated for generations, could not control her anger. She considered such damaging misrepresentation an insult to Chinese women, who have been poets, writers, and artists in their own right. But this kind of misinformation was widespread, as Chen noted: "Instances like this happened over and over again during my six years of study in the U.S.A., until they succeeded in strengthening the prejudice that had already existed in my mind against missionaries."[2]

Chen wrote of such hurtful experiences in 1934, when China was one of the largest and most significant mission fields. Protestant missionaries first arrived in China in 1807, and when the treaties of Tianjin (1858) and Beijing (1860) allowed missionaries to build churches and erect schools anywhere in China, mission boards on both sides of the Atlantic competed to gain a foothold in this ancient country. The establishment of local missions and churches and the deployment of missionaries were often described in military terms, modeled after Western powers' scramble for "spheres of influences" on Chinese soil. It is noteworthy, for example, that the detailed and meticulous 1922 survey of churches and missionary personnel was entitled *The Christian Occupation of China: General Survey of the Numerical Strength and Geographical Distribution of Christian Forces in China.*[3]

If military troops were deployed to serve imperialistic interests in those days, the "Christian forces" were commissioned under much nobler causes. One such cause was to save brown women from brown men, which some have called "colonialist feminism."[4] This chapter explores how saving brown women functions as a colonial ideology helping to camouflage the violence and brutality of colonialism by sugarcoating it as a form of social mission. Popularized by colonial and missionary literature, the notion of saving brown women becomes deep-seated in white women's consciousness and resurfaces in feminist religious discourse. Using *Gyn/Ecology: The Metaethics of Radical Feminism* by Mary Daly as an example, I demonstrate how colonialist representations are reinscribed in her text, though such a problem is by no means unique to her work alone. Daly's book provides examples of some epistemological assumptions with which other Western feminists operate either consciously or unconsciously.

Saving Brown Women

The conversion of "heathens" to Christianity and the spread of Western civilization and values have been considered "the white men's burden." Gayatri Chakravorty Spivak, a leading feminist literary and cultural critic, points out that such a burden has a gender dimension. With specific reference to her Indian context, Spivak formulates the masculine-imperialist ideological formation as "white men saving brown women from brown men."[5] Similar to Freud's using women as a scapegoat in his rewriting of incest and sexual abuse as "the daughter's seduction," colonial discourse has legitimized the violent subjugation of the Other, as if such action was called for and demanded by brown women's situation. Spivak does not collapse colonial conquest with domestic abuse, but she recognizes similar mechanisms at work in Freud's psychological discourse and in colonial discourse: the denial of guilt, scapegoating, the finding of excuses, and projection onto the Other. Thus she argues: "The masculine-imperialist ideological formation that shaped that desire into 'the daughter's seduction' is part of the same formation that constructs the monolithic 'third-world women.'"[6]

Under the pretext of saving brown women, colonial desire and imperialistic advances have been masked and collectively reconstituted in a blatant reversal as "social mission." The perceived backwardness, illiteracy, and promiscuity of native women were contrasted with the Victorian ideals of womanhood, such as education, hygiene, and sexual restraint. The "barbaric" practices of footbinding, polygamy, *sati*, and veiled women were seen as further symptoms of the inferiority of native cultures, and as calls for colonial or missionary intervention. One frequently cited example of the benevolent acts of the British Empire was the abolition in 1829 of *sati*, the practice of burning widows alive upon their husbands' funeral pyres. Spivak comments on that historical incident, "The abolition of this rite by the British has been generally understood as a case of 'White men saving brown women from brown men.' White women—from the nineteenth-century British Missionary Registers to Mary Daly—have not produced an alternative understanding."[7] As I wrote this chapter in early 1999, the joint forces from NATO and the United States were bombing Kosovo to save ethnic Albanians from persecution by the Serbs. Politicians appealed to popular support by referring time and again to the systematic raping of Albanian women when they were living in Kosovo as well as when they were forced to flee the country. Whether it is right or wrong to bomb Kosovo is a seperate question; this recent event shows the luring power of the script "white men saving brown (Other) women from brown (Other) men."

The focus on the goodwill and action of white men completely mystifies the complex political configurations and cultural politics of situations imbued by a power imbalance shaped by race, class, and gender. In the case of *sati*, Lata Mani reminds us that the intense debate on the issue took place from 1780 to 1833, a period when the British gradually expanded their control from their foothold in Bengal to much of the Indian subcontinent. Her careful analysis shows that the colonial intervention in *sati* was not based on some kind of Christian benevolence horrified by a practice so cruel to women. Instead, the official debate on *sati* during that time focused on two points. First, it revolved around the political feasibility of carrying out such a law in the face of popular opposition. Second, the officials went to great lengths to show that the abolition of *sati* was not an imposition of foreign values, but consonant with the scriptural tradition of the Hindu religion. Through an Orientalist study of scriptures, a Hindu past was reconstituted as a lost ideal, which contrasted sharply with the present degeneration of India. At the same time, the British were shown to have a knowledge of scripture superior to that of the Indians and could better interpret the Indian past. The abolition of *sati* was not aimed to save Indian women from suffering, as Mani observes:

> Constituting the problem of *sati* primarily as a matter of scriptural tradition contributed greatly to the marginalization of widows, whose interests and suffering were, as will become evident, remarkably absent from these proceedings, calling into question its characterization as a debate on the status of indigenous women.[8]

If the colonial script of saving brown women from brown men masks the motives of white men, it also glosses over the complex and ambiguous relationship between brown and white men. As the attempt to abolish *sati* clearly shows, the British were careful not to provoke Indian men to such an extent that colonial rule would be undermined. The relationship of the colonizers and the colonized was not always confrontational, because the dominant had to pacify and appease the subjugated to assure collaboration and submission. In many instances, the British tolerated indigenous religious and cultural practices that were deeply patriarchal, such as dowry, polygamy, and male inheritance, to avoid social unrest and the stirring up of anticolonial sentiment. As a result, the colonial process further reinforced patriarchal structures and male dominance in the indigenous culture.

Another problem of such a masculinist script is that it renders completely invisible the roles played by white women in the colonial era. White women who settled in the colonies were discriminated against because of their gender, but benefited from class and racial privileges and were protected by white institutions. Such contradictory subject positions of white women disrupt the simple homology of man is to woman as colonizer is to colonized, just as the metaphoric usage of women as "slaves" has been challenged as overlooking the actual material conditions of life under slavery. Laura Donaldson criticizes "women=colonized" because of its "imperialist cross-referencing" and its denial of the material realities of colonialism and of women. She writes: "The man=colonizer, woman=colonized metaphor lacks any awareness of gender—or colonialism, for that matter—as a contested field, an overdetermined sociopolitical grid whose identity points are contradictory."[9]

The contradictory positions of white women in colonial communities have been widely recognized by scholars engaged in studies of white settlements in colonial settings. With the arrival of large numbers of white women, there arose the need for their protection and a clear demarcation of racial boundaries. The white women supposedly needed more bourgeois amenities and native helpers to release them from the burden of household chores. As Ann Laura Stoler has said, "White women needed to be maintained at elevated standards of living, in insulated social spaces cushioned with the cultural artifacts of 'being European.'"[10] On the one hand, they were charged to reproduce Western domesticity in a strange land and to be guardians of Western morality and religious piety and to pass these on to the young. On the other hand, they were described in several studies as clinging more to their class and racial privileges, and displaying more racial intolerance than the white men did. Their abuse of the servants and their jealousy of sexual liaisons of white men with native women widened the racial gulf and created rifts and tension with the natives, as well as divisions among the whites themselves. The racist behaviors of white women and the social cleavages they created have been interpreted by some as contributing to the difficulties and eventual breakdown of colonial rule.[11]

Whether white women are considered to have bolstered the colonial regime through maintaining European cultural standards or to have contributed to its demise because of their racism, these studies unequivocally demystify the essentialist notion that women, by nature, are gentler, more loving, and more compassionate than men. Caught in a highly politically charged situation structured by race and class, over which they often had not much control, white women were shown to be as racist, if not more so, as white men. White women were not shown to be natural allies of brown women, nor did their sameness of gender help the two groups to bond easily. White women's power was dependent on the white men's, and they constantly feared that brown women would usurp their position. Because of insecurity and the need to protect their identity, it was to their advantage not to stress commonality because of gender, but to exaggerate racial and class distinctions. Moreover, gender is not fixed, but constructed; the different constructions of gender in the West and in indigenous cultures contributed to misunderstanding and ill feelings between white and brown women.

But the most problematic aspect of the masculine-imperialist ideology concerns the monolithic and biased construction of brown women. The script "saving brown women from brown men" simultaneously constructs brown women as victims of male oppression and objects of compassion by Westerners. As Sophia Chen has observed, such construction homogenizes women in the Third World, suppressing their differences according to family background, region, ethnicity, class, and religion. Furthermore, they were to be saved from patriarchal oppression by brown men, without any mention of their suffering under imperialism. Brown women constructed as pitiful victims played into the superiority complex of Western audiences, without challenging their complicity in colonialism. Stereotypical images of brown women as ignorant, filthy, and poor flooded missionary literature because of their appeal to the sensibilities of middle-class Christians, who contributed generously to support "women's work" by missionaries in foreign lands. Missionary religious journals, memoirs, and travel writings, reaching to grassroots women sitting in the pews, were important sources of information about Third World women at the turn of the nineteenth century. The condescending attitude toward women of other parts of the world and the missionary impulse to save them remains deeply lodged in Western women's minds even to the present.

As passive victims, brown women were not allowed to speak. For Spivak, the female subaltern, as the silent/silenced bearer of the burdens of racism, sexism, classism, and imperialism for thousands of years, cannot speak for herself: "Between patriarchy and imperialism, subject-constitution and object-formation, the figure of the woman disappears, not into a pristine nothingness, but into a violent shuttling which is the displaced figuration of the 'third-world woman' caught between tradition and modernization."[12] The subaltern woman has been written, represented, argued about, and even legislated for, but she is allowed no discursive position from which to speak. By speech, Spivak has in mind access to symbolic and political power. If the subaltern can speak, she says in an interview, "the subaltern is not a subaltern anymore."[13]

Spivak's pessimistic conclusion has been subjected to criticism because she seems to cast the subaltern woman forever as a silent object, with no possibility of escaping from the totalizing discourse of Western and patriarchal domination. Critiquing her elitist understanding of "speech," Benita Parry, for example, argues that the woman has spoken, though in ways that the academy and postcolonial theorists may not understand.

> Since the native woman is constructed within multiple social relationships
> and positioned as the product of different class, caste, and cultural specifici-
> ties, it should be possible to locate traces and testimony of women's voices
> on those sites where women inscribed themselves as healers, ascetics, singers
> of sacred songs, artisans and artists, and by this to modify Spivak's model of
> the silent subaltern.[14]

In response to mounting criticism, Spivak has somewhat revised her position, saying that the important point is not whether the subaltern can speak, but whether she can be heard, and under what conditions.[15]

In the last three decades, there has risen in the U.S. academy a proliferation of "minority discourse," which takes as its aim precisely to articulate and theorize the voices of the subjugated: colonized Other, racial minority, women, and gays and lesbians. Challenging universalist humanism in the West for its tendency to negate differences and for its false inclusion, minority discourse emphasizes culture as a site of struggle for survival. According to Abdul R. JanMohamed and David Lloyd, one of the tasks of minority discourse is the recovery and mediation of cultural practices that continue to be subjected to "institutional forgetting," which is a form of control of memory and history. The other is to create an alternative space to evaluate the contributions of cultural expressions of "minorities," which often entails scrutinizing the critical tools and methods, as well as epistemology, aesthetics, and politics learned from the dominant culture.[16]

With the mushrooming of minority discourses and the resurrection of suppressed histories and knowledge, the gradual process of the displacement of the West as the universal "center" has begun. At the same time, the cultural differences among those who claim to be the Other are increasingly recognized. This acknowledgment changes both the conceptualization of the Other as well as the Other's relationship to Western hegemony. Rey Chow has argued that "it has become clear that 'otherness' as the site of oppression, alternative subject formation, and alternative value, is hardly a unified essence."[17] While oppositional discourses in the past have had a tendency to valorize or even essentialize the repressed characteristics of dominant culture, such as blackness and femaleness, current scholarship has moved toward investigating diversity among the subjugated.

Mary Daly's *Gyn/Ecology*

Gyn/Ecology was written at a critical juncture of Daly's career, after she had published two books exposing sexism and the church and condemning the irredeemably androcentric symbolisms of Christianity.[18] In *Gyn/Ecology*, she looked outside her Western context to find out how patriarchy enacted itself as a global phenomenon. She discussed Indian *sati*, Chinese footbinding, African genital mutilation, European witchburning, and American gynecology and psychotherapy as examples of sadocratic rituals done to women's bodies and minds. Audre Lorde has commented on the chapter on Africa, and Uma Narayan, the chapter on India.[19] I will focus on the chapter on Chinese footbinding to show how "saving brown women" resurfaces in Daly's religious discourse. The choice of Daly's text is not to "attack" her or trash her work. Among the foundational figures in feminist theology, Daly stands alone in her early attempt to study women in other cultures and in her investigation of patriarchy from a cross-cultural perspective. Her text raises significant issues for subsequent feminist debates and highlights the ambiguities of the intersection between white feminist religious discourse and postcolonial criticism.

Daly begins her global investigation of atrocities done to women by discussing *sati*, footbinding, and genital mutilation. Her representation of these foreign practices is troubling, as Audre Lorde has pointed out: "Then I came to the first three chapters of your Second Passage, and it was obvious that you were dealing with noneuropean women, but only as victims and preyers-upon each other. I began to feel my history and my mythic background distorted by the absence of any images of my foremothers in power."[20] Daly's inablity to see Third World women other than as victims is not a simple oversight, because such images are deeply rooted in past colonial history and colonialist representations, as I have discussed above. Without a serious challenge of the colonial mind-set and its production of the Other, Daly and other Western feminists may work with the assumptions of the same epistemological framework without even being conscious of it.

Daly's chapter on footbinding begins by observing: "The Chinese ritual of footbinding was a thousand-year-long horror show in which women were grotesquely crippled from very early childhood. . . . All of the components of the Sado-Ritual Syndrome are illustrated in this atrocity" (135–36). The practice immobilized women, she continues, and made them dependent on men for their livelihood and for their knowledge of the outside world. The three-inch "lotus-hooks," a symbol of good upbringing and feminine virtue, were to make the woman more desirable and marriageable. Daly finds it appalling that the tiny mutilated feet were supposed to arouse the sexual desire of men and to satisfy their erotic fantasy. Moreover, footbinding alienated women from one another, she maintains, as mothers and close female relatives carried out the torture, branding upon the little girl's mind, "Never trust a woman."

Daly is not the first Westerner to critique the custom of footbinding. More than a century ago, some Protestant missionaries in China condemned footbinding as a grotesque practice that is detrimental to women's health and inflicts unnecessary pain. J. Dudgeon, a Christian medical doctor in Beijing, wrote in 1869: "As it originated, in a desire, and is probably partly maintained or at least found, to create and excite lustful and licentious feelings."[21] John Kerr, of Canton Hospital, went further to say: "The custom is established and fostered by pride and lust, both of which are condemned by our holy religion." He indicted the practice as a "sin against God, and a sin against man" that Christians should condemn.[22] The missionaries' condemnation of footbinding was part of the colonial discourse, which justified foreign aggression and reinforced their cultural superiority. Daly's indictment of footbinding is different from that of the nineteenth-century missionaries for she is not oblivious to patriarchal control in her culture. Yet, she does not take care to distinguish her position from the terms and representations of colonialist discourse, nor does she seem to be aware of the danger of repeating the kind of "colonialist feminism" set in place by such a political and discursive background.[23] Her radical feminist stance does not immunize her from sharing some problematic viewpoints common in a colonialist stance.

For example, she presents a picture of China as unchanging and timeless, and the practice of footbinding as remaining quite the same for one thousand years. She notes that footbinding began between the Tang and Song dynasties, and became widespread in the twelfth century (139). She does not specify that the practice gained popularity when Neo-Confucian doctrines were institutionalized during the reconstruction of gender in the Song dynasty. While footbinding has been condemned by Westerners as barbaric, it was, ironically, a means to accentuate the contrast between genteel Chinese and their uncouth rivals in the North.[24] Throughout the long millennium, people's attitudes toward footbinding changed, and the Manchu government even issued an unsuccessful fiat to ban it in 1662. But as one reads Daly's chapter, one would have been led to believe that footbinding was an ancient custom that remained unchanged over hundreds of years. Similar to her representation of *sati*, her discussion of footbinding replicates "a 'colonialist stance' because it reproduces a Western tendency to portray Third-World contexts as dominated by the grip of 'traditional practices' that insulate these contexts from the effects of historical change."[25] Colonialist representation assumes that while Western history progressed over time, Third World societies either remained woefully unchanged or caught in dynastic cycles, until forced to change by the West.[26]

Daly also fails to provide information about the variance of the practice according to region, class, and ethnicity, and thus portrays a China that is abstract and monolithic. She makes general statements that the practice spread from the upper to the lower class (139), but offers very few other details, especially on how the practice affected women's health and their reproductive function, women's labor and economic involvement, and domestic and public roles. The practice was more prevalent in the central and northern part of China and less popular in the south coastal provinces of Guangdong and Fujian, where wet rice was grown. Footbinding became a status symbol for women of the upper and middle classes, but working-class women who dreamed of upward mobility through marriage also had their feet bound. While footbinding was common among Han Chinese women, Mongolian, Manchu, and Kejia women had natural feet. Contrary to Daly's impression that the bound feet kept women at home, survival and economic reasons compelled many to work in the field, helping out with lighter farm work. Women also contributed to productive labor by sewing, spinning, embroidering, and weaving at home.[27] The information on the variance of the practices among different groups of Chinese women is important not to lessen the horror of footbinding, but to counteract colonialist impressions of a monolithic China and to provide necessary knowledge for understanding Chinese women's social history.

Not being a specialist in Chinese history, Daly obtains her knowledge about footbinding through the works of Western men, and inadvertently reinscribes their ethnocentric and even colonialist attitudes. Daly's chapter relies heavily on the "standard" works of Howard Levy and Robert Van Gulik[28] and, amazingly, cites no single Chinese author, man or woman. Although she criticizes these Western authors for their patriarchal biases, she leaves their colonialist positions intact. For example, Daly criticizes Levy's deceptive description of footbinding as a "curious erotic custom" for "it fails to convey the fact that sexual desire is aroused precisely by mutilation" (145). But she does not question Levy's ethnocentrism in his exoticizing the curious custom and his constant comparison of Chinese culture with Western culture in a derogatory manner. While she accuses Van Gulik of minimizing the effects of footbinding on women's health (148), she does not ask why Van Gulik would be interested in studying Chinese erotic picture albums and bedchamber manuals in the first place.[29] Commenting on Van Gulik's work, historian Charlotte Furth writes: "In light of late twentieth-century western feminist standards, it is easy to recognize Van Gulik's androcentrism, and to see that the reader is being offered a familiar Orientalist fantasy of an exotic, eroticized 'other' women of the East."[30] Although in 1978 Daly might not have been able to identify the Orientalist tendency, as the debate on Orientalism had barely begun, her failure to question the colonialist stances of the authors leads her to blindly follow their interpretive framework: footbinding represents a curious erotic desire of Chinese men. Thus, Chinese women remain invisible in her study because they are the passive objects of male desire. As objects of male erotic fantasy, Chinese women are eclipsed in Daly's elucidation of white men's colonialist discourse on the desire of brown men.

Since Daly constructs Chinese women as victims, she allows no Chinese women to speak. In her chapter, Chinese women are discussed by Western men, Chinese men, and Western women, but they cannot speak for themselves. That Daly suppresses the voices of Chinese women knowingly is clear, because Levy's book has a whole chapter on Chinese women and men opposing the custom.[31] Chinese women did not remain silent over the atrocities committed against them and spoke out when circumstances permitted them. The anti-footbinding movement represented the first organized effort of Chinese women to challenge the patriarchal system. In 1874, some sixty Chinese women gathered in a Christian church in Xiamen to form an anti-footbinding society. They condemned the practice that crippled women and caused suffering. Early support came from women missionaries and the missionary schools, which urged mothers not to bind their daughters' feet. During the late nineteenth century, many Chinese women joined the Natural Feet Society, unbinding their own feet and persuading others to do so.[32] The first Chinese female medical doctors, Shi Meiyu and Kang Cheng, advocated natural feet through writings, educational campaigns, and medical practices. The radical revolutionary martyr Qiu Jin had natural feet and organized women into military bands to topple the Manchu regime. Contemporary Chinese women remember footbinding as a symbol of women's subordination, and unbinding the feet symbolizes the liberation of women's bodies and minds. Because Daly does not cite Chinese voices against footbinding, the chapter seems to suggest that only she and Andrea Dworkin are sufficiently enraged to attack such a horrendous practice. The erasure of Chinese women's agency in their long struggle for freedom is troubling, as Narayan observes:

> Third-world feminists would find the implicit suggestion that only West-
> erners are capable of naming and challenging patriarchal atrocities commit-
> ted against Third-World women to be a postcolonial replication, however
> unintentional, of the "missionary position" of colonial discourses, including
> that of "imperial feminism."[33]

If the colonial script has been "white men saving brown women from brown men," then Daly has only changed the gender of the agent, rendering a Western feminist script of "white women saving brown women from brown men." Brown women are still considered bound objects, waiting to be set free. Daly's failure to articulate the roles played by Chinese, Indian, and African women in subverting and challenging patriarchy is especially prob-lematic because later in her book, she urges women to be Active Voicing agents, speaking for themselves to confront sadocracy (340). The book gives the impression that women around the world are unable to remember or speak until summoned by Daly to do so. It is Daly who enables them to name their oppression and recall their suffering. Such a condescending attitude bespeaks the unequal power of women both in terms of sociopolitical status and knowledge production.

In Daly's museum of horror, Indian, Chinese, and African women are silent objects on display. Their burned, bound, and mutilated bodies can be seen, but their screams, protests, and laments cannot be heard. There has been a long history of "exotic" displays in the West, from "cannibals" at world exhibitions, "uncivilized" Africans in Tarzan films, to "authentic" Third World arts in museums. This history of displaying "primitive" people in "civ-ilized" places, as James Clifford indicates, "provides a context of enduring power imbalance within and against which the contact work of travel, exhibi-tion, and interpretation occurs."[34] As a result of such asymmetry of power, these "exotic" people or artifacts become cultural spectacles, consigned to or coerced into performing identities highly scripted, usually not of their choos-ing. As we can see in Daly's display, Indian women become immolated sub-jects loyal to their husbands, Chinese women become eroticized subjects of male fantasies, and African women become genitally mutilated subjects.

The viewers Daly has in mind are undoubtedly white people living in met-ropolitan centers, who frequent places like the American Museum of Natural History or the Museum of Modern Art.[35] The way Daly orients her Western viewers is noteworthy, showing how she establishes sameness and difference for the different exhibits. At the first stop in India she says although Western society does not customarily burn its widows alive, *sati* has similarity with Western rituals (114–15). At the end of the exhibit on footbinding, she provides the link that the familiar story of Cinderella might have its origin in China, since it is about a girl with tiny feet, the symbol of beauty (152). To prepare the viewers psychologically for African genital mutilation, she reminds them that clitoridectomies and other mutilations have been inflicted by American gynecologists (155). Thus, what seems strange becomes cozily familiar in her downplay of cultural specificities in order to advance a transhistorical account of patriarchy.

Yet, the way the exhibits are staged and the sequence of Daly's tour point to differences between foreign and domestic practices. Daly discusses customs in "foreign" places—India, China, and Africa—before she analyzes the practices in Europe and America. From a postcolonial perspective, the sequence suggests either a narrative of affinity: "they," versus "we," or a narrative of temporality: "ancient" culture versus "modern" culture. These two narratives mutually reinforce one another to marginalize the Other through a subtle valorization of the "modernized we." Whereas *sati*, footbinding, and genital mutilation are portrayed as ancient traditions of timeless and changeless cultures, witchburning in Europe and American gynecology are newer variants, occurring at particular moments of Western history because of changing social and historical circumstances detailed in her book. Her choices of modern medicine and psychotherapy to represent "American" sado-ritual are also telling because other atrocities, such as forced sterilization of Native and black women, could have been considered.

Daly is certainly not the first or only scholar to display women from other parts of the world and to inscribe her *theories* on their muted bodies. The cultural practices of *sati*, footbinding, and genital mutilation have often functioned as screens for Westerners to display their fantasies and for scholars to project their theories. Let me use again the example of footbinding for illustration. About fifty years before Daly, Freud in his 1927 essay on "Fetishism" observed that footbinding was a symbol of the "castration of women."[36] Julia Kristeva further developed Freud's argument around the same time when Daly was writing on footbinding. In *About Chinese Women*, Kristeva used footbinding to show that the Chinese way of organizing sexual difference is distinct from that of the West. In Western society, it is circumcision, inscribed on a man's body, which is used to signify social and symbolic prohibition. In China, the analogue is footbinding, inscribed on the bodies of women, who derive suffering and masochistic pleasure from it, in exchange for the superior and symbolic knowledge of sexual difference.[37] Chinese cultural critic Rey Chow has criticized Kristeva's utopian and convoluted understanding: "Reading *with* her, we would think that the Chinese practice of maiming women's bodies is Chinese society's recognition, rather than denial, of woman's fundamental claim to social power."[38] Unlike Kristeva, Daly considers footbinding as exemplifying all the characteristics of sado-rituals. But as one journeys with Daly, one wonders if she is more concerned with proving her transcultural theory of patriarchy than with the real suffering of Chinese women.

Like a curious curator collecting and displaying diverse cultural specimens, Daly needs to find a plausible explanation for the global phenomenon of patriarchy, manifested in these cross-cultural sado-rituals. Following Durkheim and Nietzsche, Daly suggests that rituals reenact religious myths and create a collective memory (109–10). For her, the horrifying and routinized sado-rituals are a means to reenact the dismemberment of the Goddess (110–11), whose replacement by the patriarchal God of Christianity contributes to the global subordination of women. Without checking whether such a bold claim fits with Indian, Chinese, and African cultures, she superimposes her post-Christian interpretation of religious history onto others. Within such a framework, the patriarchal trinitarian Christian God displaced the goddesses of Rome, Greece, Egypt, and Asia Minor, while adopting their symbolisms (74–83). This theory gains currency through Gerder Lerner's book *The Creation of Patriarchy*, though Lerner admits that her data are drawn from one region and her hypothesis is offered for Western civilization.[39] Such qualifications are necessary because the cultures of India, China, and many societies in Africa have not been shaped historically by the Christian myth and need no post-Christian deconstruction. Moreover, Daly will be surprised to know that goddesses are much alive in these people's myths and memory. Ironically, it is not the murder of the Goddess, but the veneration of her in some cases, which is deployed to justify the marginalization of women in these societies. As we can see, the post-Christian myth, when universalized, can be as dangerous as Christian imperialism in terms of its totalizing effect.

The Dream of a Common Tapestry

In the last section of *Gyn/Ecology*, Daly evokes the powerful image of a cosmic tapestry to be spun and woven by self-identified women of all races, nations, and colors (385–424). The image remains strong in *Pure Lust*, though by this time she has become more aware of the divisions among women:

> For it is clear that Lusty women are profoundly different from each other. Not only are there ethnic, national, class and racial differences that shape our perspectives, but there are also individual and cross-cultural differences

of temperament, virtue, talent, taste, and of conditions within which these can or cannot find expression. There is, then, an extremely rich, complex Diversity among women and within each individual. But there is also above, beyond, beneath all this a Cosmic Commonality, a tapestry of connectedness which women as Websters/Fates are constantly weaving. The weaving of this tapestry is the Realizing of a dream, which Adrienne Rich has Named "The Dream of a Common Language."[40]

Daly's dreams of a cosmic tapestry and cosmic commonality of women have been criticized by feminist theorists, who label her an essentialist for assuming a common essence of women and for glossing over differences. She and Adrienne Rich have been labeled as influential proponents of cultural feminism, which is defined by Linda Alcoff as "the ideology of a female nature or female essence reappropriated by feminists themselves in an effort to revalidate undervalued female attributes."[41] For cultural feminists, the enemy of women is masculinity itself, and they seek to create a women's culture free from masculinist values. It is ironic that Daly would be called a *cultural* feminist since she neither pays attention to cultural specificity nor engages theorists in cultural analysis.

The problem of universalizing and overlooking difference is not only found in Daly, but is also pervasive in the early works of Western feminist theorists, cutting across diverse theoretical frameworks. Meyda Yeğenoğlu argues that this is not a careless oversight or an example of theoretical naiveté, but rather demonstrates the contradictions in Western women's construction of an imperial subject for themselves. She points out that universalism has close liaisons with masculinism, and women can enter this privileged space only by assuming a male position and by denying their difference. Western women's claim of universalism replicates the masculinist stance they criticize and dangerously colludes with colonialism:

> Although feminist theory has successfully revealed the phallocentric bind of the claims for neutrality and universality, it has nevertheless, by privileging sexual difference to other forms of difference, itself remained blind to the imperialist and ethnocentric bind of such a gesture. The relegation of the pretensions of universality only in the domain of sexual difference carries the risk of phallocentric gesture in representations of cultural difference and the ethnocentric bind of phallocentrism. . . . The apparently benign appeals to a common good for universal womanhood and the presumption that all women are being spoken for in the name of global sisterhood are not free from colonial and masculinist fantasies of attaining a sovereign subject status.[42]

The problem is compounded when such global sisterhood is couched in the ultimacy of religious language and in apocalyptic terms. In *Apocalypse Now and Then*, Catherine Keller offers an eschatological reading of Daly's Cosmic Commonality and the Second Coming of Women. Keller delineates a tradition of appropriating the language of apocalypse among American feminists, from women who gathered in Seneca Falls in 1848 to the present moment. Keller invites us to attend to the complex rhetorical devices and the rich metaphorical field embedded in Daly's text, arguing that Daly's satire, parody, and prophecy are fine examples of the apocalyptic genre. In both *Beyond God the Father* and *Gyn/Ecology*, she notices that metaphors such as the end of phallic morality, feminists as Antichrist, new time/space, and the Second Coming of Women abound. On Daly's eschatological hope, Keller writes:

> Yet the language of an inevitable and imminent revolution of history, in which the demonic forces are defeated and the good enshrined in radiant Presence, poses the only alternative to doom. Daly stands here within the heritage of apocalypse, summoning the force of Second Coming and Final Judgment to foreclose, if not on history, then certainly on "this age."[43]

Daly's apocalyptic language projects a powerful vision of the Armageddon showdown and the final victory of women over the tyranny of patriarchy. But the dream of an abstract new heaven and earth ruled by the Global Sisterhood may also camouflage actual differences in the present. It also fails to pinpoint the important fact that not all women are included, but only those enlightened Hags and Crones who are conscientized and share Daly's vision and travel along in her outerworld journey to this new time/space.

While Keller reads Daly in a more sympathetic and playful way, I would like to offer a postcolonial reading of Daly's dream for commonality and interconnection, based not on essential female nature or an apocalyptic hope, but on the concrete colonial history that has shaped much of our "common" memory. One of the most important insights of postcolonial criticism is that the colonizers and the colonized mutually inscribe each other. Postcolonial critic Stuart Hall writes: "One of the principal values of the term 'postcolonial' has been to direct our attention to the many ways in which colonisation was never simply external to the societies of the imperial metropolis. It was always inscribed deeply within them—as it became indelibly inscribed in the cultures of the colonised."[44]

We are used to thinking of colonization as a one-way process, with the powerful dominating the powerless at will. Instead, Hall argues that colonization must be seen as a transnational and transcultural "global" process, which challenges a simple binary construction of they/we, there/here, then/now, and home/abroad. Five hundred years of colonial history have linked women in the imperial metropolis and the colonies in numerous ways, from fashion to cooking curry, from manufacturing myths of one another to appropriating other's symbols.

A postcolonial reading of *Gyn/Ecology* would suggest that women are linked not only by patriarchy, but also colonialism. From the fifteenth to the seventeenth century, the "discovery" of the Americas, the sailing around the Cape, the increased encounter with native peoples, and early mercantilism in Europe created transformation and immense anxiety in European society. Witchburning might be not only the "purification of the Body of Christ" as Daly suggests (186), but also the sanitization of a nascent colonial order. Later in the nineteenth century, the medicalization of European and American white women's bodies was carried out in the name of protection of children and the future of the bourgeois order, while *sati* was outlawed by the British, and footbinding and genital mutilation were condemned to reinforce racial superiority. Freud's phallocentric psychology not only showed his contempt for women (266–68), but also reinforced the necessity for male sexual control and adjustment to protect the "bourgeois body" of the Victorian Empire. Embedded in the rhetoric of moral superiority of the West, Freud's post-Oedipal bourgeois men were seen as better able to control their libido than the "infantile" natives, who still indulged in gratifying themselves with such "primitive" practices as *sati*, footbinding, and genital mutilation. The natives, therefore, were considered morally unfit and culturally unprepared for ruling themselves and had to be subdued.

Such an interpretation aims to rewrite Daly's script, opening new space to discuss the construction of gender as a device to justify racism, genocide, and colonization. It connects European witchburning and American medicine and psychotherapy with *sati*, footbinding, and genital mutilation in a new way. It shows that the same colonial ideology undergirds both the control of white women's bodies and sexuality at home and the seemingly contradictory practice of "saving brown women" abroad. A postcolonial interpretation does not name all men as the enemy in an essentialist manner, but acknowledges that some men and women have more power than others. It simultaneously challenges colonial discourse on *sati*, footbinding, and genital mutilation, as well as patriarchal constructions that reinforce gender hierarchy. Such postcolonial rewriting is one of many learning devices to glean new insights from our "common" history. And there are many possible rewritings.

As the global market is more integrated and the survival of the destitute as well as refugees becomes a major issue for the twenty-first century, it is strategic that women acknowledge and celebrate their differences without losing the hope for working together. To create a common future, women of color and Third World women must not essentialize the qualities repressed by the dominant culture (black, Hispanic, or Asian). To participate in weaving the common tapestry, European and Euro-American women must first decolonize their minds and save themselves from the state of unknowing. Like the unbinding of our feet, this is indeed a long, long process.

Notes

The epigraph from Sophia H. Chen is taken from *Chinese Recorder* 65 (1934): 114. Page references to Mary Daly's *Gyn/Ecology: The Metaethics of Radical Feminism* are given in parentheses in the text.

1. Chen, "A Non-Christian Estimate," 111.

2. Ibid., 112.

3. M. T. Stauffer, ed., *The Christian Occupation of China: General Survey of the Numerical Strength and Geographical Distribution of the Christian Forces in China, 1918–1921* (Shanghai: China Continuation Committee, 1922).

4. Leela Gandhi refers to this as "the colonialist deployment of 'feminist criteria' to bolster the appeal of the 'civilising mission.'" See her *Postcolonial Theory: A Critical Introduction* (New York: Columbia University Press, 1998), 83. See also Ania Loomba, *Colonialism/Postcolonialism* (New York: Routledge, 1998), 171–72.

5. Gayatri Chakravorty Spivak, "Can the Subaltern Speak?" in *Marxism and the Interpretation of Culture*, ed. Cary Nelson and Lawrence Grossberg (Urbana: University of Illinois Press, 1988), 296–97.

6. Ibid., 296.

7. Ibid., 297. The Missionary Register was published by the Church Missionary Society based in London, and Daly discussed the abolition of *sati* in *Gyn/Ecology*, 114.

8. Lata Mani, *Contentious Traditions: The Debate on Sati in Colonial India* (Berkeley: University of California Press, 1998), 15.

9. Laura E. Donaldson, *Decolonizing Feminisms: Race, Gender, and Empire-Building* (Chapel Hill: University of North Carolina Press, 1992), 6.

10. Ann Laura Stoler, "Carnal Knowledge and Imperial Power: Gender, Race, and Morality in Colonial Asia," in *Gender at the Crossroads of Knowledge: Anthropology in the Postmodern Era*, ed. Micaela di Leonardo (Berkeley: University of California Press, 1991), 65.

11. Ibid., 64–67.

12. Spivak, "Can the Subaltern Speak?" 305.

13. Gayatri Chakravorty Spivak, "The New Historicism: Political Commitment and the Postmodern Critic," in *Post-Colonial Critics: Interviews, Strategies, Dialogues*, ed. Sarah Harasym (London: Routledge, 1990), 158.

14. Benita Parry, "Problems in Current Theories of Colonial Discourse," *Oxford Literary Review* 9:1–2 (1987): 35.

15. Spivak responded to her critics more fully in her recent book, *A Critique of Postcolonial Reason: Toward a History of the Vanishing Present* (Cambridge, Mass.: Harvard University Press, 1999), 308–11.

16. Abdul R. JanMohamed and David Lloyd, introduction to *The Nature and Context of Minority Discourse*, ed. Abdul R. JanMohamed and David Lloyd (New York: Oxford University Press, 1990), 6–9.

17. Rey Chow, *Ethics after Idealism: Theory—Culture—Ethnicity—Reading* (Bloomington: Indiana University Press, 1998), 3.

18. Mary Daly, *The Church and Second Sex* (Boston: Beacon Press, 1968) and *Beyond God the Father* (Boston: Beacon Press, 1973).

19. Audre Lorde, "An Open Letter to Mary Daly," in *Sister Outsider: Essays and Speeches* (Trumansburg, N.Y.: Crossing Press, 1984), 66–71; Uma Narayan, *Dislocating Cultures: Identities, Traditions, and Third World Feminism* (New York: Routledge, 1997), 43–80.

20. Audre Lorde, "An Open Letter," 67.

21. J. Dudgeon. "The Small Feet of Chinese Women," *Chinese Recorder* 2 (1869): 93.

22. J. G. Kerr, "Small Feet," *Chinese Recorder* 2 (1869): 169–70.

23. Narayan, *Dislocating Cultures*, 55.

24. The Mongols and Manchus were considered "uneducated" and "barbarian," and they rejected footbinding.

25. Narayan, *Dislocating Cultures*, 48–49.

26. See Paul A. Cohen, *Discovering History in China: American Historical Writings on the Recent Chinese Past* (New York: Columbia University Press, 1984).

27. C. Fred Blake, "Foot-binding in Neo-Confucian China and the Appropriation of Female Labor," *Signs* 19 (1994): 676–712.

28. Howard S. Levy, *Chinese Footbinding: The History of a Curious Erotic Custom* (New York: Walton Rawls, 1966); R. H. Van Gulik, *Sexual Life in Ancient China* (Leiden: E. J. Brill, 1961).

29. Van Gulik originally wanted to write a preface for a Ming erotic album he intended to publish. See *Sexual Life*, xi.

30. Charlotte Furth, "Rethinking Van Gulik: Sexuality and Reproduction in Traditional Chinese Medicine," in *Engendering China: Women, Culture, and the State*, ed. Christina K. Gilmartin, Gail Hershatter, Lisa Rofel, and Tyrene White (Cambridge, Mass.: Harvard University Press, 1994), 128.

31. Levy, *Chinese Footbinding*, 65–103.

32. Kwok Pui-lan, *Chinese Women and Christianity, 1860–1927* (Atlanta: Scholars Press, 1992), 110–15.

33. Narayan, *Dislocating Cultures*, 57.

34. James Clifford, *Routes: Travel and Translation in the Late Twentieth Century* (Cambridge, Mass.: Harvard University Press, 1997), 197.

35. For insightful cultural criticism of these two museums, see Mieke Bal's *Double Exposures: The Subject of Cultural Analysis* (New York: Routledge, 1996), 13–56; James Clifford, *The Predicament of Culture: Twentieth Century Ethnography, Literature, and Art* (Cambridge, Mass.: Harvard University Press, 1988), 189–214.

36. Sigmund Freud, "Fetishism," in *The Standard Edition of the Complete Psychological Works of Sigmund Freud,* vol. 21 (London: Hogarth, 1961), 149–57.

37. Julia Kristeva, *About Chinese Women,* trans. Anita Barrows (New York: Urizen Books, 1977), 83–85.

38. Rey Chow, *Woman and Chinese Modernity: The Politics of Reading between West and East* (Minneapolis: University of Minnesota Press, 1991), 6.

39. Gerder Lerner, *The Creation of Patriarchy* (New York: Oxford University Press, 1986), 11.

40. Mary Daly, *Pure Lust: Elemental Feminist Philosophy* (Boston: Beacon Press, 1984), 26–27.

41. Linda Alcoff, "Cultural Feminism Versus Post-Structuralism: The Identity Crisis in Feminist Theory," *Signs* 13 (1988): 408.

42. Meyda Yeğenoğlu, *Colonial Fantasies: Towards a Feminist Reading of Orientalism* (Cambridge: Cambridge University Press, 1998), 105–6.

43. Catherine Keller, *Apocalypse Now and Then: A Feminist Guide to the End of the World* (Boston: Beacon, 1996), 245.

44. Stuart Hall, "When Was 'the Post-Colonial'? Thinking at the Limit," in *The Post-Colonial Question: Common Skies, Divided Horizons,* ed. Iain Chambers and Lidia Curti (New York: Routledge, 1996), 246.

3

Sartorial Fabric-ations

Enlightenment and Western Feminism

MEYDA YEĞENOĞLU

Lifting the Veil, Modernizing the Woman

Within the grim picture of the Orient, the situation of its woman, who is secluded behind her veil, looked even more gruesome to the Western colonial gaze. Her situation thus required a much more serious working, for the most essential features of the culture are assumed to be inscribed onto her; she is taken as the concrete embodiment of oppressive Islamic traditions which the Orient desperately needed to break up in order to reach the level of development the West achieved a long time ago. In fact, one of the central elements in the ideological justification of colonial culture is the criticism of the cultural practices and religious customs of Oriental societies which are shown to be monstrously oppressing women. Hence, the barbarity of the Orient is evidenced in the way cultural traditions shape the lives of its women.

This Enlightenment rhetoric (in its feminist career) took "backward" and "barbaric" Islamic customs, which are assumed to be central in the enslavement and imprisonment of Muslim women, as the target upon which to work. It was believed that the conditions that perpetuate the non-modern social structures and values of Oriental cultures needed to be uprooted for new and modern conditions to be put in place to produce the desired effects in women's status in the Middle East. Therefore, the systematic breakdown of the "backward" cultural, economic, and political conditions was essential if these cultures were to be improved in the direction of modern Western ideals. Ruth Frances Woodsmall, in *Women in the Changing Islamic System,* first published in 1936, is confident that the West can provide the desired model in this process: "Change behind the veil is being made along lines of Western imitation in clothes with a steady improvement in taste and more discrimination as to suitability in dress . . . Social life within the harem now definitely follows the European model."[1]

As in all other Orientalist texts, the temporal problematic, which Johannes Fabian calls "pushing the Other back in time," is one of the defining characteristics of anthropological texts on Middle Eastern women. As I mentioned above, it is also the founding principle in the construction of the universality of Western time and progress. The essential difference between the East and the West is premised on this temporal lag. Such societies are by definition deemed "stagnant"; their temporality and dynamism are not understood to be simply different. This difference is negated, denied, pushed back in a temporality which is construed in linear and progressive terms. As Edward Said exemplifies in the case of Massignon, within the Orientalist imagery, "the essence of the difference between East and West is between modernity and ancient tradition."[2] The time lag that characterizes the religious/traditional Orient is its despotic time which remains practically stagnant. Woodsmall expresses this widespread tendency in the following way:

> In the East the social system has until the last decade remained practically unchanged throughout the centuries. The Islamic world, with its integrated system of religion and society, has preserved with little if any variation, the social customs of the seventh century. Between the social practices of the East and of the West, there has always been until recently the cleavage of centuries.[3]

Even when Eastern societies undergo social transformation, the situation of women is assumed to remain the same. As Leila Ahmed notes, Western civilization has produced volume after volume regarding the supposed backward and oppressive conditions under which Muslim women live. The unchanging condition of women in these societies is expressed by Juliet Minces, writing in the 1980s, in the following way:

> What is particular and problematic is that while women elsewhere gradually liberated themselves—to some extent—from the total supremacy of men, *most women in the Muslim world continued to be totally subordinate. They live under a system which has barely changed despite the undeniable*

evolution of their societies and of certain would-be "revolutionary" governments to grant women greater equality and rights, in keeping what we
would call desire for "Modernization."[4] (emphasis added)

It is striking that although there is a forty-year time span, there is no difference between the observations of Minces and Woodsmall. It seems that both
observations were made within the same representational framework. In the
identification of the locus of change, the question of woman gained particular
importance. The ability of the Orient to modernize itself is assumed to be possible only by its radical break from tradition. The oppressive and unfree condition of the Oriental woman is not only morally condemned, but also she is
transformed into, as Partha Chatterjee notes in the context of India, "a sign of
the inherently oppressive and unfree nature of the entire cultural tradition of a
country."[5] The metonymic association between the Orient and its women, or
more specifically the representation of woman as tradition and as the essence
of the Orient, made it all the more important to lift the veil, for *unveiling and
thereby modernizing the woman of the Orient signified the transformation of the
Orient itself.* It is this metonymic association between tradition and woman
that can explain the continual obsession with and the fundamental weight
given to women's unveiling as the privileged sign of progress. Taken as the
most visible marker of tradition and religion, the veil provided the benevolent
Western woman with what she had desired: a clinching example that inter-
locks "woman" and "tradition/Islam" so that it could be morally condemned
in the name of emancipation. The veil is taken as the sign of the inherently
oppressive and unfree nature of the entire tradition of Islam and Oriental cultures and by extension it is used as a proof of oppression of women in these
societies. When the necessity to modernize these cultures was taken for
granted, there was no hesitation in morally condemning the practice of veiling, for it was regarded as an impediment to modernization.

It is no coincidence that the desire to unveil the Oriental woman coincided with the broader agenda of "progress" and belief in the incompatibility
of Islam with Western models of modernity and reason. Within this continual quest for a modern and civilized identity for Oriental women, Islam
gained centrality in debates concerning the "woman question." The subordination of Oriental women was read off mainly from the Islamic cultural practices. Conceived as the indisputable emblem of Islamic culture's essential
traditionalism, the veil was consistently seen as a problem, and its lifting as
the most important sign of reform and modernization. Within this constructed imagery of Muslim cultures, the harem, veil, and polygamy were
highly charged symbols, and they all functioned as synonyms of female

oppression and nourished the colonial female desire with a most exquisite example for designating the target of change.[6] Grace Ellison, an English-woman writing in the early 1920s, expresses this very widespread trend in her representation of Turkish women: "The slavery of ages cannot be set aside in a few months, and the ladies continue to wear their thick black canvas veils over their faces."[7]

The privileged place accorded to woman within such discourses reveals what Lata Mani has convincingly demonstrated in the context of the debates on *sati* in colonial India: "women . . . became the site on which tradition was debated and reformulated. Thus, what was at stake was not women but tradition";[8] she is constructed as representing the inner, sacred, spiritual, and inviolable locus of the true, authentic identity of the culture. And it is precisely by being such a locus that she embodies the tradition and represents the nation's innermost essence.[9] Therefore, if a fundamental rupture from this traditional identity is to be achieved, the ideals of progress and modernization have to be meticulously inscribed onto her; she has to be remade.

It is from this modernist position that Ruth Frances Woodsmall speaks in *Women in the Changing Islamic System*. The book's main focus is on Muslim women's adjustment to the modern world. In a chapter typically entitled "Lifting the Veil," after declaring the veil as "the barometer of social change in the Moslem world," she identifies the progress and achievement of freedom with women's unveiling: "although there is no concerted move to discard the veil, one is conscious of a very strong urge for freedom which is symbolized by unveiling. . . . Although there is little unveiling as individuals, there is a growth in freedom in collective unveiling."[10]

Among all the "signs of advancement," it is the native's conviction of the necessity of abandoning traditional customs which is regarded as the indisputable way to foster social "progress." Woodsmall regards women's and men's recognition of veiling as a problem more important than the unveiling itself: "that purdah is recognized by men and women alike as a national problem is the most helpful sign of advancement."[11] Such a recognition is fundamental not simply because it ensures that the desired change will be achieved, but it has also the power of bestowing an illusive agency onto the native herself and thereby making her the agent of her own subjection to Western norms of progress.

The association between the unveiling of women and the modernization of the Orient recalls the inner/outer distinction Chatterjee talks about.[12] The veil represents for the colonial gaze the Orient's/woman's mask; it is an exterior surface which is assumed to conceal the site of interiority, the essence of the culture—that is, femininity as the embodiment of culture's authentic core. Like the female sphere of domesticity, which connotes "interiority," the veil signifies the true self of the Islamic culture, its spirituality, its quintessential and unchanging essence. I am referring here to a colonial fantasy structured or (over)determined by binary oppositions of the inside and outside or veiled and unveiled. And it is within such a condensed totality of signifiers that woman becomes, to borrow a phrase from Radhakrishnan, "the mute but necessary allegorical ground" for the discursive operations of imperial feminists. In turning woman to a signifier of interiority through associating her with tradition and by advocating the necessity of transforming the oppressive Islamic cultural practices by unveiling her, the discourse of imperial feminism in turn generates the divided topography of inside versus outside, and tradition versus modernity.

Allegedly, it is Western feminists who have, with their achievements of freedom, inspired and prepared the ground for the liberation of Oriental women. Woodsmall is a typical example of the attitude that takes Western feminist ideals as the norm:

> In this movement towards the freer life of to-day, Eastern women have received much from the West. Social freedom, educational advance, economic independence, political privilege and participation in public life, the widening range of interests and activities of Eastern women—in short, the whole forward movement towards a free life for women has been inspired by the advance of women in the West. The feminist struggle in the West, to establish the principle of equality, has in no small measure prepared the way, so that men of affairs, nationalist leaders of the East to-day, have accepted equal opportunity for women as an inseparable element of Western progress.[13]

What is at stake in the unequivocal acceptance of Western feminists' lives and achievements as democratic, advanced, emancipated, in short as the *norm*, is the positing of a universal subject status for themselves, for after all it is their condition which represents the highest achievement of humanity. For example, despite her "awareness" of the possible dangers of Eurocentrism, Juliet Minces wants to retain the Western feminist ideal as a universal one:

> Can the evolution of the condition of women in the Arab world be evaluated by the same criteria as in the West? Is it not Eurocentric to put forward the lives of Western women as the only democratic, just and forward-looking model? I do not think so. The demands of Western feminists seem to me to represent the greatest advance towards the emancipation of

women as people. Ideally, the criteria adopted, like those for human rights generally should be *universal.*[14] (emphasis added)

Minces declares Western feminist achievements as the universal ideal without any further discussion of the content and context of specifically Western feminist ideals. This desire for a direct expression of universal feminist ideals in Western feminism is typical. The question here is not simply to criticize this, but also to understand what is at stake in such bold, dogmatic assertions. What kind of discursive or ideological mechanism is operating here? As Gayatri Chakravorty Spivak suggests, it is by erasing his/her role as an investigator that the imperialist subject denies his/her own worlding and renders his/her own position transparent.[15] This preempting of their particular position provides the discursive ground for the constitution of the universality of the Eurocentric subject. The assertion of a universal norm could not have been possible without designating the achievements of Western women as the yardstick against which one can measure and define the goal other women must achieve. In other words, the declaration of an emancipated status for the Western woman is contingent upon the representation of the Oriental woman as her devalued Other, and this enables Western woman to identify and preserve the boundaries of self for herself. The deliberate confusion of their particularity and specificity with universalist norms has crucial implications for the subject status these women occupy. To be Western here implies feeling that one is entitled to universalize one's particular achievements and interests. The effacement/erasure of the particularity of Western women in the name of universality has the effect of legitimizing the colonial-feminist discourse as an act of generosity and as an act of conferring upon Middle East women the privilege of participating in Western women's universalism rather than a denial and negation of difference. As Spivak puts it, "if there is one universal, it cannot be inclusive of difference."[16] The attribution of a universal subject status to Western women should be understood as nothing but a "particular becoming dominant";[17] it is a particular that masquerades as universal. But it should be emphasized that not any particular has the power to enforce itself as universal. Nor is the command of the universal simply a result of prior attainment of such a status, but it is a consequence of an oppositional and hierarchical ordering of the universal and the particular. And, as Joan Scott points out, it is important to recognize the effect of power in this ordering. Relegation to the status of the particular does not happen because difference and otherness is discriminated against. Rather, in following Scott, we can suggest that such discrimination occurs precisely because difference is relegated to the status of particularity and, more important, the particularity of difference is a product or effect of power and discrimination. It is "a process that establishes the superiority or the typicality or the universality of some in terms of the inferiority or atypicality or particularity of others."[18] This is a process which not only establishes a standard to exclude those who are different by defining them as other than the norm, but operates first and foremost as a means of registering the relationship of difference and thereby as a means of securing a sovereign status to the subject of representation in a relation of contrast. It is a process that allows setting the self off from the particular, and this is nothing other than centering oneself as universal. As David Lloyd cogently describes, the alleged neutrality and universality is at the same time a process that secures a sovereign status for the subject:

> [T]he position occupied by the dominant individual is that of the Subject without properties. This Subject with 'unlimited properties' is precisely the undetermined subject. . . . Its universality is attained by virtue of literal indifference: this Subject becomes representative in consequence of being able to take anyone's place, of occupying any place, of a pure exchangeability. Universal where all others are particular, partial, this Subject is the perfect, disinterested judge formed for and by the public sphere.[19]

A similar universalizing gesture can be found in the collaborative work of Nicki Keddie and Louis Beck. In a striking statement, Keddie and Beck explicitly state that they are not interested in whatever satisfactions and positive aspects Middle Eastern women's lives may contain. In advance of a possible objection, they insist that they will keep the West as standard:

> [T]here is, by current Western standards and possibilities, something lacking in the lives of most Middle Eastern women, whatever satisfactions and positive features these lives may often contain. . . . What most Middle Eastern women lack when compared either with their wealthier and better educated compatriots or with Western women of many social classes, is freedom of choice regarding basic life decisions.[20]

It is not surprising that such an ethnocentric representation reveals itself as the illusion of freedom of choice. It is always the "absence" of Western principles of progress and freedom that marks the Orient. What is lacking in Oriental women is indicative of a general deficiency in the culture at large. The result is not only the identification of what is Western with what is universal, but also the creation of an essentialist typology in which the distinction between East and West is conceived of as constitutively contrary and profoundly different. It is this absolute and systematic difference between the

West and the Orient that is repeated (and evidenced) in the respective positions of their women.[21] In Woodsmall's words:

> The social systems of the East and West are established on *diametrically dif-*
> *ferent principles*. The pivotal difference is the difference in the position of
> woman. In the *East* society has always been *based on the separation of the sexes*
> *and seclusion of women,* limiting their sphere to the home. Perhaps their
> power within this limited world has been considerable, but there are bound-
> aries beyond which they have not been free to go. The *West* has *not sharply*
> *differentiated between the world of women and that of men.* Western society is
> built on the basis of unity, which may not mean equality, but which does not
> definitely place women in a sphere apart.[22] (emphasis added)

Woodsmall's discourse exemplifies here a typical feature of Orientalism,
the creation of an absolute or radical difference between the West and East
(what Said calls "epistemological and ontological distinction") in a way in
which the East is seen as the negative opposite (characterized by lack,
absence, etc.) of the West. This is indeed a *profoundly phallocentric* gesture, if
we see phallocentrism not simply as "men oppressing women" but understand from it *a particular structuring of discourse where the law of the one oper-*
ates. The association of the West with modernity, progress, development, and
freedom, and the East with the opposites of these features is indeed a phallocentric gesture which is characterized by a binary logic of oppositions. Such a
gesture, which associates the Orient with negativity, simultaneously construes
it as that which is other than the established norm. In this respect the actual
content of the terms of the opposition is less important than the logic that
posits the two as contrary and profoundly different. Within this oppositional
structure, the Orient and the condition of its women are represented as the
sites of devalued difference. Such a gesture provides the ground for the production and legitimation of a normative discourse where the West and the
"free" and "liberated" condition of its women are taken as the norm. If the
position of the Orient and its women are represented within such a dualist
logic, then it follows that the colonial nature of this "feminist" discourse is
not an exception but rather part of a system that requires the representation
of difference as negativity to be able to posit the positivity of the norm. *There-*
fore, the colonial and phallocentric nature of such a feminist discourse is not an
aberration, but rather a structural necessity of a discourse that represents otherness
and difference as negativity. The representation of the other as negativity, as
devalued difference, remains a constant in Western thought. The logic that is
operative here can be understood as the law of the one. There is a paradoxical
mixture of "the same and yet different" in the logic that recognizes the

Eastern woman's difference insofar as it is other than the Western woman as the norm. In other words, the law of the one, the phallocentric gesture *par excellence*, is operative as long as a norm is erected.

The Veiled Embodiment: Sartorial Fabric-ation of the Muslim Woman's Body

How can we think of the veil and embodiment together? Can we read veiling simply as an instrument of oppression? Or should we conceive of veiling and unveiling in terms of the bodily affects such practices imply? How should we conceptualize the relationship between discourses, practices, norms about dressing and the embodiment? What kind of an understanding of the body can enable us to understand corporeality in culturally and sexually specific terms, in their concrete specificities? What kind of presumptions about subjectivity and body need to be scrutinized and challenged so as to posit the bodily roots of subjectivity?

Feminist theory is witnessing heated discussions about the status of the body. Increasingly, emphasis is placed upon the need for a materialist conception of the body, for the embodied nature of subjectivity and sexual difference. Feminist theorists who emphasize the usefulness of poststructuralism for feminist theory, such as Elizabeth Grosz, Judith Butler, Rosi Braidotti, Vicki Kirby, and others, point to the need for understanding the body as an effect of historically specific technologies of power. Michel Foucault's analysis shows how the body does not stand in an external relation to power, but is marked, stamped, invested, acted upon, inscribed, and cultivated by a historically contingent nexus of power/discourse; that is how it is brought into being by power.[23] Power is the productive principle through which the materiality of the subject is constituted. Such a constitution takes place through processes of training, shaping, cultivation, and investment of the body by power. Power takes the body as its target, the object, the medium to extract information so as to transform, remake, reinscribe, and subject it to the functioning of power. However, the subjection and control of the body within the field of power must not be understood through a model of repression. The Foucauldian approach challenges the understanding of subjection of the body to power as a simple process of subordination or as a repression of its desires and instincts. As Butler, following the Foucauldian insight, puts it, "this 'subjection', or *assujettisement*, is not only a subordination but a securing and maintaining, a putting in place of a subject, a subjectification."[24] Therefore, the formation and regulation of bodies in their materiality cannot be understood separately from their subjectification, for subjectification implies both a creative and a coercive process simultaneously. As Foucault argues:

> [T]he body is also directly involved in a political field; power relations have an immense hold upon it; they invest it, mark it, train it, torture it, force it to carry tasks, to perform ceremonies, to emit signs. This political investment of the body is bound up, in accordance with complex reciprocal relationships, with its economic use; it is largely as a force of production that the body is invested with relations of power and domination; but on the other hand, its constitution as labor power is possible only if it is caught up in a system of subjection . . . the body becomes a useful force only if it is both a productive body and a subjected body.[25]

Understanding power as a productive and formative process requires a questioning of the presumptions of paradigms that conceive of the subject in terms of the primacy of mind and the concomitant assumption of the body's naturalness and precultural status. As Elizabeth Grosz persuasively argues, bodies are not ahistorical, precultural, or presocial: they are in no way natural, but always already marked, inscribed, and engraved by social pressures.[26] In emphasizing that bodies cannot be adequately understood if they are seen as impregnable by cultural, social, and historical factors, Grosz's aim is to underline the fact that power produces bodies always as a *determinate* type; bodies are neither universal nor neutral, but always culturally, sexually, racially specific. To liberate the body from its colonization by the paradigms that privilege the mind in understandings of subjectivity will not only enable us to posit its *materiality* but also foster an understanding of bodies in their sexual, cultural, and racial *specificities*. In a way, raising the question of the *specificity* of the body requires simultaneously raising the question of its *materiality*, for questions regarding the differences between bodies can be meaningfully asked only if the corporeality of bodies is no longer seen as biological, natural, and neutral, but always as a product, an effect of power relations that constitutes them in their specificities.

To be able to develop a materialist conception of the body, the body as an effect of power/knowledge nexus, we need to formulate theories that have the force and capacity to overcome the various dualisms through which the body is traditionally envisioned. As Grosz shows, among the most pertinent oppositions that need to be displaced for exploring and developing an understanding of the body other than that offered by traditional philosophical and phallogocentric understanding are the body-mind, nature-culture, and discourse-referent.[27] Following Grosz, we can suggest that the constituted nature of the body does not imply that the effectivity of discourses (among all of them medicine and biology occupy a privileged place) on the body should be seen as limited to the shaping and influencing of the mind, for such an understanding implies that there is a biological, natural, real, material body on the one hand, and there are various cultural and historical representations of it. The controlling, making, and marking of bodies are not realized through the control of ideas. Such inscriptions are not merely added to a body that is naturally and biologically given. If a materialist notion of corporeality implies that power operates by constituting the subject's biological makeup, then positing the body's naturalness as prior to its inscription needs to be seen as an effect of power. As Butler notes, the representation of the body as preceding signification is itself an effect of signification and of power: "the body posited as prior to the sign, is always *posited* or *signified* as *prior*. This signification produces as an *effect* of its own procedure the very body that it nevertheless and simultaneously claims to discover as that which *precedes* its own action."[28] The notion of a biological or natural body is the very discourse that neutralizes and universalizes the cultural, racial, sexual specificity of different bodies. In fact such a universalizing and neutralizing gesture is the gesture of phallogocentrisim which preempts the embodied nature of the masculine subject, a gesture that conflates the human with masculine and thus marks women as the site of embodiment. As Rosi Braidotti notes:

> Simone de Beauvoir observed fifty years ago that the price men pay for representing the universal is a kind of loss of embodiment; the price women pay, on the other hand, is a loss of subjectivity and the confinement of the body. The former are disembodied and through this process gain entitlement to transcendence and subjectivity, the latter are overembodied and thereby consigned to immanence.[29]

The notion of the body as the stuff of inscription of social norms, practices, and values can be extended to the discussion of veiling and the possibility of Muslim women's bodies within Western representations. We can bring a different perspective to the taken-for-granted presumption about the cruelty and primitiveness of veiling when we recognize the possibility of the inscription of bodies through various practices of adornment, clothing, cosmetics, and so on. If veiling can be seen as a specific practice of marking and disciplining the body in accordance with cultural requirements, so can unveiling. In other words, the practice both of veiling and unveiling are culturally specific procedures of corporeal inscriptions, conditioned by specific cultural histories. What needs to be examined here is the presumption of the truth and naturalness of the unveiled body that the discourse of colonial feminism is predicated upon. However, if veiling is a specific practice of situating the body within the prevailing exigencies of power, so is unveiling. Therefore, the unveiled body is no less marked or inscribed; rather a whole battery of disciplinary techniques and practices have produced Western women's bodies, and therefore not-to-veil needs to be seen as one among many practices of corporeal inscriptions. In other words, there is nothing natural about unveiling, and therefore not-to-veil is no less inscriptive than being veiled. Not-to-veil is also another way of turning the flesh into a particular type of body. However, the body that is not veiled is taken as the norm for specifying a general, cross-culturally valid notion of what a feminine body is and must be. Hence the presumption of the naturalness of not-to-be-veiled has come to secure the truth of bodies and is used as the universal norm to yield Muslim woman as a knowable and comprehensible entity for the West. In other words, it is the naturalness and truth of the unveiled body that legitimates and endorses colonial feminist sentiments and certitude in the necessity of interventionist action against Muslim women's veiling. Although the beliefs and values about not veiling are also incorporated in the existential and embodied being of Western women, the fact that this is a culturally specific inscription is effaced in colonial feminist representations. Such an effacement ensures that the beliefs and values that produce Western women's bodies stand in for the truth of women universally. They are used as the explanatory norm to unravel the desires and pleasures of bodies that are located in other histories and cultures: one culture's coding of bodies becomes the template through which all bodies are conjured. Veiling is one of those practices that irritates the Western, especially feminist cognizance; it is one of those practices, like incision and various other body markings, that incite anxiety. Practices and processes by which other bodies are marked have appeared to the Western eye to be excessively violent, barbaric, and indisputable proof of the cruelty to which Muslim women are subjected. The disciplinary techniques and procedures that inscribe, control, and train Muslim bodies are distinguished from the "civilized," Western techniques and practices by the degree of barbarism inflicted upon the former. Emphasizing the culturally specific nature of embodiment reveals, however, that the power exercised upon bodies by veiling is no more cruel or barbaric than the control, supervision, training, and constraining of bodies by other practices, such as bras, stiletto heels, corsets, cosmetics, and so on.

If bodies are produced through various cultural practices, then their desires, pains and pleasures must be specific to particular cultures. If this is so, then the truth of veiled women and their bodies cannot easily be retrieved within the terms of the colonial feminist discourse, for it is a discourse which is already a cultural product, enabled and conditioned by dominant discourses. The foreignness of the veiled body is assumed to be deciphered by being translated and neutralized within an economy of universal truth.

The body is the medium through which power operates and functions, and knowledge is the major instrument power utilizes for this operation. It is also through the exercise of power that knowledge from bodies can be extracted, and this knowledge in turn functions as the main instrument in the control, inscription, and training of bodies. Following Foucault on the issue of the power/knowledge nexus, we can suggest that power and knowledge are the condition of existence of each other. Power is transformed, altered, modified, intensified in accordance with the diversification and alterations in the order of knowledges.

The intertwined relation between power and knowledge can be extended to the ways in which Muslim women's bodies are positioned within colonial discourse. The exercise of colonial control implied in unveiling was a way of seizing hold of Muslim bodies. This seizure required knowledge and information to be extracted about them. But this knowledge required rendering them visible in the first instance, for as I have argued above, visibility in the Enlightenment ideology is regarded as the precondition of the possibility of true knowledge. It was only by rendering Muslim women's bodies visible that they became capable of being recodified, redefined, and reformulated according to new, Western codes. The regime and control involved in colonial power need the creation of docile, obedient subjects. This is indeed a fundamental characteristic of colonial power which the commanders of the French army articulated in their own way. The following are the words of a French general in his study of the lessons of the Dahar insurrection in North Africa in the nineteenth century:

> In effect the essential thing is to gather into groups this people which is everywhere and nowhere; the essential thing is to make them something we can seize hold of. When we have them in our hands, we will then be able to do many things which are quite impossible for us today and which will perhaps allow us to capture their minds after we have captured their bodies.[30]

Although the general's body-mind distinction is rather non-Foucauldian, the essence of his argument can be understood only through a Foucauldian approach. In his discourse, the people appear to be veiled indeed: they are visible and invisible, everywhere and nowhere. The fundamental question is to "seize hold of them," and the capture that the general articulates does not aim at repression in a simple sense, but at the *production* of "minds" and of course "bodies." By conceptualizing the interlocking of bodies and discursive regimes, Foucault enables us to understand the process of subject constitution in modern society. As a body subject to modern, colonial technology of power-knowledge, the colonized should be produced as a new body and mind with certain skills, characteristics, and form; she/he needs to be remade. But to understand this remapping and reterritorialization, we need to position the body of the Other within a frame that can account for it as a historical and cultural effect of power. The Other's particular mode of corporeality is an important site for colonial inscriptions of power, as the desire to get hold of the native woman's body is evoked as the metaphor of colonial occupation (hence French colonialism's obsession with unveiling the Algerian women). If veiling is one of the instruments of coding Muslim women's bodies and their embodied nature of subjectivity, then what bodily implications might unveiling have for these women? The following quotation from Frantz Fanon is worth citing here as he describes the bodily transformations an Algerian woman undergoes when she is unveiled:

> The body of the young Algerian woman, in traditional society, is revealed to her by its coming to maturity and by the veil. The veil covers the body and disciplines it, tempers it, at the very time when it experiences its phase of greatest effervescence. The veil protects, reassures, isolates. One must have heard the confessions of Algerian women or have analyzed the dream content of certain recently unveiled women to appreciate the importance of the veil for the body of the woman. Without the veil she has an impression of her body being cut up into bits, put adrift; the limbs seem to lengthen indefinitely. When the Algerian woman has to cross a street, for a long time she commits errors of judgment as to the exact distance to be negotiated. The unveiled body seems to escape, to dissolve. She has an impression of being improperly dressed, even of being naked. She experiences a sense of incompleteness with great intensity. She has the anxious feeling that something is unfinished, and along with this a frightful sensation of disintegrating. *The absence of the veil distorts the Algerian woman's corporal pattern. She quickly has to invent new dimensions for her body, new means of muscular control.* She has to create for herself an attitude of unveiled-woman-outside. She must overcome all timidity, all awkwardness . . . and at the same time be careful not to overdo it, not to attract notice to herself. *The Algerian woman who walks stark naked into the European city relearns her body, reestablishes it in a totally revolutionary fashion.*[31] (emphasis added)

Fanon draws our attention to one of the most striking instances of the cultural violence of colonialism. He also suggests that the veil is not simply attire that covers the woman's body, but it is what transforms a little girl into a woman in Muslim society. It is because her mature female body is made by the veil that unveiling her is not simply an uncovering or change of dress, but *peeling her skin off.* In this sense, the so-called dream hallucinations which she experiences are very real sensations that have parallels in the everyday, "normal" experiences of crossing a street or simply walking out in the street. As Kaja Silverman notes, clothing (and veiling should be seen as one particular style among many) has the force of constituting identity and corporeality: "Clothing exercises as profoundly determining an influence upon living, breathing bodies . . . affecting contours, weight, muscle development, posture movement and libidinal circulation. Dress is one of the most important cultural implements for articulating and territorializing human corporeality —for mapping its erotogenic zones and for affixing a sexual identity."[32]

Following Silverman, then, we can see the veil, that sartorial matter, as not something that is external to the identity of Muslim women, but as a fundamental piece conjoined with the embodied subjectivity of Muslim woman. If we cannot comfortably assume that her body is inside the veil or the veil is something that is outside of her body and hence does not function merely as a body cover, can we then think of bringing this body outside the veil (as colonial or imperial feminism desires) without at the same time exercising another form of power? If the veil is part of her body, *part of her being-in-the-world,* then it differs from a simple cover that has an inside and an outside; its "function" cannot be captured by such categorical oppositions. The veil can indeed be understood as the Derridean reading of hymen which has "the structure of *and/or,* between *and* and *or.*"[33] As a "confusion" between a set of opposites, the veil or hymen embraces both terms; it is in-between them. As Derrida puts it, "It is an operation that *both* sows confusion *between* opposites *and* stands *between* the opposites 'at once.' What counts here is the in-betweenness of the hymen. The hymen 'takes place' in the 'inter-,' in the spacing between desire and fulfillment, between perpetration and its recollection."[34]

As the in-between of outside and inside, the veil makes both inside and outside possible. There would indeed be no inside-outside without the veil. It is what constructs a before and a behind. But there would also be no veil without the inside and outside that it makes possible by separating and constructing. In the ambiguous position it occupies, the veil is not outside the woman's body. Nor is she the interior that needs to be protected or penetrated. *Her body is not simply the inside of the veil: it is of it; "she" is constituted in (and by) the fabric-ation of the veil.* Being an undecidable text-ile, the veil interweaves the woman's skin with its threads; as the sign of fusion it stitches together the epidermus of woman with cultural codings. It is both her identity and her difference, or it is what makes her identity different. The veil is that which produces woman, or difference; it is spacing, *différence.*[35]

By assuming an interiority that is concealed by the veil, colonial gesture articulates itself in terms of the Western metaphysical or philosophical oppositions between origin and representation, essence and appearance, identity and difference. A number of writers have pointed to the fundamental continuity and homology between the structure of Western metaphysics and phallocentric order.[36] There is thus a fundamental affinity or a chain of equivalence among Western philosophical, colonial, and patriarchal discourses. This implies that any serious challenge to patriarchy cannot overlook questions of colonial discourse, for both are placed within a larger cultural project whose fundamental philosophical assumptions need to be questioned. To assume that these questions are separate from each other is the very illusion that the categorical-analytic discourse of Reason produces. A feminist discourse that tries to emancipate others should in the first place learn how to question this very process of other-ing, and what this implies for its "own" "identity" (that is to say, whether a discourse can be both a discourse of identity and sameness under the governance of Reason and Progress and a feminist one at the same time). Such a questioning should of course include the questioning of the very opposition between inside and outside as one of the fundamental cultural oppositions that constructs femininity itself.

The veil is dress, but a dress which we might consider as articulating the very identity of Muslim women. Only if we see the veiling of woman in Muslim culture as a unique cultural experience, we can then actually learn what it is to veil or unveil as woman, rather than simply re-setting the liberal scene and repeating commonsensical and clichéd standards in the name of universal emancipation. I want to argue here that such commonsensical and clichéd standards may not be so commonsensical and clichéd after all. They may, on the contrary, be part of a colonial gesture that is hard to define as colonial because, especially in a now decolonized world, it articulates itself as a universal, and politically and morally correct task.

Notes

1. Ruth Frances Woodsmall, *Women in the Changing Islamic System* (Delhi: Bimla Publishing House, 1983; 1st ed. 1936), 48.

2. Edward Said, *Orientalism* (Harmondsworth: Penguin, 1978), 269.

3. Woodsmall, *Women in the Changing Islamic System*, 39.

4. Juliet Minces, *The House of Obedience* (London: Zed Books, 1980), 14.

5. Partha Chatterjee, "Colonialism, Nationalism, and Colonized Women: The Contest in India," *American Ethnologist* 16: 4 (1989): 622.

6. Leila Ahmed, "Western Ethnocentrism and Perceptions of the Harem," *Feminist Studies* 8 (fall 1982): 523.

7. Grace Ellison, *An Englishwoman in a Turkish Harem* (London: Methuen, 1915), 61–62.

8. Lata Mani, "The Contentious Traditions: The Debate on *Sati* in Colonial India," *Cultural Critique* 7 (fall 1987): 151.

9. For an excellent discussion of this question, see R. Radhakrishnan: "Nationalism, Gender and the Narrative of Identity," *in Nationalisms and Sexualities,* ed. Andrew Parker, Mary Russo, Doris Sommer, and Patricia Yaeger. (New York: Routledge, 1992), 77–95.

10. Woodsmall, *Women in the Changing Islamic System,* 48, 49.

11. Ibid., 42.

12. Partha Chatterjee, "The Nationalist Resolution of the Women's Question," in *Recasting Women: Essays in Colonial History,* ed. Kumkum Sangari and Sudesh Vaid (New Brunswick: Rutgers University Press, 1990), 233–53.

13. Woodsmall, *Women in the Changing Islamic System,* 413.

14. Minces, *The House of Obedience,* 25.

15. Gayatri Chakravorty Spivak, "Imperialism and Sexual Difference," *Oxford Literary Review* 8: 1–2 (1986): 229.

16. Gayatri Chakravorty Spivak, "French Feminism Revisited: Ethics and Politics," in *Feminists Theorize the Political,* ed. J. Butler and J. Scott (New York: Routledge, 1992), 75.

17. Ernesto Laclau, "Universalism, Particularism, and the Question of Identity," *October* 61 (summer 1992): 83–90.

18. Joan Scott, "Multiculturalism and the Politics of Identity," *October* 61 (summer 1992): 14–15.

19. David Lloyd, "Race under Representation," *Oxford Literary Review* 13: 1–2 (1991): 70.

20. Nikkie Keddi and Lois Beck, *Women in the Muslim World* (Cambridge, Mass.: Harvard University Press, 1978), 18.

21. However, there is a fundamental assymetry here. The possibility of inferring the characteristics of a culture from the position of its women seems to be valid only for non-Western cultures. This is such a taken-for-granted belief that, for instance, the large numbers of raped or beaten women found every day in the West are not taken as typical or essential features of a specifically Western culture. There is no metonymic relationship established between Western culture and rape or wife beating. The differences between the two cultures is not complexly articulated; rather they are seen as absolute, radical, essential, profound.

22. Woodsmall, *Women in the Changing Islamic System,* 39.

23. Michel Foucault, *Language, Counter-Memory, Practice: Selected Essays and Interviews*, ed. Donald Bouchard (Oxford: Blackwell, 1977); *The History of Sexuality*, vol. 1, *An Introduction*, trans. Robert Hurley (New York: Vintage, 1990). For a useful incorporation of Foucault's analysis for feminist discussions of embodiment, see Elizabeth Grosz, *Volatile Bodies: Toward a Corporeal Feminism* (Bloomington: Indiana University Press, 1994) and Judith Butler, *Bodies That Matter: On the Discursive Limits of "Sex"* (New York: Routledge, 1993); Rosi Braidotti, *Nomadic Subjects: Embodiment and Sexual Difference in Contemporary Feminist Theory* (New York: Columbia University Press, 1994); Vicki Kirby, "Corporeal Habits: Addressing Essentialism Differently," *Hypatia* 6: 3 (fall 1991): 4–24.

24. Butler, *Bodies That Matter*, 34.

25. Michel Foucault, *Discipline and Punish: The Birth of the Prison*, trans. Alan Sheridan (Harmondsworth: Penguin, 1977), 26–27.

26. Grosz, *Volatile Bodies*, x.

27. Ibid., 3.

28. Butler, *Bodies That Matter*, 30.

29. Rosi Braidotti, *Patterns of Dissonance*, trans. Elizabeth Guild (New York: Routledge, 1991), 153.

30. Charles Richard, *Etude sur l'insurrection du Dahra* (1845–1846), quoted in Timothy Mitchell, *Colonising Egypt* (Cambridge: Cambridge University Press, 1988), 95.

31. Frantz Fanon, *A Dying Colonialism*, trans. Haakon Chevalier (New York: Grove Weidenfeld, 1965), 58–59.

32. Kaja Silverman, "Fragments of a Fashionable Discourse," in *Studies in Entertainment: Critical Approaches to Mass Culture*, ed. Tania Modleski (Bloomington: Indiana University Press, 1986), 146.

33. Jacques Derrida, *Dissemination*, trans. Barbara Johnson (Chicago: University of Chicago Press, 1981), 261.

34. Ibid., 212.

35. Carole Naggar describes the veil as a second skin. Although I would certainly agree to see the veil as a skin, I would also argue that to see the veil as a second skin, is still to assume that there is a "first," i.e. "natural" skin that comes before the cultural skin. My reading of the veil aims to question precisely this kind of binary opposition between nature and culture, body and mind. See Carole Naggar, "The Unveiled Algerian Woman, 1960," *Aperture* (summer 1990): 4.

36. Jacques Derrida and Christie V. McDonald, "Choreographies," *Diacritics* 12: 2 (1982): 66–77; Luce Irigaray, *Speculum of the Other Woman*, trans. Gillian Gill (Ithaca, N.Y.: Cornell University Press, 1985).

4

Postcoloniality, Feminist Spaces, and Religion

MUSA W. DUBE

The Postcolonial, Ethics, and Feminism

What characterizes postcolonial feminist spaces of Two-Thirds World women? In pursuit of this question, I will seek to identify some of the major categories of analysis pertinent to postcolonial feminist theorists. First, I will briefly define the term postcolonial—its rise and ethical commitment. Second, I will assess some postcolonial feminist spaces and practices as defined by various feminist theorists and writers of formerly colonized countries. Third, I will explore how the status of colonized women was affected by colonialism and the role of religion in this process. In conclusion, I will highlight how postcolonial feminist spaces and strategies of decolonization and antipatriarchalism are being defined by Two-Thirds World postcolonial feminist writers.

Postcolonial theories emanated from the rise of the Western empires in the eighteenth through the twentieth centuries, their scramble to divide the world among themselves, the strategies of subjugation and resistance engendered by colonialism, and the chain reactions that have been in motion ever since. The attempt of Anglo-European nations to order the world culturally, economically, and politically from a Euro-centric worldview and their view that this was good for everyone was a central feature of modern imperialism.[1] This mammoth task entailed ideologies that legitimized and sanctified the acts of dominating foreign nations and setting up Euro-oriented satellite economies worldwide.

The political independence of former colonies did not mark the end of colonialism. The postindependence native elites, revolutionaries, and leaders of the new nations emerged fully cloaked in the colonial garment and devoted to the structures and policies of their former colonizers. This has led to the need to evaluate and understand the making of a postcolonial subject (the colonizer, the colonized, and the collaborators) and to highlight the role of literary texts in the process of domination, resistance, and collaboration in what has become popularly known as postcolonial studies.

The modern colonizer (whether English, French, Portuguese, German, or Dutch) believed in the superiority of his religion, race, economy, and culture. This superiority called upon the colonizer to bear the vocation of converting and ordering the world toward his own identity.[2] Such an ideology was grounded in the beliefs of modernity, Christianity, and industrial advancement. The colonized (nations, races, and countries ruled by foreign imperial powers), on the other hand, were imbued with the belief that their own religion, race, economy, and culture were backward.[3] Within this dichotomy, however, there was a third space: the space of conversion or transformation. The colonized could be saved, progress, develop, become modernized, and assimilated to their colonizers in this conversion space, which had the institutions of church, public administration, school education, language, and trade at its service. In the case of Africa, by the time political independence was won, almost all the educated leaders and elites had been initiated in this transformation process through undergoing colonial educational training, inheriting colonial governments and boundaries, and, naturally, maintaining colonialist structures, now as "independent" bodies in their own countries. The economies of many countries became raw materials producers for Western industries, which, in turn, sold expensive manufactured goods back to these countries at whatever prices and terms of trade they wished to set.[4] The vicious circle of economic and cultural dependency was thus structurally established and, indeed, is now a proclamation and justification of the colonizer's claims of superiority.

Postcolonial theories highlight the complexity of imperialism. They underline that it involves something more than just foreign rule of one nation by another. Colonialism is a process that affects and permeates all the institutions of the colonized. The independence of formerly colonized nations is now recognized as a struggle that will remain in prolonged birth pangs. Indeed, it is amazing how fast the process has moved from former colonies' struggles for independence to the current phenomenon of these same nations calling for their former colonizers to come and do business in their countries in the name of "globalization." Not too long ago we were singing songs of liberation. While these liberation tunes are still fresh in our minds, globalization is knocking loudly by our doors, demanding the right to enter and to sit at the high table. Regardless of how one defines globalization, it is clear that some are actors while others are being acted upon: some are globalizing, and others are being globalized. Postcolonial theories, therefore, seek to understand the complex construction of the colonized and the colonizer: how history, geography, anthropology, travel writing, navigation, novel writing, Christian missions, and more concurred on proclaiming the superiority of West,[5] and how they concurred on converting the world to Western patterns of thought, religion, education, economy, and culture.

Postcolonial theories also highlight the various strategies adopted by colonized nations to resist this domination, to decolonize their own lands, minds, and to charter their own liberation as well as to propose better, more just forms of international relations. Placing postcolonial theories within the international framework of dominating world powers and the dominated but struggling Two-Thirds World demands an ethical commitment. It is a concern for the millions of people in various continents and nations who are economically, politically, and culturally exploited by a few world powers.[6] A postcolonial analysis is, therefore, a search for answers and change in the face of entrenched global structures of oppression and exploitation. The postcolonial consequently requires an ethical commitment to, and identification with, those struggling under global structures of domination and exploitation. It is a search for a just form of international relations.

Postcolonial theoretical consideration includes an analysis of the international relations informing ancient, modern, imperialist, and present globalization periods. It involves the so-called First, Second, and Third Worlds, which are often divided into the two opposing categories of the developed and underdeveloped. These are very broad categories that run the risk of being ignored by the particularist academician as too vague, too general, or universalist. As Angela Gilliam points out, however, there is a need for a "theoretical focus that connects local concerns with national *and* international issues."[7] The internationalist character of postcolonial studies makes it invisible depending upon where the academician is positioned: in other words, those on the dominant side are not always adversely affected by international imperialism, unless they make a conscious effort to identify with the oppressed for ethical reasons. On the other hand, those on the dominated side live with international exploitation and domination on a daily basis. In such situations, the dominated tend to blame themselves for their suffering, turn against themselves, fight for inadequate resources, or turn to the imagined stability of the past. They are further driven by established structures to subscribe to the colonial stereotypes of perpetual dependence.

While postcolonial theories cannot avoid an international character, they are also historically specific. They become specific by focusing on how the colonizer's control of former colonial centers functions in particular countries, continents, and in certain groups. For example, one can focus on how the international domination of the former colonizing centers has promoted child labor, racism, and trafficking in women as well as its effect on the lives of rural and urban women in the Two-Thirds World. One can also focus on how this remote control of colonizing centers transformed the socially acceptable values and institutions of a particular society into valueless spaces or into overtly oppressive institutions. In their specificity, decolonizing postcolonial theories employ different ways of understanding and resisting imperialism specific to various dominated continents, countries, nations, genders, races, classes, ethnic groups, and economies. The particularity of this paper is focused on feminism/s within the framework of postcoloniality. It seeks to understand how gender relations are constructed in postcolonial spaces in order to identify decolonizing feminist strategies of liberation among Two-Thirds World women. Feminism/s, as used here, defines a worldwide political movement of women and men that seeks to understand the construction of women as secondary citizens in their societies and to implement change that will reinscribe them as whole beings with full rights in their given contexts. Feminist movements are diverse in their methods of fighting for the empowerment of women. What then are the characteristics and practices of Two-Thirds World feminists within the diversity of postcolonial spaces? What are their concerns and strategies? What is the role of religion in the colonization and decolonization of postcolonialist feminist space/s and subjects? A variety of Two-Thirds World feminist scholars have examined the issue of developing postcolonial feminist spaces. I will begin my analysis of their efforts by "conversing" with Chandra Talpade Mohanty, Gayatri Chakravorty Spivak, Ania Loomba, Ifi Amadiume, and Anthonia C. Kalu.

Postcolonial Feminist Spaces

Chandra Mohanty's article "Under the Western Eyes: Feminist Scholarship and Colonial Discourses" provides significant insights into the nature of postcolonial feminist spaces.[8] As previously defined, feminism is a worldwide political movement of many colors and, like its postcolonial counterpart, consequently manifests international characteristics. Because of this, it runs the risk of generalizing and prescribing feminist perspectives from the Western centers, which are often in a better position to sell their ideas given that the markets favor them. This danger, as Mohanty notes, is easily produced by homogenizing non-Western women into one group while maintaining the superiority of Western women over against the rest. To illustrate this point, Mohanty quotes Maria Rosa Cutrufelli, who states: "My analysis will start by stating that all African women are politically and economically dependent" and proceeds to say, "either overtly or covertly, prostitution is still the main if not the only source of work for African women."[9] Cutrufelli's statement notably participates in an old and continuous colonial construction of African women and men that epitomized Africa and other worlds as paragons of evil and savagery, immaturity, and static civilizations. Her feminist analysis of the Other woman exemplifies the colonial ideology of subjugation that characterized its victims as people who needed to be saved from their own terrible shortcomings. This colonizing construction proceeds by portraying the West as the center of all cultural good, a center with a supposedly redemptive impulse, while it relegates all other cultures to the project of civilizing, Christianizing, assimilating, and developing. It works by portraying the Other negatively while it continuously underlines the superiority of the West. The colonial approach constructed both the colonizer and the colonized to accept their given places in the rhetoric of colonizing. The colonizing discourse still thrives today in various forms of media. For example, whenever Africa appears in TV or movies, it is represented by poverty, disease, war, or wild animals.[10] North America and Britain, on the other hand, are represented by the White House (or the U.S. flag) and Westminster's golden parliament.

Cutrufelli's portrait of African women also highlights the complexity of their positioning in postcolonial spaces. That is, Two-Thirds World women experience themselves as oppressed by patriarchal structures in their own societies, the patriarchal structures of their colonizers, and the imperial structures of Western men and women. Women of colonizing centers, while oppressed by various forms of patriarchy in their own contexts, also perpetuate the oppression of the Other when they operate within colonial frameworks of thinking. Mohanty thus holds that the imposition of Eurocentric feminist categories of analysis on different cultures "limits theoretical analysis as well as reinforces Western cultural imperialism."[11] This caution is a reminder to Western feminists to be self-critical and recognize that they have often not escaped colonialist representations of the "colonized woman" and the Two-Thirds World women of our day. It reminds feminists of former colonial centers that colonizing frameworks are still, by and large, in place and unless one deliberately chooses to be a decolonizing feminist, one is likely to operate within these oppressive paradigms, and consequently to reproduce them. Mohanty concludes by warning the Western feminist scholar who continues to hold that postcolonial women "cannot represent themselves; they must be represented."[12] Mohanty emphasizes the need to recognize that Two-Thirds World women must define their own realities from their own perspectives, and that the authority of their own discourse should be accepted.

Gayatri Spivak answers her own question—"Can the subaltern speak?"—with an emphatic "no."[13] Instead, Spivak enjoins the female intellectual to bear the responsibility of "representing" the subaltern. Spivak's analysis of the postcolonial space reflects a Marxist-socialist influence. She defines imperialism as a creation of the capitalistic mode of production on a global scale, holding that: "The contemporary international division of labor is a displacement of the field of nineteenth-century territorial imperialism. Put simply, a group of countries, generally first-world, are in the position of investing capital; another group, generally third-world, provide the field for investment."[14] This relationship, Spivak insists, is built not only on simplistic economic machinery but on the ideological support that has maintained its power. Therefore, when Spivak says the subaltern cannot speak, she does not mean that workers have not recognized oppression and revolted. As she points out, this is well established historically. In the case of women, Spivak does not mean Two-Thirds World women cannot or have not participated in resistance as well as in the international division of labor.[15] Rather, she refers to the fact that dominant ideology is so well girded that it always privileges hegemonic powers. Bringing gender issues into this postcolonial context of production, Spivak holds that "the subaltern as female is even more deeply in shadow," or "muted."[16] How does Spivak perceive the construction of this deep shadow? Does she provide a way out?

First, Spivak points out that the categories of "color" or "black" lose significance when they are removed from their oppositional contexts in the First World. For example, the race issue assumes pronounced forms in places like South Africa but becomes less eminent in homogenous nations.[17] Second, she points out that the retrieval of lost origins or the call for a more intensified theory common in Anglo-American feminism/s cannot serve the muted subaltern woman. Race consciousness is often insignificant because the imperialist ideology clothed itself in humanistic ideology of a mission to save, to do good, and to assimilate the Other to itself. The subaltern female, therefore, did not experience herself as being hated on the basis of her color, but as being saved, civilized, or educated for the better. Spivak illustrates her point with the case of *sati* in India, to show how the imperialists who documented its occurrence aimed at two things: first, to legitimize the sacredness of their imperialist mission to their home countries; second, to appear as saviors of brown (Indian) women from brown men. In fact, this is achieved by imposing Victorian stereotypes on Indian women.

Regarding the retrieval of lost origins or reclaiming one's history, Spivak finds that it also further subsumes the subaltern woman. The retrieval has been used to impel the subaltern woman, for example, to celebrate the most patriarchal practices such as *sati*, or that of the royal Indian women who committed suicide in the face of rape by the conquerors of their men.[18] In both cases, the subaltern woman can speak only by embracing self-erasure. Spivak points out that, while Western feminists have been paraded as saviors of Two-Thirds World women, they also subscribe to the silencing of the subaltern woman.[19] She points to Mary Daly's project in *Gyn/Ecology*,[20] as an approach that operates within the larger context of imperial discourse—that is, it presents the Other woman as a victim who needs salvation. The imperialist framework of Mary Daly's project was challenged by African-American intellectuals such as Audre Lorde, in her open letter to Mary Daly, to which the latter chose not to respond.[21] Within these competing discourses, all of which claim to be interested in liberating the subaltern woman, Spivak is forced to conclude that "there is no space from which the sexed subaltern can speak."[22] She emphatically holds that "the subaltern as female cannot be heard or read."[23] In the place of a muted subaltern woman, Spivak appeals instead to intellectual responsibility, which demands that the intellectual should be self-critical and avoid subscribing to the dominant discourses of oppression. The intellectual must use her privileged position to understand the various layers of ideological oppression expounded by both imperialist centers, nativist, and international feminist movements. The intellectual must represent the subaltern woman. Except for exposing the ideological interestedness of these competing discourses and how they mute the subaltern woman, Spivak does not provide any further answer to the question of how best to give voice to the silenced subaltern woman. Spivak is instructive in three ways, however: she points to the complexity of the feminist postcolonial space, warns against easily subscribing to many self-proclaimed liberationist movements, and points to the depth of ideological interestedness of many theories that disadvantage postcolonial women of the former colonies.

While Mohanty's critique focuses on the dangers of universalist tendencies of feminism and its Western center, Ania Loomba focuses on the categories of analysis defined by the postcolonial theorists of Two-Thirds World.[24] Among these are Frantz Fanon's black skins/white masks, hybridity, master-slave configuration, Spivak's muted subaltern, modernist/nativist, and the theory of retrieving the past. Loomba assesses these various theoretical perspectives and finds them too rigid, ahistorical, prone to romanticizing or silencing the subaltern, and, sometimes, to reinscribing the colonial discourse while it reduces this discourse to a textual struggle, having little or no contact with the practical world of the postcolonial subject. In particular, Loomba finds these categories inadequate to assess the location of a postcolonial woman. Critical of the dual polarizations, Loomba prefers to examine the interaction of the native and colonial, a collision which usually mutilates or transforms the local culture in order to reinforce the hegemony of the superpowers. Interestingly, she shows how the colonial discourses that have presented themselves as emancipators manage to reinscribe the colonized woman under a heavier yoke. Education, for example, did not exempt the Indian woman from her traditional bondage; it simply added its own English stereotypes to her image.[25]

Loomba finds that assessing the retrieval of the past as a way of locating the Indian woman in the center of resistance is an unproductive approach–especially given that revivalism and communalism return with commercialized patriarchalism. The practice of the dowry, for example, is not only retrieved, but now also emerges with full-fledged capitalistic values, thereby underlining the oppression of Indian women. Although Loomba does not offer a precise alternative, except to warn against easy polarizations of the colonized and the colonizer, neither does she locate the alternative in hybridity or nostalgic retrieval of the past for an Indian woman. She does, however, highlight that the feminist space of the postcolonial is complex, inconsistent, and resists easy polarization if placed within historical contexts. While she problematizes all three theoretical categories, Loomba finds Spivak's mute subaltern a dangerous discourse that threatens to theorize the subaltern into silence again.

In sum, Mohanty, Loomba, and Spivak agree on the complexity of defining postcolonial feminist spaces. They provide caution against easy transference of First World feminist and male theories to Two-Thirds World women. Such transferences tend to translate themselves into other imperialist discourses that believe in the diffusion of Eurocentric civilizations to its peripheries. The return to the origins or color analysis are seen as inadequate, depending on the context,[26] to serve the interests of some feminists of former colonies. None of these three provides any specific way for the postcolonial feminist. Mohanty seems to say, Let the postcolonial woman (of former colonies) represent herself. Spivak, on the other hand, says the postcolonial subaltern woman cannot represent herself, but must be represented by a highly educated and self-critical intellectual. Loomba is content to caution against easy polarization, nostalgic retrieval, or hybridity theories, but she does not offer any particular alternative. This theoretical opaqueness, characterized by exposing the insufficiency of the available theories without offering any alternative, speaks of the difficulty that surrounds postcolonial feminist space.

I shall now look at how African women were constructed and socially affected during colonial times and the role of religion in the process. In order to understand the interaction of colonial discourse with some aspects of Setswana religion, I will focus on V. Y. Mudimbe, an African male philosophical writer; Ifi Amadiume, an African female sociologist; and Anthonia C. Kalu, a Nigerian literary feminist.

Mudimbe: Colonization and Religion

In his book *The Idea of Africa*, Mudimbe has a chapter entitled "Domestication and the Conflict of Memories."[27] In this chapter he focuses on the former Belgian Congo, the current Democratic Republic of Congo (henceforth DRC), to analyze how the colonial subject was constructed in the nineteenth and twentieth centuries. He uses archival information to show how the colonization of the DRC began as a planned meeting in Belgium in 1876, where the king expressed an interest in exploring Central Africa in order "to stop slavery practices and also to bring light to these areas."[28] The pope, who had earlier expressed an interest in the work of civilization, "thought that missionaries could contribute to [his] oeuvre."[29] His plan approved by the king, the pope blessed Bishop Lavigerie in February 24, 1878, and "put him in charge of evangelizing and converting equatorial Africa."[30]

Of note here is that the colonization of the DRC was intricately intertwined with religious agendas of conversion, which was expressed as an ethical goal of arresting slavery. By 1911, the Belgian Congo was divided into ten ecclesiastical regions, which also served as political regions. By 1939 there were 1,631 missionaries of different Catholic orders, all of which were primarily Belgian. As Mudimbe points out, the missionaries were expected "to carry out in Central Africa the obligations of the Church and political objectives of the king."[31] This understood and the missionaries well positioned, the mission showed "a will to convert, to transform, to change radically a space and its inhabitants."[32] This transformation of space involved the construction of the colonial subject according to Eurocentric specifications. It required conversion of the physical geography as well as the spiritual and mental space of individuals. Geographically, the transformation of the DRC took the form of Westernized architectural projects: the building of a mission city, which consisted of a church, a school, hospitals, missionary residences, orphanage, and garden. Moreover, missions were symbolically positioned apart from local settlements, yet close enough to the main village. Thus positioned, they became centers that disseminated a Eurocentric worldview and motivated the locals to yearn for and strive to accept their purported superior values.

The transformation of the individual required a transformation of the mind, which began with spiritual conversion. This was underlined by Western education in seminaries, attaining literacy in the language of the master, access to official work in the church or colonial administration and finally assimilation, which declared one a qualified French or Belgian citizen. To encourage more Congolese people to desire such transformation, church services were structured so that parishioners sat according to their ranks. The first space was reserved for the clergy and the second for white people. After this came the greater nave, the space of black Christians. Finally came the lowest nave of catechumens so that, as Victor Rolens puts it, "they can feel excluded from the celebration of the most sacred mystery and thus experience better their inferiority vis-à-vis the Christians."[33] Once the missionaries had won a few followers, the rigorous training of some local male professionals began. It entailed withdrawing young boys from village life for long periods. These trained indigenous individuals became liaisons between their people and the colonizers. They became agents of transforming their own people by becoming living models of what it means to be civilized, its advantages and how it can be attained. While this seems to espouse some form of equality, Mudimbe points out that "a general policy of acculturation situated these chosen ones between their black brothers and the white colonizers, without reducing them to one or the other group."[34] This policy explains why despite African subjects' conversion (and that of other colonized peoples) to Christianity and Western ways they did not attain equal faith status with their masters. The program from the beginning meant to win itself devotees, not equals. This tension created an intense identity crisis for the colonized Congolese and other colonized Africans, for they were neither African nor European.

In the initial stages of colonization, the African patronage was regarded as total. Most colonizers could not even perceive that Africans might revolt and demand their own independence. Mudimbe's archival research indicates that after World War II, when indigenous revolutionaries began to agitate against colonization, the missionaries held a consultation among themselves and reorganized their strategies so that they would appear to be on the side of indigenous people. By the 1960s, the period when most African states attained independence, many of the emergent leaders were former seminarians. They belonged to a class that stood between the colonizer and the colonized. They were a group of elites prepared to yearn for and to imitate the superior colonial center as well as to lead their nations along this path of yearning.

The colonial transformations of spaces and individuals operated by setting up tensions between indigenous life and the supposedly superior new European life. The tensions created and maintained conflicts by proclaiming the superiority of the new system and devaluing the social, economic, and political structures of the indigenous African societies. It thus became socially more advantageous to be Christian than not, to be educated in the European fashion than in indigenous schools, to work in the church and colonial administration offices than to manage one's own farm. A middle class consisting of professional workers was created. Large areas of land were converted to the production of cash crops, and working as a laborer for wages rather than working one's own land became normal. This marked the beginning of a landless class of workers in an economy reconfigured to a capitalistic structure. The African elites who came into power inherited colonial boundaries, religions, school curricula, languages, ideologies, and economies geared to supply Europe with raw materials. To this day, Africa is still demarcated as "Anglophone Africa," "Francophone Africa," and "Lusufophone Africa" because the languages of their former colonial masters continue to function as official languages.

Where did Congolese women fit in this transformation, however? Their absence from Mudimbe's analysis attests to their systematic exclusion. The Catholic church was and remains an intensely patriarchal institution, as was the colonial administration system of the DRC. The first locals to be trained were to serve these two institutions. In short, a structural exclusion of women was inaugurated through the school, the church, and the colonial administration. For an analysis that does focus on women in the colonial transformation, Ifi Amadiume's book, *Male Daughters, Female Husbands* is instructive.[35]

Colonization, Religion, and the Status of African Women

Amadiume's sociological research focuses on one African ethnic group in Nigeria, the Igbo, particularly in Nnobi. Here the erasure of African women was met and resisted by militant women, who rioted and even fought a war, on their own, against the British colonial administration in 1929.[36] To account for their militancy and resistance, Amadiume presents her research in three parts: precolonial, colonial, and postcolonial. The presentation allows us to observe how colonial transformation affected Igbo women.

Amadiume begins by assessing the myths of origin, ecology, production, wealth, economic activities, and their relation to gender among the precolonial Igbo. In general, Amadiume finds a society built upon "flexible gender construction." For example, land was owned and inherited by males, but in the absence of a male heir, a daughter could be termed "male daughter" and inherit the land. Crops were evenly distributed among men and women. Yams were cultivated by males while the production of cassava was assigned to females. Both sexes could excel in the production of their respective crops and earn titles of success such as Ogbuefi and Ekwe. Both women and men were entitled to sell their surplus products and to keep their profits. The market, however, was a woman's place. Women sold men's yams in the market and made extra profit out of it. Thus flexibility was built into a division-of-labor system that did not completely privilege a man over a woman in terms of public spaces of power and ownership of property.

Igbo gender construction had its own supporting myths and spiritual world that recognized female divine power through the goddess Idemili. Female industriousness and economic self-help were traced to such figures and used to reinforce a gender ideology that demarcated male and female social spaces. Under this framework, men tended to specialize in certain crops, ritual knowledge, and craft, while women produced their own crops, planted their own gardens, processed and preserved food, and dominated the marketplace. This gender construction, though certainly not egalitarian, had strength in its flexibility: it did not completely exclude women from the spheres of power. How did the colonial times affect this gender system? Amadiume says colonial invasion suppressed indigenous institutions through the imposition of Christianity, Western education, and new economic and administrative systems. The immediate impact corroded the flexible gender constructions of the Igbo and introduced "strong sex and class inequalities supported by rigid gender ideology and constructions."[37] In terms of Christianity, Amadiume documents Igbo women's resistance to its arrival because it was an apparent threat to the goddess worship, a religious practice that gave titles of prominence to women in the society. In its initial stages, therefore, Christianity was a male discourse with very little support from women—or from men. The support of the British colonial government aided the dissemination of Christianity and its institutions. Once established, Amadiume notes: "Church and school were synonymous. Classes were held in church buildings and no one was admitted into the school who had not converted to Christianity."[38] In addition to required conversion, the school lessons condemned indigenous religious practices, and proclaimed that their Christian God, who is male, was the creator of the whole universe. This systematic condemnation of the goddess, followed by the belief in the male God and his son, had economic consequences. As Amadiume points out: "Not only did Christianity condemn the goddess religion, but it also banned the Ekwe title. In a short space of time, the focal symbols of women's self-esteem were shattered. At the same time, women found themselves divided in their families . . . and torn by the different denominations to which they belonged."[39]

Concepts of female husbands and male daughters that allowed for gender flexibility and the rise of women were condemned as incompatible with the Christian gospel. The condemnation was brought into effect through the manipulation of local administration and the censorship of the school. The church owned and controlled most of the schools in those days, hence every mission-educated student passed through a systematic dislocation and self-alienation. Every educated student had been initiated into a gendered educational structure that relegated women to private spaces, devoid of public powers. Amadiume's analysis demonstrates that the colonial mission school also carried and constructed rigid gender roles. Boys were trained for carpentry, trade, priesthood, and printing, while girls were taught domestic services such as cleaning, cooking, sewing, and child care. Advanced educational levels were accessible only to boys. This was dictated by the fact that newly professionalized posts such as colonial clerks, church ministers, and military service privileged men over women.

Through these systematic changes in religion, economy, administration, and school, Amadiume's documentation demonstrates that a rigid gender construction was established, which relegated women to a secondary position in the Igbo society. The missionary education for girls equipped them to be housewives, not public players. Women could enter the job market as domestic servants and in what were regarded as women's jobs. Igbo women were now void of supporting myths and divine symbols of power since the Christian ones privileged men over women. This social debasement of Igbo women was met with continuous resistance from women, finally leading to the Women's War in 1929. However, the rigid gender construction was well set and structurally supported.

As noted earlier, most new African governments of the independence era kept their inherited colonial systems. Their social, economic, and political structures had been established as satellites to the Western economic and cultural systems. Amadiume shows continued resistance of Nigerian women up until the early 1980's when the increasingly militant governments of Nigeria sealed male power. Nigerian women remained dominant in the trade market, but have been educationally ill-prepared to compete with international companies of the global age. This example is specific to the Igbo women of Nigeria, but it finds many echoes among African women from the southern, central, and eastern regions of Africa.[40] I will illustrate this by briefly examining the Setswana spiritual structure and how it was colonized and gendered in the colonial era.

The Setswana Spiritual Space, Colonization, and Gender

Among Batswana,[41] and most ethnic groups of Southern Africa, there were no goddesses or gods. However, one finds a gender system that included women and men in its spiritual and social structures. Modimo, the High One (God), is neither male nor female in the Setswana cultures and other Southern African groups. The Badimo, the High Ones or Ancestors are the sacred figures residing next to Modimo; they consist of women and men who were once members of the society, but who are now the living dead. The word *Badimo* is always gender neutral and plural. It does not denote male or female sacred figures. The Badimo continue to care for their survivors; they pray for us and present our cases before Modimo, ensuring that we are blessed with all that we need. In society, the human intermediaries were Sangoma and Wosana (spirit mediums) as well as Ngaka (diviner herbalist). All these priestly figures who act as liaisons between humans and Badimo and Modimo could be male and female.

Colonial Christianity reduced the Badimo, Sangoma, and Ngaka to negative powers.[42] The Badimo were given the roles of demons in the Setswana Bible and dictionaries of colonial times. The Ngaka, on the other hand, was dubbed a witch doctor. While the closest term to translate the role of Jesus would have been *ngaka*, biblical translators preferred to use *moprista*, derived from the term for "priest." Modimo, the High God, was retained and accepted as the good God, appearing in the Setswana translations of the Bible as the equivalent of Yahweh. However, Modimo was transformed from a gender-neutral figure to a male one: *rara wa rona*, "our father" (Matt. 6:9) and the father of Jesus, his only son. The colonization of the Setswana religious system introduced a rigidly gendered system that stripped women of their power; they could hardly count themselves among Badimo, who were now demons, or freely claim the Sangoma and Ngaka positions, for these were now construed as the position of witches. The colonization process alienated the Batswana from their cultural symbols of power and particularly marginalized indigenous women; men could at least identify with Modimo, the Father God, and his son, who functions as the head of the church just as the men function as heads of the home (Eph. 5:22). This new gendered divine space was complemented by the colonial schools and public offices that favored men and relegated women to the positions of powerlessness.

In his paper "Missionary Wives, Women, and Education: The Development of Literacy among Batswana, 1840–1937," Patrick Mgadla shows that in precolonial times Batswana women's occupation was in ploughing and producing crops, and men's occupation was herding the cattle. What is notable about this observation is that both men and women were involved in economic production outside the home. In missionary education, women's industrial education focused on domestic services such as lace making, knitting, crocheting—subjects that did not necessarily equip them to occupy public work places, teaching being the only exception.[43] As I have noted elsewhere, some African women and men who resisted this colonizing hierarchical separation of the religions embraced what they found life affirming from both African Religions and Christianity to form what is today termed African Independent Churches (AICs).[44] Southern African women in the AICs claimed the indigenous priestly roles, which were not exclusively male, in order to become prophets, church leaders, healers, and bishops.

Amadiume's Igbo women, along with other Southern African women, help to define African postcolonial feminist spaces. Women in precolonial African gender systems have always participated in production, controlled markets, and possessed religious myths upholding economically strong and independent women. According to Antholia C. Kalu: "African reality . . . sees the woman as an active participant in all aspects of economic, political, social, and cultural existence."[45] This does not mean that African societies are or were egalitarian. It does, however, mean that their feminist quests for the empowerment of women must depart from a different angle from other feminists by virtue of their cultural differences and historical experiences. Kalu argues that it is "imperative that the African woman be restored to her precolonial status as integral participants in political, economic, social and cultural existence."[46] Unlike Spivak and Loomba, she apparently embraces some retrieval and restoration as a viable postcolonial feminist strategy.[47]

Kalu also discusses the role of Christianity in the erasure of African women. She holds that "the silencing of Africa was originally cloaked in the colonizer's goodwill messages of enlightenment and Christianity," and that African women were "walled off by Christian dogma."[48] Kalu concurs with Mudimbe and Amadiume in the role played by Christianity in the conversion of African spaces and the subjugation of women. Christianity, therefore, deserves a closer scrutiny and analysis from a postcolonial African feminist perspective. In postcolonial Africa, Christianity now exists together with indigenous African religions, and it should not continue to operate as a suppressor of women and indigenous cultures. African postcolonial feminists must therefore ask: How does Christianity continue to buttress the secondary position of African women today? How can the restoration of indigenous religious figures such as the goddess Idemili and Badimo counteract the negative impact of Christianity? How might these two religious traditions enrich each other and affirm women? Such questions and answers must be articulated in the light of both past and present oppression, and with a well-defined agenda to empower women of former colonies to become agents of their own lives within the contexts of their own societies and the larger global arena.

Conclusion: Two-Thirds World Feminist Spaces and Strategies

What, then, are the characteristics of the postcolonial feminisms articulated by Two-Thirds World Women? What are some of their practices and strategies? The above review of postcolonial feminist writers indicates that the answers to these questions will differ depending on ethnicity, nationality, gender, race, class, continents, and the type of colonialism they experienced. For example, Spivak and Loomba, speaking from their different Indian backgrounds, reject any form of nostalgia and retrieval of the past, whereas Kalu advocates the "restoration" of the African past as a viable postcolonial feminist strategy. Yet even within their various forms and practices, postcolonial feminisms display a number of recognizable strategies and concerns in their decolonizing and depatriarchalizing practices. First, postcolonial feminists operate within the parameters of past and present international oppression, which continues to exert its forms of oppression in their lives. Second, they indicate that the international oppression of the former colonies has exerted its greatest influence on colonized women. Thus, postcolonial feminist practices recognize the interaction of two or more patriarchal structures on colonized women: the imposed patriarchal structures of the colonizer and the indigenous ones. Working within this gendered space of oppression, postcolonial feminists of the Two-Thirds World may begin by investigating how colonial constructions reduced a woman to silence, either by replacing prevailing flexible gender systems with rigid and dualistic ones or by reinforcing indigenous patriarchal systems. Postcolonial feminists recognize that the mechanisms of subjugating women of the former colonies were often engineered through projects that proclaimed themselves as redemptive, but which must now be subjected to a decolonizing feminist analysis. In their feminist practices of reading and writing, Two-Thirds World women call for the decolonization of inherited colonial educational systems, languages, literary canons, reading methods, and the Christian religion, in order to arrest the colonizing ideology packed in claims of religious conversion, Western civilization, modernization, development, democratization, and globalization.

Third, as exemplified by Kalu's argument, the decolonizing practices of Two-Thirds World feminists are accompanied by a willingness to embrace and confront indigenous religious and cultural worldviews. This includes the willingness to pronounce them legitimate and adequate wherever possible, to reinterpret them where necessary, and to avoid the colonizing strategy of dismissing as negative all social systems of the colonized. Decolonizing feminists are keeping Audre Lorde's words in mind; namely, that "the master's tools can never dismantle the master's house." That is, postcolonial feminists cannot allow themselves to depend solely on the religions, languages, and educational programs of their former colonizers and expect to avoid subscribing to their own colonization. If the goddess Idemili is a divine symbol of social and spiritual empowerment for Igbo women in Nigeria, its rejection by Eurocentric/imperialistic rhetoric should not be allowed to hinder her restoration. Similarly, if Ancestor Veneration, Badimo, represents a gender-inclusive divine space that empowers women and men in the social and spiritual spaces of Southern Africans, then the system must be maintained and reinterpreted at various times rather than allowing it to be lost in an embrace of the exclusive rhetoric of Western Christian imperialism. Further, if imperialism is seen as a project impelled by the fear of difference and an attempt to organize the world according to the Western image, then reasserting diversity in international cultural, economic, and political systems is a crucial strategy in the decolonizing feminist spaces. The Western reorganization of the world into its own image gives the First World an unlimited global market space for its goods, services, and ideas. It is, therefore, vital for postcolonial feminists to assert their differences in the face of universalizing forces of globalization and colonization. A decolonizing feminist practice must also assess how this international domination renders women of former colonies politically invisible, economically impoverished, and culturally suppressed while it highlights diverse ways of resistance and liberation.

Fourth, postcolonial feminist strategies must confront oppressive aspects in one's own indigenous systems of gender. Oppressive practices such as genital mutilation and *sati* are confronted and rejected, without joining the colonizing discourse of rejecting or demonizing every aspect of indigenous cultures. A total rejection of one's culture, for whatever reasons, closely befriends imperial strategies of colonizing. Since no culture is absolutely negative or wholly pure, room should always be made for reinterpreting the old, promoting the good, and imagining the new in the hybrid spaces of the native culture. In these decolonizing spaces, postcolonial feminist analysis wrestles with the restoration of some aspects of the indigenous cultures and reinterprets others for the empowerment of women and all people.

Fifth, in their decolonizing feminist spaces, Two-Thirds World women also adopt hybrid means of resistance and liberation. While colonialism thrived by promoting the West as the center of all good, and portraying the rest as needing conversion, development, civilization, assimilation, and so on, decolonizing Two-Thirds World women adopt hybridity as a strategy of resistance. This hybridity also resists the nationalist call for colonized women to preserve indigenous cultures without question. This hybrid strategy refuses to endorse the stringent binary opposition that often relegates women to subordination and invisibility. Two-Thirds World feminists allow themselves the right to reap from both fields, from that of the colonized as well as the colonizer, and use whatever they find life affirming. Christianity and indigenous religions are thus not seen as competing opposites but as mutual traditions that enrich each other. In so doing, hybridity becomes a decolonizing feminist strategy, since it erodes the oppressive patriarchal demands of both imperialism and nationalism.

Broadly speaking, postcolonial feminist spaces are inscribed within the worldwide international relations of domination, suppression, and resistance. Postcolonial feminisms focus on how women of different backgrounds were, and are, affected by colonialism in addition to their own indigenous patriarchal systems, and how Two-Thirds World women can chart their ways through the various forms of the postcolonial condition. While there seems to be an unrelenting international domination, the strategy of postcolonial feminists is that of *aluta continua*. That is, the struggle continues in many different and small ways to seek for justice and empowerment of women and men within the national, international, and religious structures of the world.

Notes

1. See V. Y. Mudimbe, *The Invention of Africa: Gnosis, Philosophy and the Order of Knowledge* (London: James Currey, 1988), 1–3.

2. See Edward Said, *Culture and Imperialism* (New York: Alfred A. Knopf, 1993), 17.

3. In cases of Asian civilizations, the policy of colonialism was to believe that there was something lacking in Asian developments. See James M. Blaut, *The Colonizer's Model of the World: Geographical Diffusionism and Eurocentric History* (New York: Guilford Press, 1993).

4. See David Basil, *Modern Africa: A Social and Political History* (London: Longman, 1989), 11–20.

5. See Said, *Culture and Imperialism,* whose study shows how imperialism was a cooperation of many schools. There were those who had to go to the colonies and bring information while others stayed home, wrote books, arranged talks, and sponsored missionaries, who made the whole project legitimate.

6. Basil in *Modern Africa* points out "that colonial system aimed successfully at taking wealth out of Africa: by means of cheap mining labor; by paying prices to export crop farmers that were lower than prices on the world market" (19).

7. Angela Gilliam, "Women's Equality and National Liberation," in *Third World Women and the Politics of Feminism*, ed. Chandra Talpade Mohanty, Ann Russo, and Lourdes Torres (Indianapolis: Indiana University Press, 1991), 215.

8. See Chandra Talpade Mohanty, "Under the Western Eyes: Feminist Scholarship and Colonial Discourses," in *Colonial Discourse and Post-colonial Theory: A Reader*, ed. Patrick Williams and Laura Chrisman (New York: Columbia University Press, 1994), 196–220.

9. Quoted by Mohanty from Maria Rosa Cutrufelli, *Women from Africa: Roots of Oppression* (London: Zed Books, 1983), 13, 33.

10. Even a movie such as *Coming to America* subscribes to the colonial stereotype that characterizes Africa as a place of wild animals.

11. See Mohanty, "Under Western Eyes," 214.

12. Ibid., 216.

13. See Gayatri Chakravorty Spivak, "Can the Subaltern Speak?" in *Colonial Discourse and Post-colonial Theory*, 66–111.

14. Ibid., 83.

15. Ibid., 82.

16. Ibid., 83.

17. This tends to depend on the types of colonialisms. Settler colonialisms such as those of South Africa, Zimbabwe, Australia and North America exhibit strong racist edges.

18. Spivak, "Can the Subaltern Speak?" 101–3.

19. Ibid., 93.

20. Mary Daly, *Gyn/Ecology: The Metaethics of Radical Feminism* (Boston: Beacon Press, 1978).

21. See Audre Lorde, *Sister Outsider: Essays and Speeches* (Trumansburg, N.Y.: Crossing Press, 1984), 66–71.

22. Spivak, "Can the Subaltern Speak?" 104. It is more persuasive to say the subaltern cannot be heard. Most people speak in their various situations and times; the difference is that the powers of hegemony may not allow them to be heard.

23. Ibid.

24. See Ania Loomba, "Overworlding the 'Third World' " in *Colonial Discourse and Post-colonial Theory*, 305–32.

25. Ibid., 315–16.

26. While the ideology of superior races (colonizer) and inferior ones (colonized) is cen-

tral to the strategy of colonialism, this lost most of its significance after independence, for locals had power to assert themselves.

27. V. Y. Mudimbe, *The Idea of Africa* (Indianapolis: Indiana University Press, 1994).

28. Ibid., 104.

29. Ibid., 106.

30. Ibid.

31. Ibid., 109.

32. Ibid., 107.

33. Ibid., 112. Interestingly, white and black Christians were not mixed, that is, racism was maintained within the Christian church.

34. Ibid., 121.

35. See Ifi Amadiume, *Male Daughters, Female Husbands* (London: Zed Books, 1987).

36. Ibid., 140. Their revolt was characterized by the attack and destruction of the white man's symbols such as courts, factories, foreign goods in the markets and warrant chiefs, which displaced Nigerian women's power in the society.

37. Ibid., 119.

38. Ibid., 121.

39. Ibid., 25–38.

40. See Robin Morgan, ed., *Sisterhood Is Global: The International Women's Anthology* (New York: Doubleday, 1984). Most African women contributing to this anthology are of the view that the majority of African women, married or not, were not dependent on men. They also point to the negative impact of Western civilization on women, as they were summarily defined as secondary citizens during colonialism. A study of African mythology's portayel of women's image and role agrees with this view. Basically their gender structures were not constructed on a rigidly exclusive worldview.

41. The word *Batswana* refers to the people of Botswana, while Setswana refers to the language and culture of the country.

42. For a detailed analysis of this colonizing construction, see Musa W. Dube, "Consuming a Colonial Cultural Bomb: Translating Badimo into Demons in the Setswana Bible," *Journal for the Study of the New Testament* 73 (1999): 33–59.

43. See Patrick Mgadla, "Missionary Wives, Women, and Education: The Development of Literacy among Batswana, 1840–1937," *Pula: Botswana Journal of African Studies* 11:1 (1997): 70–81.

44. See Musa W. Dube, "Readings of *Semoya*: Batswana Women's Interpretations of Matt. 15: 21–28," *Semeia* 73 (1996): 111–29.

45. Anthonia C. Kalu, "Those Left in the Rain: African Literary Theory and the Reinvention of the African Woman," *African Studies Review* 37: 2 (1994): 82.

46. Ibid., 91.

47. Although the return to precolonial times is frightening and is rejected by many, one should consider Audre Lorde's saying, "the Master's tools can never dismantle his house." Holding on to the received traditions is indeed holding on to limiting master's tools. In his article "Native American Perspective: Canaanites, Cowboys, and Indians," Robert Allen Warrior, reflecting on the participation of Christianity in the oppression of American Indians, concludes by saying, "Maybe, for once, we will just have to listen to ourselves" (*Voices from the Margin: Interpreting the Bible in the Third World*, ed. R. S. Sugirtharajah [Maryknoll, N.Y.: Orbis Books, 1991], 205).

48. Kalu, "Those Left in the Rain," 92, 94.

Part Two

Rethinking Texts and Traditions

5

The Prostitute's Gold

*Women, Religion, and Sanskrit in
One Corner of India*

Laurie L. Patton

Preliminaries

A retired professor of Sanskrit from Cotton College, Assam, a woman
in her early seventies, tells this story about her most beloved teacher:

> In the early decades of this century, he was a young man, a devoted
> Hindu and teacher of Sanskrit, who became involved in the Freedom
> Fighter movement in Assam. He was asked to deliver a message from
> one fellow Freedom Fighter to another, and was on his way through
> the streets of Gohati, Assam, to do so. He began to feel ill, and col-
> lapsed by the roadside. When he awoke, he found himself in the back
> room of a house, tended to by various women who came and went.
> When he finally recovered after a day or two, the women came to him
> with a large, heavy bag. One of them said, "We know who you are,
> and what your work is. We would like to donate this to the cause."
> The bag was filled with gold jewelry, and he realized that he had been
> in the back room of a brothel. "Because those women saved my life,
> and helped me to complete my errand, I will always be indebted to
> women. That is why I teach Sanskrit to women."

I begin with this story of feminism, postcoloniality, and religion to illustrate one situation in India that holds some intriguing tensions I want to focus on in this chapter. The women in the story are indeed the subalterns who will never have a name, and yet they helped change the course of colonial history by enabling the Freedom Fighter to remain healthy and continue his work. He, in turn, in a classical reformist move, bestows the privilege upon the dispossessed—the privilege of access to the hegemonic language of Sanskrit. This move, in turn, helps to create a lineage which is part of the postcolonial legacy—the bestowal, and later abandonment, of the privilege of learning elitist languages to women. Women thus become the holders of an abandoned and romanticized Sanskrit past. This past, in turn, acts as the sign of postcolonial Hindu nationalists, who are simultaneously void of actual monetary commitment to the study of Sanskrit. This is an ambivalent empowerment indeed.

Sanskrit, as a result of this postcolonial legacy, has become a marker of the Hindu religiosity of women as well as of men. In certain places it will soon become entirely the prerogative of women. This has happened without the help of postcolonial theory or secular feminism, either Indian or Western. It will continue without that help. And yet engagement between, even transformative conversation among, postcolonial and feminist theorists and traditional Sanskritists might afford a way of interpreting elitist texts and altering hegemonic languages in an entirely new way. In this chapter I make no attempt to excuse the elitism; rather, I attempt in some small ways to dislocate it, to misplace Sanskrit and place its cultural heritage in new and unsettling contexts. This dislocation partially reveals some of the transformative possibilities and impossibilities of reading in one literate, elitist sphere of postcolonial Indian culture.

I do this by providing a very preliminary description of my conversations with women Sanskritists, all of whom I count as my teachers. I learned from them both formally and informally, and their words are an account of what I learned.[1] For purposes of clarity, let me define my terms as I use them in this chapter: When I use the term *feminist*, following Chandra Talpade Mohanty, Sara Suleri, and Samir Dayal,[2] among others, I try to move away from the voice of a "hegemonic monolinguistic culture who makes everybody's life miserable by insisting on women's solidarity at her price."[3] While some commonality between women Sanskrit scholars is inevitable, I try to enter into a diverse conversation with the multiple voices of women who are joined together only by virtue of their previous exclusion from a sacred language.[4] When I use the term *postcolonial*, I use it as a historical marker, as

Arif Dirlik does, "the description of a condition of the period after colonialism."[5] When I use the term *postcolonialism*, or *postcolonial theory*, I follow Gauri Viswanathan in meaning that attitude or position from which "the decentering of Eurocentrism may ensue."[6] Finally, I use the term *religion* to mean that set of practices that are defined as Hindu by the women with whom I am speaking.

Some Facts

Let us turn now to review some intriguing facts. There are indeed exceptional people like the one above who changed the study of Sanskrit for women earlier this century. However, in at least one area of India, the landscape of the study of Sanskrit is rapidly changing when it comes to gender. Let me begin with some facts about Maharashtra, the area where I did my preliminary research. In Maharashtra, Sanskrit is alive and well within the educational system—with eight major independent research institutes in Pune and Bombay; six universities that offer master's and doctoral degrees; thirty-three major Sanskrit manuscript collections; and nine Indological journals published in the state.[7] The personnel needed to maintain this large educational tradition is quite large.

This corps of personnel increasingly consists of women. With one retirement, the Department of Sanskrit of the University of Pune will consist entirely of women. The ratio of male to female students registered for the M.A. in Sanskrit in 1999 was 1 to 6. In the Deccan College Dictionary Project, Pune, there are seven women and two men on the regular research staff. Fifty percent of the researchers on staff at the Bhandarkar Oriental Research Institute are women. The number of *stri-purohits*, or women ritual specialists, is growing rapidly, and, according to one report by V. L. Manjul,[8] women now outnumber men in certain neighborhoods in Pune. On a nationwide scale, six of the chairs of the major universities—Delhi, Madras, Nagpur, Pune, Calcutta, and Hyderabad—are women.

These are preliminary facts in the first stages of my research project. This revolutionary gender shift in the study of Sanskrit has happened with very little ideological war; it has happened because the sons of famous Sanskritists of the previous generation have turned to science, engineering, and computer programming as more lucrative and prestigious means of employment. To put it clearly: there is no male hegemony in the field of Sanskrit in Maharashtra; instead there is a gender shift of gargantuan proportions in a single generation—a shift that deserves to be pondered.

I have completed sixteen out of a projected thirty oral life histories of women in the field of Sanskrit in Maharashtra, using as my starting point (and my starting point only!) the questionnaire outlined in my review of the data below. The conversations were long and meandering, lasting two to three hours each. They were conducted mostly in my native language of English, some in my conversational Hindi (which is good enough for about a half hour of conversation), and some with occasional phrases in conversational Sanskrit (which I can partly understand but have only a rudimentary level of speaking.) All the conversations except two were recorded. The results, I think, are fascinating. I will begin with a review of the numbers; I will then turn to an assessment of the trends that emerged and the significant factors for these women in their study of Sanskrit. These trends and factors are far different from what I had expected to find going into the project. I will end with a discussion of the themes of this book in light of my data: the tensions and relationships between feminism, postcoloniality, and religion. As we will see below, they reveal intriguing relationships between precolonial and postcolonial India; the ideologies of gender, both feminist and Hindu; and the role of Sanskrit as an indicator of Hindu religiosity.

I interviewed three M.A.'s and thirteen Ph.D.'s. Three women were age thirty-five and under; ten were between the ages of thirty-five and sixty; three were sixty and older. Two were research assistants; five were readers or professors at the university level; six were researchers hired by institutes and universities; two were retired teachers; and one was a librarian.

Let us begin with question 1: "When was the first time you encountered Sanskrit?" Thirteen of the sixteen women had been raised in households where chanting *Subhashitas* and other songs, *shlokas* from the *Ramayana* or *Gita*, were significant childhood memories. Thirteen of the women describe the experience as positive. "The pronunciation of my father was so pure, I could feel the serenity of it," said one. "It was as if Sarasvati was there." "We worshiped without *murtis* (images), and therefore sound was the only thing we had," a senior woman recounted. "If you knew the *Shlokas* you were part of the family, and that indeed was a great comfort to me," said one long-term researcher. "You feel better from the sound itself."

Those who experienced the sound of Sanskrit as negative were driven by the discouragement and derision they felt from others. Kumud Pawde, retired professor of Nagpur who is also a Dalit, writes, "It was this [Brahmin] disgust [for me] that inclined me towards Sanskrit. . . . Even at [a] young age, this emotion of disgust taught me to think."[9] Others were discouraged because their brothers were considered to be more appropriate to learn Sanskrit, even though they would never take it as a profession. And one remembered: "My father made us memorize, and we were scared. That fear has never left me."

Interestingly, however, the influence of parents is divided fairly equally in terms of gender. Eleven were influenced by their fathers and eight by their mothers. Many fathers, in addition to being scholars of Sanskrit or university teachers in other fields, had artistic or alternative occupations of some kind: a royal photographer, a ritual adviser, an activist for the Freedom Fighter movement, an artist. The mothers tended to use Sanskrit instruction as part of the activity of the home. "When my mother dusted, she would take me around and help me chant *Shloka*s as we did the housework." A retired teacher said, "The ladies in the neighborhood took me to the temple and treated me as their own daughter. I learned a lot of Sanskrit in their homes." Nine out of the sixteen knew the meanings of the Sanskrit verses they learned as children; six were influenced by the sound alone and did not have access to the meaning until later.

Several intriguing facts emerge in response to question 2: "Who was your first Sanskrit teacher? What do you remember about him or her?" Again, there is no gender differentiation in terms of the influence of teachers. Eight of the women had women teachers, and eight had men teachers. Thirteen of the women were encouraged to do science instead of being Sanskritists: this, in fact, is the only trace of rebellion I could find during my interviews. Moreover, thirteen out of sixteen mentioned nontraditional ways in which their teachers taught them. Two of the teachers were blind and focused on the sound of the language. One blind teacher asked the students to close their eyes as well. Two used reenactments of Puranic stories or Sanskrit dramas. Another teacher used regular household tasks as a way of teaching the student simple Sanskrit sentences. Another drew huge tables on the blackboard, with each sound representing a different country on the map.

In response to question 3, "What was your biggest challenge in learning Sanskrit, and how did you overcome it?" again there was no universally common hindrance to these women's Sanskrit education. Six described marriage and child rearing, one a violent husband, and one caste barrier. Eight described more intellectual challenges such as English versus Marathi medium classes, the use of *vibhakti* (grammatical cases) and so on. Twelve out of the sixteen described themselves as having a mediocre intellect, inferior to the previous generation.

In response to question 4, "What was the topic of your dissertation, and how did you choose it?" fourteen responded; two had not written dissertations. Eight chose Vedic topics, four topics in Sanskrit philosophy, and two topics in Sanskrit grammar; all of them except one were guided by their mentors' suggestions and advice on topics. The range of these topics also reflects the senior scholars who were working in the field at the time of the dissertation writing.

Question 5 asked "Who was your biggest intellectual influence outside of your dissertation guide?" Twelve women mentioned other teachers as major influences, six of whom were traditional male pundits. The nature of their influence tended to be based on the simplicity, accessibility, and kindness of the person, as well as his breadth of knowledge. Two named their circle of friends as their major intellectual influence—groups of women for whom knowledge and friendship went together. Intellectual influence tended to be perceived as pragmatic and ethical in nature. One woman described an event in which her mentor publicly defended a woman whom he knew had been deriding him behind his back; this act of selflessness impressed her greatly. Another mentioned pundit Padurang Shastri Athavale, the Hindu activist who advocates reading of the *Gita*, and his use of Sanskrit in daily life.

Question 6 was "How do you see the connection, if any, between your research and your teaching?" Here the sample was too small and the kinds of work too varied to remark upon particular trends. Some Sanskritists interviewed were exclusively teachers, others were exclusively researchers, and so on. Question 7, "What is your current teaching post?" is answered in my descriptions of the various occupations of the women above.

Question 8, "Do you teach Sanskrit in the same way that you learned it? If not, why not?" reveals an even split between traditional and innovative teaching methods. Only three women emphasized teaching methods different from those of their own teachers, regardless of whether those teachers were traditional or innovative. Those who insisted on traditional methods all volunteered additionally that there was no substitute for memorization. Those who emphasized innovation tended to remark upon the necessity of audiovisual tools and interdisciplinary focus in teaching.

In response to question 9, "What is your current research interest, and how did you develop it?" the research interests of the women reflected no real change from the dissertation topics. However, in response to this question I received an overwhelming number of unsolicited arguments for involving Sanskrit in public education programs and public intellectual life. I will discuss this issue in more detail below.

The women's responses to the final three questions revealed the most interesting narratives and images of the questionnaire. Question 10 was "What is the future of Sanskrit study in India as you see it?" Half of them thought the state of Sanskrit was getting better; half thought it was the same or worse. "Society now demands it but we don't have the supply of the experts," said one professor. "Nationalism has changed everything. We now have opportunities to educate in the way we didn't before. We are in a stage of awakening, and if the government sponsors us, we will do well." Two independently remarked that the government had adopted pro-Sanskrit rhetoric, but had failed to come through with any actual monetary support. Those who felt that the state of Sanskrit was the same or worse focused on the hardship of the struggle. They worried that Sanskrit would be eradicated from school-level education completely. Another mused philosophically, "Sanskrit is always a question mark. It is always a question whether it will be studied or not. Even in Patanjali's time it was not relevant."

Despite the split in assessing the present state of Sanskrit, question 11 elicited a very clear and uniform response ("What is the biggest change you have seen in the study of Sanskrit during your career?"). The biggest change in Sanskrit study tended to be the fact that teaching methods were less stringent (8). A close runner-up to that response was the observation that many more women than men were teaching now, and that the field needed men (7); finally, that the study of Sanskrit was becoming more integrated into other disciplines (6). The Sanskritists who were more than sixty years old tended to see the change in terms of the political significance of Sanskrit.

The answers to the final question were also quite strongly uniform, and the illustrations and elaborations very intriguing indeed. ("How do you view the role of women in the study of Sanskrit?") Fifteen out of sixteen women saw women's roles as crucial in building the culture and the academic study of Sanskrit. Only one saw no significant role for women. I will discuss these views below.

Trends

What is the overall profile from these numbers if we define, for the moment, a "trend" as existing when twelve out of sixteen women give the same answer? First, we can note the places where trends did *not* occur: there is very little gender differentiation in terms of the influence of parents and teaching. This fact also undermines the forced assumption of female solidarity mentioned above, about which many postcolonial and feminist thinkers have written. Both mothers and fathers influenced these women; both genders taught these women. I think this pattern might reflect the fact that the change in gender has taken place without ideological war, but rather with ideological place shifting: "It is now better for boys not to take up Sanskrit, but take up other professions suited to their nature and responsibilities." Moreover, there is very little distinguishable pattern as to the choice of topic for dissertation or present research. Most of the women follow the prescriptions of their dissertation guides, which would reflect the variety of interests of the previous generation. One clear trend to note in this regard, however, is that while formative intellectual influences may have been both men and women, dissertation guides per se have tended to be men from the previous generation of Sanskritists.

All of the trends that *did* occur can be thought of in terms of religious identity and deserve much richer elaboration. They are caste and Sanskrit, the public culture of Sanskrit, and the role of women in shaping the future study of Sanskrit.

Caste

Let me begin with caste, for as many Indian postcolonialists continually point out, discussions of caste and class are absolutely necessary to any discussion of gender in India. Thirteen of the sixteen women identified brahmin families as a positive preserver for Sanskrit in the present environment. Moreover, they spoke of the brahmin heritage as a vehicle for knowledge. While the issue of making Sanskrit available to the culture at large was mentioned constantly, as we will discuss below, very rarely were specific other castes or religions mentioned. Mention is made by Kumud Pawde herself, whose driving metaphor for her Sanskrit learning is the fact that she is a Dalit. Her own horrifying relationship with the "Splendid People" is the memory and motivation for her learning. And her Dalit status is forever the referent in her professional adult life after that; she struggles with being a "token" in a number of ways.

The second instance is that of the daughter of a well-known scholar in Vedic studies, who was a young girl at the beginning of the making of J.A.B. Van Buitenen's film on an early Indian sacrifice. (J.A.B. Van Buitenen was a famous scholar of early Indian religions and translator of Sanskrit texts.) At one point during the filming of the ritual, an *adivasi* (An *adivasi* is an "original inhabitant" of India, and thereby low-caste, or beyond caste, to a brahmin.) rode in a chariot race, and she and her younger sister were asked to ride in the chariot with the *adivasi*. "I was so proud of this; we each had a job; my brother had the job of distributing the *ladhus* (sweets), and I had the job of riding with the *adivasi*." The *adivasi* was placed in a symbolic role and was welcomed as a source of prestige. Intriguingly, she mentions later that her family often had pundits over who would not take food cooked by the lower castes. The final mention of caste is that of a professor at the University of Bombay, who found herself in difficult personal circumstances after the breakup of a marriage. She went to a village to teach Sanskrit to support herself. In addition to her regular responsibilities, she started a class for Dalits, and found that to be one of the most rewarding experiences of her career.

"My students loved it. They took care of my son, and I taught them Sanskrit. I regard that school as the biggest achievement of my life."

It is important to note here that these stories are the exceptions, and not the rule of the women's response. Brahmin caste consciousness, then, is an implicit and integral part of Sanskrit study. Intriguingly, it was not made explicit ideologically, except insofar as brahmins were characterized as the guardians of traditional learning. If this small sample of women is any indication, it is clear that caste matters more than gender, and this is a topic to which we shall return in our conclusions.

Second, all of these women, no matter what their caste, enjoy middle-class status. Their focus on hard work, their sense of pride in their achievements, their capacity as breadwinners for the family, and their relative sense of freedom to move about within the public social spheres comes directly from that economic status. On a relative scale, university professors and researchers in India do not earn salaries as high as most First World scholars (postcolonialists included), and their economic status is decidedly in the middle of middle class.[10]

Sanskrit and Public Culture

A second striking trend is the commitment of the women to their roles as public intellectuals and as bearers of a tradition. As mentioned earlier, thirteen of the women were participating in some kind of activities to integrate Sanskrit learning into the larger culture. One woman writes a regular column for the Pune Marathi language daily newspaper on *Subhashitas* in Sanskrit, presenting and explaining a different *Subhashita* (Sanskrit aphorism) each week. Another does a regular program on *mangalacaranas* (auspicious invocations) for the local high school near her neighborhood. Another is involved in an adult education program for Sanskrit at Somaiya Vidya Vihar College in Bombay. Moreover, she used the Hindu devotional poet Jnaneshwari as the main text for inter-religious dialogue with a recent delegation sent by the Vatican on Hindu-Christian dialogue. Another sees the *Shaiva Purana*, a medieval religous text, as a source of education for environmental consciousness in India, and has developed a traveling lecture series on this topic. The youngest is very involved in publicity for the Sanskrit-speaking movement of Krishnashastri, based in Delhi, but with camps all over India. "Speaking is the only way we can prove that Sanskrit is not a dead language: we didn't call it a dead language, the Europeans did. . . . In our magazine, and in our organization, anyone and everyone is welcome."

Several of the women assisted as *stri-purohits*, or women ritual specialists, in particular ritual occasions. Five women mentioned participation in the annual government-sponsored elocution and composition contests. There they have participated as judges as well as contestants. Giran Vagvani is the association for speaking Sanskrit in Pune; Gita Mandalam a discussion group about Sanskritic texts and topics. Veda Sastra Sabha is the vehicle for popular understanding of the Veda in Pune. The women I interviewed were members or staff of all these organizations, and several were involved in writing for the national magazine, published by Krishnashastri's organization, that promotes Sanskrit learning in Sanskrit.

Sanskrit and Stridharma

Third, and perhaps most important for our purposes, in addition to this cultural promotion of Sanskrit, there is a clear trend toward understanding Sanskrit as the positive responsibility of women. Sanskrit learning is a heritage that they now must take up. To put it even more strongly, they see it as a form of *stridharma*, or women's religious duty, written about in many classical Sanskrit texts and criticized by both Indian and Western feminists.[11] While many admit that the linkage between *stridharma* and the study of Sanskrit is not historically the case and has, in fact, been a rather hostile relationship, nonetheless the way they speak about their work now is in terms of dharmic obligation: "Generally, in India, girls offer Sanskrit ("offer" here is like "take" in American English). If they become ideal mothers, as they should, they can pass on the message of Sanskrit in the home. That will be their great contribution." "The future of Sanskrit is safe in the hands of women. They are the ones who can create generations; this is *adistridharma*." "In Cotton College there was never anything like patriarchy. Mostly women carried on the tradition; my teacher was right in his instincts to teach women." "We create Sanskrit classes for women in the afternoon, and not during the religious festivals; we know that most women are performing their duties for the festival of Navaratri, for instance, and that those duties are the reasons why we are teaching Sanskrit in the first place." "Women can teach their children at home, while they do the housework. What better way to keep Sanskrit is there?"

It is worth noting here that the study of Sanskrit does not imply the single life or a state of *brahmacarya* (celibate studentship) for these women. For them, *stridharma* still includes and emphasizes marriage; it has just expanded to include Sanskrit in the household. All of the women except two were either currently married or widowed.

One woman who had studied Mimamsa, the early Indian ritual philosophy, had the most eloquent way of talking about the dharma of women and Sanskrit: "The great commentator Sabara always wanted our sacred tradition to be *apaurusheya*—not from the human. But now we can see a new meaning to his words: Sanskrit has become *apaurusheya*—no longer from the gents!"

Moreover, the hardships that some endured in their first years of learning were overcome with kind of dharmic stoicism: "Before, when I first started to learn Sanskrit, I was told that 'you and your teacher will go to hell.' Now, all the ladies are learning. It was our own womanly instinct to advance in every field." Said another: "Women are more sincere, devoted to work, and they listen to other people. They face more difficulties on their own. Because of this, Sanskrit will not spoil in the hands of women." Some put it even more boldly —that Sanskrit improves character, perseverance, and purity: "When someone offers you *prasad* (sacred food tasted by the gods), and it has a stone in it, then you have to eat it, even when there is a stone. Modern people reject the stone that is in the *prasad* of Sanskrit, and they forget that it is *prasad*." Another, more senior woman said: "If your mind is accepting the *samskaras*, then you have better *samskaras* in Sanskrit. It gives the discipline of mind." Finally, one woman saw Sanskrit as a kind of sacred opportunity in the shape of animal: "If there is a cat in the courtyard, the older woman will call it *behin-ji* (sister). The modern girl will only say, 'Cat, go away.' But Sanskrit is the cat that has visited the women's courtyard."

Generational Images

The final trend I will mention is the remarkable correlation between a woman's generation and the way she views Sanskrit study. For the three younger women I interviewed, Sanskrit was an ideology that helped to revive parts of a lost culture. The stories of the cat and the *prasad* were told to me by a younger woman who longs for the women of her generation to hold on to traditional ways. Only one of the three had an explicit alliance with the Hindu nationalist Bharatiya Janata Party (BJP) that she was willing to talk with me about. The majority of the women I interviewed were of the middle generation; for them, maintaining the status of Sanskrit was most often spoken of in terms of maintaining the status of the household. None of these women spoke of her political allegiances directly, although I inferred from at least three of them that they were involved with BJP and Vishva Hindu Parishad (VHP) sponsored organizations. Most were reluctant, out of discretion or wisdom, to talk about their political affiliations directly. One woman said rather bluntly, "Every Westerner who comes here to study Sanskrit is pro-Muslim, so why bother to talk politics?"

For the three women over sixty years of age, Sanskrit was clearly a source of nationalist pride that had the potential to give dignity to all Indians, of whatever walk in life. We saw this in our opening story of the Freedom Fighter and the prostitute's gold. That same woman learned her first syllable of Sanskrit in the daily recitations of the *Gita* among those who gathered in her father's home before they began their resistance work. One woman had begun Sanskrit before Pune University had even been established. She said of her childhood: "Sanskrit was a symbol of all that we could be as a culture, superior to the West, even though they ruled us. Sanskrit was *svaraj* (self-rule); we had one Sanskrit teacher who bicycled through the whole of India just to show us how important it was to unite the country against the British."

Moreover, these older women speak about the ways in which Sanskrit recitation gives them the ability to deal with loss. One woman recited verses from the *Gita* as she nursed her mother through the last stages of a terminal illness: "My mother didn't have a voice, so I gave her one through the *Gita.*" Said the seventy-year-old scholar: "Even now, because of my childhood, I know I can face the future when I recite Sanskrit. It gives me knowledge of God's grace to me; I recited it when my husband died last year, and I knew I could continue. I carry the ideal of Mahatma Gandhi, and now I live in *sandhyacaya* (shadow-twilight) and I am not afraid of it. I know I can pass through *sandhyacaya* very calmly. I am not afraid of it because I know Sanskrit." Finally, one librarian wrote: "We can call Sanskrit 'the father language,' but I would prefer to call it *athibhashya*—*athi* is grandmother in Marathi, and I am now a grandmother. It gave birth to our languages, and therefore it is like a grandmother."

Tentative Conclusions

I hesitate to draw any particular conclusions at this stage of the work—although I know I will probably call the final book resulting from this research "Grandmother Language." I will end simply by posing some important questions.

To begin with, in the beginning phases of this study we have a rather stunning example of the "pink-collar" phenomenon,[12] whereby a profession becomes populated by women because it has become less lucrative and prestigious for men to choose it. In this sense it is no different from the arts and humanities in many Western cultures.

However, some particularities do emerge for women and Sanskrit. The sketch I have so far suggests that, as mentioned above, gender was not at all an important factor in the decision of these women to take up Sanskrit—the influence of male and female parents and teachers is decidedly equal. Nor did feminism even register on the scale. Pessimism and optimism about the future of Sanskrit were evenly balanced. Instead, as we saw earlier in the chapter, the most influential factors were (1) family/brahmin identity, (2) innovative teaching methods of mentors, and (3) the fact that Sanskrit was seen as a positive alternative to science.

Most important for our purposes, women seem to place a heavy emphasis on using Sanskrit to create culture and public intellectual life. In addition, they see the study of Sanskrit as part and parcel of their religious obligation as women, married women who follow *stridharma*. Finally, and relatedly, there are clear generational differences in the ways in which the significance of Sanskrit is viewed: for the elder women, it is a vehicle for national dignity; for the middle generation, a vehicle for creating culture; and for the younger women, a vehicle for the preservation of something that is disappearing with modern ways. They share with the older generation an emphasis on nationalism, but it is the nationalism of Advani, not of Gandhi and Nehru.

Two final and important notes as I continue my research. First, it is clear that the relationship between women and Sanskrit must be studied regionally. The situation for women Sanskritists is vastly different in Maharashtra than it is in Orissa or Kerala or Uttar Pradesh. Maharashtra's strong heritage of educational reform for women (Ramabai, Lakshmibai, the Karve Institute, the first *stri-purohits*, etc.) makes it very different from other regions. Second, it is clear that one might keep in mind the complex relationship between caste and gender. With the exception of Kumud Pawde, the move to include women in the study of Sanskrit has not included women of non-brahmin castes. This fact leads one to the uneasy question of whether, in fact, the inclusion of brahmin women in the study of Sanskrit is an occasion for celebration at all; might it not be a way to keep the study of Sanskrit within brahmin boundaries?

Exploring the Tensions

What are the theoretical implications for this study, in terms of the tensions between feminism, postcolonialism, and religion, outlined in this book? First, the lack of feminist ideology in the study of Sanskrit might give us a kind of "empowerment by abdication," in which the world women inherit is tarnished as unwanted, and where the decidedly postcolonial male-dominated cybertechnology and scientific careers win out over the more cultural careers dominated by women. Perhaps because of these reasons, to date the worlds of Sanskrit interpretation have existed in a kind of intellectual apartheid. Western and Indian feminists have interpreted the texts in occasionally similar and occasionally different ways. Hindu women in charge of

much of the Sanskrit legacy very rarely talk to feminists, and their traditionally religious conception of their inheritance of the Sanskrit legacy would be
anathema to most feminists. Thus the apartheid continues.

Second, what we might traditionally term "empowerment" can and does
happen for many women Sanskritists despite the absence of ideological feminism, and this in turn creates a fascinating tension vis-à–vis patriarchal Hinduism. Many of the women spoke of their newfound public voices as writers,
teachers, spiritual and ritual leaders, and breadwinners for the family. As Sanskrit, the harbinger of moral virtue and piety, is more and more allied with
women, it can itself be a kind of resistance to the corrupting power of male
dominance. Many women spoke of the "domestication" of Sanskrit, and the
stronger moral qualities of women, as a corrective to the current system of
education. Thus their worlds exist in a highly ambivalent space between critique and support of patriarchal learning.

Third, the generational differences among these women teach us that Sanskrit was clearly a force of resistance in precolonial India, and a place of tem-
porary empowerment for women, albeit in a Rosie-the Riveter-like way. The
use of Sanskrit in that period was clearly postcolonialist in nature and intent,
in that it afforded a position from which to decenter Eurocentrism. And yet,
in postcolonial India, Sanskrit is also a place from which to consolidate
majority Hindu rule, and thus has a Janus-like quality in that it can be used
for resistance of either the foreign Other or the non-Hindu Other at home.

Relatedly, postcolonialism and Hindu nationalism dance an ambivalent
dance of alliance in their common resistance to Eurocentrism. However, Sanskrit is still a hegemonic language to most subalternist thinking, and therefore cannot be used as part of the ongoing postcolonial critique. The work of
Purushottama Bilimoria,[13] Sheldon Pollock,[14] as well as Gayatri Spivak's
recent interest in the Dharmashastras,[15] are the exceptions to this rule. Interestingly, the demise of Sanskrit is a direct result of the very cyber and technological capitalism that is decried by postcolonial writing; today Sanskrit no
longer signifies livelihood prestige, but only knowledge prestige. It is ironic
that this is one loss that would not be mourned by many postcolonialists.

Models for Reading

Such tensions and nonalliances beg the question of what *is* possible in the
matrix of ideological forces behind the present position of Sanskrit. In what
follows I would like to suggest three possibilities: (1) that postcolonial theories and feminisms have committed themselves to criticizing or ignoring
hegemonic languages, but not to transforming them, (2) that such transfor-

mation needs to be one of the next steps in the study of Sanskrit, and (3) such transformative moments are possible in small, modest, collective acts of reading. These moments are transformative in that they help some readers unlearn the privileges that they have, and others take on the privileges that they do not have.

I am not speaking here of a final, or even a tentative, resolution between postcolonialism, feminism, and Hindu religiosity. I am suggesting rather what Marxist anthropologist Johannes Fabian[16] called in a recent article "moments of recognition," whereby readers might see the Other on a mutual plane. This momentariness is the key to avoiding what Fabian calls a naive dialogical ethnography,[17] whereby implicit and explicit expectations of permanent reconciliation between "others" are set up—expectations that the system of the production of knowledge itself can never fulfill. While such a resolution may never happen, there can nonetheless be an accumulation of these smaller moments of change, including changes in the practices of reading themselves. This transformative process is what Elizabeth Long refers to in her article "Reading as Collective Action,"[18] and whose current work addresses the link between women's reading groups and social change.

What would these changed moments of reading look like? I can offer three scenarios from my own fieldwork for the reader's consideration. The first has to do with *the commitment to reading elitist texts transformatively.* In my work with one Sanskritist, I learned that she was working on medical terms in the *Jaiminiya Brahmana,* a very obscure Vedic ritual text, which has been incompletely translated and in very expensive books produced in Europe. My colleague was working on the issue of whether same-sex relations were condoned or not in the medical terminology about the production of embryos. She wanted to know more about lesbian theory and gender theory as we argued and discussed the various Sanskrit compounds related to her work. She was preparing a paper for a conference in Marathi on Sanskrit literature and was very timid about presenting her explorations. I learned a huge amount from her about medical terminology, and in a form of intellectual barter, I shared with her some of my background in lesbian theory and gender studies more broadly. She was working with unpublished manuscripts as well as the published Sanskrit editions and English translations. We were collaborating in a project which transformed the *Jaiminiya Brahmana* into a text that could be relevant to a number of disparate audiences, all of it written in a vernacular Indian language. While anxious to the end, my colleague ended up winning the prize for the best paper at the conference. This is one example of reading elitist texts transformatively. It involved close philological discussions of the meaning of a compound; it involved the barter of intellectual information; it involved the correction of her assumptions about Western lesbians and mine about the ability of the Marathi judges to see the value of her work. This was a moment of postcolonial exchange in which feminism, religious sensibilities, vernacular and hegemonic languages worked in transformative fashion. There was no denial of the politics of race and of gender, only a small and stumbling attempt to change them in the act of conversation itself. It was the beginning of "Reading as Translation" from one culture to another.[19]

Second, in transformative textual reading, there can and should be a committed refusal to use the terms "Western" and "Indian" in an intellectually determinative fashion. (Spivak also raises doubts about using nationalist terms to describe intellectual agendas in chapter 2 of her *Outside in the Teaching Machine*, although she does not have the same hesitations, as I would, about using the term "white feminism.") At best, such descriptors are ill-founded conclusions about intellectual character, and at worst, they are nothing more than sophisticated and thinly disguised ethnic slurs. This refusal to use such terms can lead to moments of recognition. I experienced this refusal to speak in such categories in the work of a Sanskritist colleague, who is using Sanskrit and Latin as a basis for conversations between Hindus and Christians in Orissa and elsewhere in India. In her Sanskrit classes, she gives students other names, and does not ask their real names until the end. This way she encourages Muslim and Dalit students to stay in the class without the added social pressure of revealing their social backgrounds. This too, is a refusal of intellectual determinism, a refusal which can be potentially transformative of hegemonic languages. This does not mean that we deny the politics of race and gender, nor that we give up our social and religious identities in favor of some creeping perennialism or Vedantic soup. Rather, in transformative collective reading we refuse to allow the label of social backgrounds to be determinative conclusions of intellectual worth, whether we are engaging in so-called liberational postcolonial discourse, neocolonial Pepsi wars, or arguments about the translation of a Sanskrit compound.

Finally, the hegemonic language of Sanskrit might be transformed by avoiding the "frozen example of success." No one single moment of change can stand as an "example" of a power structure being resisted so that we can turn our attention elsewhere. (This is also Kumud Pawde's resistance to being paraded as the "example" of the Dalit Sanskritist.) To take one small illustration: a Hindu woman from a small college in India was giving a paper on family relationships in Vedic texts. She was berated at the end because she did not use the most recent publication from America on the topic; she explained calmly that her college's library could not afford to buy the book. Such conferences will always be filled with interactions where economics and intellectual worth are joined in a stark and indisputable way. The politics of the situation stopped the conversation. The next day the postcolonialist feminist man who berated her, comfortably employed in the West, began to explore the possibility of funding for her library, duly embarrassed at the previous exchange. This gesture might indeed have changed some practices of reading, but it could not suffice as the example of success which allowed all of us to turn our attention elsewhere. The imbalance of intellectual resources is endless, partly because libraries in Europe and America have not bought Indian vernacular language works, and partly because libraries in India cannot afford to buy books produced in the West. Only in an ongoing, systematic attempt to address such an imbalance, an attempt which refuses to freeze at each example of success, will such transformative reading be possible.

The story of the prostitute's gold, then, is an important link to these questions about postcolonialism, feminism, and religion, as I move into the next phase of my research: can the study of Sanskrit reach across the outer realms of caste and gender, as it did in that story, or can it only do so momentarily, in times of nation-forming struggle? In one way, the study of Sanskrit has changed more in the last decade than it had in 3,500 years. Yet even with the new role for women, it is not clear whether it will simply remain the coveted, but ultimately irrelevant, possession of a learned caste elite, or whether, like the prostitute's gold, it can be melted down to achieve new and valuable shapes.

Notes

I am grateful to all of the women Sanskritists, my teachers with whom I spent time in 1993, 1995, 1997, and especially in the summer of 1999. I am also grateful particularly to Ganesh Thite, Maitreyee Deshpande, Deepika Bahri, Saurab Dhube, Arshia Sattar, Madhavi Kolhatkar, Gayatri Chatterjee, Medha Kotwal Lele, Purushottama Bilimoria, Renuka Sharma, Wendy Doniger, Joyce Flueckiger, Paul Courtright, Parimal Patel, Tara Doyle, and Shalom Goldman for their comments on earlier drafts of this essay. For the sake of accessibility in this book, I have dispersed with my usual practice of using diacritics.

1. Although I am averse to the methodological throat clearing and pseudo-confessionalism that is also called "situating one's scholarship," nonetheless I will do what I think is necessary in this note: I am a white woman who reads and writes about Vedic texts, who remains engaged by postcolonial writing, and who loves and argues with the Sanskrit teachers from whom she has learned, in long years both in India and in the United States.

2. Chandra Talpade Mohanty, "Under Western Eyes," in *Third World Women and the Politics of Feminism*, ed. Chandra Talpade Mohanty, Ann Russo, and Lourdes Torres (Bloomington: Indiana University Press, 1991), 333; Sara Suleri, *Meatless Days* (Chicago: Univesity of Chicago Press, 1989), 20; Samir Dayal, "Style Is (Not) the Woman," in *Between the Lines: South Asians and Postcoloniality*, ed. Deepika Bahri

and Mary Vasudeva (Philadelphia: Temple University Press, 1996), 250–69.

3. Gayatri Chakravorty Spivak, *Outside in the Teaching Machine* (New York: Routledge, 1993), 192.

4. As Spivak notes in *Outside in the Teaching Machine*, only the condition of "dominant and subordinate gendering" give us some reason to focus on women's texts. She writes:

> Let us use the word "woman" to name that space of parasubjects defined as such by the social inscription of primary and secondary sexual characteristics. Then we can cautiously begin to track a sort of commonality in being set apart, within the different rhetorical strategies of different languages. But even here, historical superiorities of class must be kept in mind." (*Outside*, 103)

Following this train of thought, I do not assume that all women Sanskritists are concerned with women's issues, as indeed my conversations with them show. Nor do I assume that all research conducted by women in Sanskrit is "good" (following Spivak, *Outside*, 188).

5. Arif Dirlik, "The Postcolonial Aura: Third World Criticism in the Age of Global Capitalism," in *Critical Inquiry* 20 (winter 1994): 332.

6. Deepika Bahri and Mary Vasudeva, "Pedagogical Alternatives: Issues in Postcolonial Studies: Interview with Gauri Viswanathan," in *Between the Lines*, 54–63.

7. See V. N. Jha, "Sanskrit Studies in Maharashtra," in *Sanskrit Studies in India*, ed. K. K. Mishra (Delhi: Amar Printing Press, 1997), 185–93.

8. V. L. Manjul, "Striya aur Adhikar" in *Veda Pradipa*, April 4, 1998; and "Changing Patterns of Priesthood in Maharashtra," unpublished manuscript.

9. Kumud Pawde, "The Story of My 'Sanskrit'," in *Subject to Change: Teaching Literature in the 90's*, ed. Susie Thar (Hyderabad: Orient Longman, 1998), 88.

10. I am grateful to Parimal Patel for conversation on this matter. Also see Deepika Bahri on the situation in the United States: "The erasure of considerations of class . . . are masked by academic gestures of acceptance of the visible difference presented by displaced Third World postcolonial intellectuals." See her "Coming to Terms with the Postcolonial," in *Between the Lines, 53*.

11. The list of authors who have written on this concept is myriad; the classics are Julia Leslie, *The Perfect Wife: The Orthodox Hindu Woman According to the Stridharmapaddhati of Tryambakayajvan* (New York: Oxford University Press, 1989); more recently *Women and the Hindu Right*, ed. Tanika Sarkar and Urvashi Butalia (New Delhi: Kali for Women, 1995); and Srmati Basu, *She Comes to Take Her Rights: Indian Women, Property, and Propriety* (Albany: State University of New York Press, 1999); and the essays in my *Jewels of Authority: Women and Textual Tradition in Hindu India* (New York: Oxford University Press, 2001).

12. See the essays in *Pink Collar Blues: Work, Gender, and Technology*, ed. Belinda Probert and Bruce W. Wilson (Carlton, Victoria, Australia: Melbourne University Press,

1993) for a description of pink-collarization, the phenomenon whereby women's entrance into a field lowers its status.

13. See among many other sources, his *Sabdapramana: A Doctrine in Mimamsa-Nyaya Philosophy* (Dordrecht: Kluwer Academic, 1988); "Mimamsa Doubts about God," in *Philosophy of Religion Reader* (Melbourne: Deakin University Press, 1987); "Sruti and Apauruseya: An Approach to Religious Scriptures and Revelation," *Journal of Dharma* 3:3 (1982): 275–91.

14. Among his many relevant writings, his now classic "Deep Orientalism? Notes on Sanskrit and Power Beyond the Raj," in *Orientalism and the Postcolonial Predicament*, ed. Carol A. Breckenridge and Peter Van Der Veer (Philadelphia: University of Pennsylvania Press, 1993), 76–133. Also "Sanskrit and the Rise of Regional Literature," presentation at the University of Pennsylvania, 2000; and "India in the Vernacular Millennium: Literary Culture and Polity, 1000–1500," *Daedalus* 127: 3 (summer 1998): 41–74.

15. Spivak herself writes about exploring the Dharmashastras without much reference to classical Indology, as if no Sanskritist had ever worked on the issue of ethics and Dharmashastra before. The many critiques of Said have taught us that surely the legacy of classical Indology can teach us something other than Orientalism and Deep Orientalism. See, for instance, Albrecht Wezler's useful article, "Towards a Reconstruction of Indian Cultural history: Observations and Reflections on 18th and 19th Century Indology," in *Studien zur Indologie und Iranistik* 18 (1993): 305–29. Also see Richard LaRiviere's excellent "Protestants, Orientalists, and Brahmanas: Reconstructing Indian Social History," *1994 Gonda Lecture* (Netherlands: Royal Academy of Arts and Sciences, 1994).

16. Johannes Fabian, "Remembering the Other: Knowledge and Recognition in the Exploration of Central Africa," *Critical Inquiry* 26 (1999): 49–69.

17. Ibid., 69.

18. "Reading as Collective Action," in *Ethnography of Reading*, ed. Jonathan Boyarin (Berkeley: University of California Press, 1993).

19. While I did not surrender to the vernacular Marathi, in Spivak's terms, nonetheless parts of this encounter might be what Spivak means by "reading as translation." One hopes that she might better address the transformative possibilities of reading hegemonic languages.

6

Multiple Critique

Islamic Feminist Rhetorical Strategies

Miriam Cooke

The authors of the 1998 Sisterhood Is Global Institute manual for the elimination of violence against women and girls in Muslim societies declare: "The most important feature of contemporary Muslim women's struggle for rights is that they reject the proposition that they cannot be both free and equal with men and good Muslims at the same time. This they deny. On the contrary, they insist that a woman becomes an authentic Muslim only when she has achieved freedom and equality as an individual and citizen."[1] Some Muslim women today are claiming the right to freedom and equality with men at a time when they seem to the outsider to be so far from both. In this chapter, I shall identify who these women are and how they are constructing new identities and negotiating a new presence in places where before they had been invisible.

Social, economic, military, and political failures in postcolonial Arab countries have galvanized reactionary religious responses to Western domination and globalization and the corrupt values they are thought to spread. Islamist groups from Morocco to Bahrain are calling for the establishment of an Islamic state governed by Islamically sanctioned gender norms and values. How and why are women dealing with the growing conservatism in their communities? How do Islamic feminists adapt their convictions that women have certain rights with the perceived need to subsume them to the community interest? How will the ways in which they position themselves to assert responsibility for the construction of their own new religious identity change the face of Islam?

Why do I use the word *feminism* when many object to its Western, activist, and even separatist associations? I do so because I believe that feminism is much more than an ideology driving organized political movements. It is above all an attitude, a frame of mind that highlights the role of gender in understanding the organization of society. Feminism provides the analytical tools for assessing how expectations for men's and women's behavior have led to unjust situations, particularly but not necessarily only for women. Feminism provides a crosscultural prism through which to identify moments of *awareness* that something is wrong in the expectations for women's treatment or behavior, of *rejection* of such expectations, and of *activism* to effect some kind of change.

None of these three terms is teleological. They are not progressive stages that culminate in their totality. Put otherwise, the activist has not necessarily first understood how the situation she is working to change has been damaging to women. She may never have said no to anyone before she joined a movement. Activism might precede awareness. So might rejection. Awareness might never develop beyond itself; rejection might never be informed by a specific agenda. Activism might never pass through the negativity of rejection and remain positive and focused on constructing new systems.

If feminism can be many changing states of consciousness, each reflecting women's understanding of themselves and their situations as related to their social and biological conditions, then it is not bound to one culture. It is no more Arab than it is American, no more Mediterranean than it is Northern European. Feminism seeks justice wherever it can find it. It is this definition of feminism that I am using.

Islamic Feminist Rhetoric

Many Muslim women would reject the term *feminist* as Western and neoimperialist. Some Western feminists, on the other hand, will reject outright the possibility of women working subversively within a deeply patriarchal institution. However, the separatist option they advocate would likely change little while they create their alternative, segregated, and probably irrelevant worlds. Separatism is not an option for Islamic feminists who believe in the possibility of creating the conditions in which multiple identities, including the religious, can coexist in safety and dignity.

Islamic feminists are choosing to work within the systems that are trying to marginalize them. Is it not more significant that some Muslim women are today becoming publicly visible and audible "*in ways that were earlier unobtainable to them and on conditions they define and choose for themselves . . .* than the specific characteristics of the associations they partake in when it comes to promoting women's empowerment in a long term perspective?"[2] Yet outsiders continue to see Muslim women and especially those within Islamist movements as victims. Few are exploring what lies behind their apparent capitulations. Dutch anthropologist Wilhelmina Jansen, however, warns against unthinking dismissal of women as victims when they "take over the idiom of their oppressors and limit their freedom of dress and movement, simplify reality and exalt their domestic activities." Their behavior tells more than the story of what they are doing, it provides a way to understand "the rise of Islamism and the meaning of Islam for women's identity."[3]

During the past decade, some women in Muslim communities have been asserting their identities as feminists concerned with Islamic epistemology. Saying no to those who claim to speak for them, these Islamic feminists are engaging in public debate about the proper roles and duties of Muslim men and women. Who are these Islamic feminists? What do I mean by "Islamic feminists"? Are Islamic feminists creating a space of power as they emerge from the margins into representation?

Many would protest that Islamic feminism is an oxymoron. Is it? Or is it rather emblematic of the ways in which postcolonial women elsewhere also are jockeying for space and power through apparently incompatible, contradictory identities and positions? The term Islamic feminism invites us to consider what it means to have a double commitment: to a faith position on the one hand, and to women's rights both inside and outside the home on the other hand. The label *Islamic feminist* brings together two epithets whose juxtaposition describes the emergence of a new, complex self-positioning that celebrates multiple belongings. To call oneself an Islamic feminist is *not to describe a fixed identity but to create a new, contingent subject position.* This location confirms belonging in a religious community while allowing for activism on behalf of and with other women. This linking of apparently mutually exclusive identities can become a radical act of subversion. In the introduction to his study of identity construction in what he calls the Black Atlantic, Paul Gilroy writes that people who occupy the space between identities that "appear to be mutually exclusive trying to demonstrate their continuity" are engaging in "a provocative and even oppositional act of political insubordination."[4]

Those who position themselves as Islamic feminists, even when they do not explicitly label themselves thus, may well be political insubordinates.

They are refusing the boundaries others try to draw around them. They are claiming that Islam is not necessarily more traditional or authentic than any other identification nor is it any more violent or patriarchal than any other religion. They are claiming their right to be strong women within this tradition, to act as feminists without fear, so that they may be labeled Western and imitative. They are highlighting women's roles and status within their religious communities while at the same time declaring common cause with Muslim women elsewhere who share the same objectives. They are linking their religious, political, and individual gender identities in order to claim simultaneous and sometimes contradictory allegiances even as they resist globalization, local nationalisms, Islamization, and the pervasive patriarchal system.

Islamic feminist performances and practices are situated somewhere on a continuum between the ascribed identity of "Muslim" and the achieved identity of "Islamist." To be a Muslim is to be born into a particular religious community, to carry an identity card that fills in *Muslim* next to the category "religious identity." Those to whom a Muslim identity is ascribed participate in a Muslim culture and community without necessarily accepting all of its norms and values. Muslims might be secular, occasionally observing some ritual—for example, fasting for the month of Ramadan while not necessarily praying regularly. Muslims might even be atheists. Islamists, on the other hand, achieve their sometimes militant identity by devoting their lives to the establishment of an Islamic state. The Islamic identification connotes another form of achieved identity, one which is highly volatile and contingent. "Islamic" bridges the two poles of Muslim and Islamist identifications. It describes a particular kind of self-positioning that will then inform the speech, or the action, or the writing, or the way of life adopted by someone who is committed to questioning Islamic epistemology *as an expansion of their faith position and not a rejection of it.* Someone who writes a novel or a memoir as an Islamic feminist may choose another speaking position when she gives a speech or writes an essay. An excellent example is Zaynab al-Ghazali. As leader of the Egyptian Muslim Ladies' Association, the female counterpart of the Muslim Brothers, she positioned herself as a gender-neutral Islamist in her Quranic exegesis,[5] but as an Islamic feminist in her prison memoirs.[6]

Whenever Muslim women offer a critique of some aspect of Islamic history or hermeneutics, and they do so with and/or on behalf of all Muslim women and their right to enjoy with men full participation in a just community, I call them Islamic feminists. This label is not rigid; rather it describes an attitude and intention to seek justice and citizenship for Muslim women.

Islamic feminists are objecting to the fact that the Qur'an has been interpreted and history has been recorded and passed down almost exclusively by
men. Egyptian-American historian Leila Ahmed adds another layer to male
domination of the religious sphere: men have excluded women not only from
the production of history and hermeneutics, but also from the spaces of religion. Thus emerged two Islams, the one for women and the other for men.
Women worked out their own understandings of Islam "as a broad ethos and
ethical code and as a way of understanding and reflecting on the meaning of
one's life and of human life more generally"; whereas men's official, arcane,
mostly medieval Islam, "in which sheikhs are trained," paid little mind to
what is central to women: "Mercy, justice, peace, compassion, humanity, fair-
ness, kindness, truthfulness, charity."[7]

Women's protest against male hegemony in the production of official
Islamic knowledge is not new. Already in the 1920s, the Lebanese author
Nazira Zayn al-Din (1908-1976) noted with dismay in her *Unveiling and
Veiling* (1928) and its sequel *The Girl and the Shaykhs* (1929) that Islamic prescriptions for women have been historically framed by men. In 1998, the Syr-
ian critic Bouthaina Shaaban edited and reissued these texts.[8] In the
introduction she points out that although these books were very well received
at the time of their publication, within less than fifty years this woman's radical interpretations—the first of their kind—had fallen out of circulation.
Why? Because they posed harsh questions about social norms and juridical
practices that male authorities had both shaped and perpetuated.[9] In the view
of feminists concerned with Islamic discourse, women should have equal
access to scriptural truth, and their works are showing what difference the
gender of the author makes.

Scholars and social commentators agree that if women opt out of these
debates, the only texts on the market will be those that insist on the need to
hide women's shameful bodies. In order to enter public discourse and to
debate effectively without fear of being silenced, women must position themselves beyond their immediate circumstances. Rooted in their specific places
but speaking out transnationally as part of the world Muslim community,
they are more likely to have an impact because their interventions cannot be
so easily silenced by kin or other authorities opposed to their message. How
can they find this speaking position that is both local and global? How does
engagement with the norms and values of Islam as a cultural and religious
practice and discourse allow for transnational self-positioning? In what follows, I argue that Islam provides the symbolic capital for the construction of
such an apparently contradictory rhetorical space.

The Transnationalism of Islam

Religions theoretically transcend geographical boundaries. This is particularly true for Islam. Its very material connection to Arabia, where it found its beginnings, provides unusual possibilities for constructing a territorialized transcultural identity. Until the emergence of the modern nation-state, religion often assumed primary importance in indigenous self-identification as civic rights came to be associated with religion. For example, in the Maghreb, the colonized Muslim and Jewish communities assumed the characteristics of national cultures; they were *musulmans* or *juifs indigenes* and not Algerians, Tunisians, or Moroccans. To be Jewish meant at a certain stage that one qualified for French citizenship. The Muslims did not. When the French government gave Jews in the Hexagon as well as in the colonies preferential treatment by progressively assigning them French citizenship, they complicated national-political loyalties established over centuries of coexistence. The French racialized and politicized religion, turning what had been transnational into an ethnocultural affiliation that coincided with geography and history. In other words, religion became the key element in indigenous identity. In the postcolonial period, the memory of belonging was to a religion. Islam has served as a kind of spiritual, ritual nation, which then provided the site of resistance to the West and above all to Western notions of "progress." This was the rhetoric then, during the fight for independence; it is the rhetoric today.

Islam provides the symbolic capital otherwise unavailable to many of today's new nations. In contrast with their claims for pure blood, Muslims can invoke and indeed do have easy access to the pure origins of the Muslim nation. No matter how contaminated by local domination, Muslims seeking an unadulterated past have scriptures as a recourse. Islam as a religion may evolve and change as interpretations of its texts proliferate, but the *sources* of these interpretations remain intact. The Muslim nation is an expedient invention whose obliteration is safe from the anxiety produced by territoriality. When the Muslim nation disintegrates, its citizens may and often do retain the religious tag, but it is demoted into second position, its "essence" sublimated into the spiritual realm. As new borders are drawn, Muslim communities may find themselves politically split while remaining culturally and symbolically connected with coreligionists with whom they continue to live through a transnational imaginary. At home in the border zones that have assured actual and cultural survival, they are like today's migrants and refugees. Unlike them, however, they have not *become* migrants moving constantly across national borders; rather, this geographically flexible identity, which oscillates between diaspora and origin, characterizes Muslim identity.

Muslims can think transnationally while continuing to live locally, recognizing themselves as citizens of the world while retaining deep connections with a specific place, whether it be of birth, of choice, or of compulsion. Travel and cosmopolitanism are a necessary part of all Muslims' spiritual and material identities, as Eickelman and Piscatori explain:

> Muslim doctrine explicitly enjoins or encourages certain forms of travel. One is the express obligation to undertake the pilgrimage to Mecca (*hajj*). Another, *hijra*, is the obligation to migrate from lands where the practice of Islam is constrained to those where in principle no such constraints exist. Visits to local or regional shrines (*ziyaras*) and travel in search of knowledge (*rihla*) provide further examples of religiously inspired travel. Yet other forms of travel unrecognized in doctrine can have equal or even greater significance. For example, Muslims have often mixed travel for trade purposes with religiously motivated travel.[10]

Travel, whether literal or symbolic, always anticipates return to "a mythical realm where home, the 'fixed point' of departure and return, is reimagined and further travel inspired."[11] Travel, in whatever sense, is a necessary part of every Muslim's daily reality, and "has contributed significantly to shaping the religious imagination in both the past and the present."[12] Islam's insistence on actual and symbolic travel allows for simultaneous self-positionings in the local and the global and then back to another local, in the present and the past and then back to a transformed present.

Muslims have two apparently contradictory stories with territory. The first is transnational and deterritorialized. Pointing *forward*, it narrates social fragmentation and occasional consociations. Muslims are scattered throughout most countries of the world; they are not members of a single nation. At least once in the lifetime of each Muslim there is awareness of this radical internationalism, when the individual performs the sacred duty of pilgrimage to Mecca. During the month of the *hajj*, Muslim pilgrims from all corners of the world, each national group in its national delegation, converge on two Saudi Arabian cities. Mecca and Medina become microcosms of the multicultural Muslim world.

The second Muslim story is national and, looking *backward*, it roots itself in a specific territory. Despite the fact that they are citizens of most countries of the world, Muslims can invoke the unifying politics of *umma*, known in the modern period as pan-Islamism. In so doing, they link the transnational with the national story by projecting themselves as the "diaspora" of a seventh century bedouin tribe in the Arabian Peninsula. This diaspora has been held together by its historical links with this simulacric origin. These links have been forged through Arabic language. Although they are overwhelmingly non-Arab, and few Muslims outside the Arab world know Arabic beyond an acquaintance with scripture, Muslims' common identification, their cultural nation, is a text, the Qur'an, God's word revealed in Arabic. For the elite, social hierarchy underscores the Arabia-centeredness of Islamic identity. To be *sharif*, or noble, in Muslim terminology is to be able, wherever one was born and lives, to trace roots back to a single place and a single language, those of the Prophet and his family. Genealogy thus becomes another deterritorialized means of connecting to place. Placed within this context of founding Muslim national, genealogical, and linguistic heritage, the *hajj* may be interpreted as something other than the exceptional gathering of different races, ethnicities, and cultures in two Saudi Arabian cities. It can be seen rather as an occasion when Indonesians, Americans, and Senegalese join their Arab cousins to make the sentimental journey "home" to Mecca, a return they daily anticipate when they orient themselves toward Mecca to perform their five daily prayers.

Multiple Critique

How can women take advantage of this transnational/national, at once historical and a-historical Muslim identity without risk of being silenced because they are women? How can they critique the global system, their own political regimes, and religious and family contexts and the patriarchal vein that runs through them all and still remain wary of others' desires to coopt their struggle? Can they do all this and retain historical agency while being considered loyal and effective citizens in each domain? I believe that they can because of the specific strategies some of them are developing and which I call "multiple critique."

I have a double hypothesis underlying the term *multiple critique* that I have coined to describe Islamic feminists' critical rhetorical strategies. First, women who have been consistently marked as victims and who have only recently started to speak for themselves may be able to situate themselves transnationally because of the global nature of the institutions with which they have had to contend. Second, women who have learned as feminists to form principled and strategic alliances which allow them to balance their religious, specifically Islamic loyalties with national, local, class, ethnic, or any other allegiances may be able to invent a contestatory, but also enabling, discourse within the global context that will not be easily coopted. They may thus initiate new forms of conversations across what were previously thought to be unbridgeable chasms.

Since the end of the cold war, Arab intellectuals have been preoccupied with the problem of how to position themselves in a globalizing universe without submitting to the violent politics of extremist religious movements. The Tunisian philosopher Fathi Triki points to the dangers that postcolonial Arabs face as they try to find themselves a niche in the global economy. He warns against the uncontextualized invocation of collective identities such as Islamism, Arabism, Nasserism, or Baathism. Without a clear sense of who they are beyond the slogan, these groups may slip into identitarian politics,[13] thereby running the risk of self-destruction. It is essential for them to learn how to situate themselves in this "new geo-political landscape of a world that remains divided, contested and conflicted." Sloganeering as self-affirmation is "not a way of avoiding transnationalism or of opposing globalization," especially if it happens in what Triki calls "a dangerous void."[14] The challenge, he writes, is to be free and responsible individuals who belong and submit to the values of their various communities.

Islamic feminists may be the ones best equipped to take up Triki's challenge because they are learning how to balance their collective and individual identities while interacting with multiple others. They are beginning to play the pivotal role Homi Bhabha has claimed for marginalized groups as they emerge from unexpected places, position themselves in the world, affirm their identities and thus disturb "the calculation of power and knowledge, producing other spaces of subaltern signification."[15] I am not trying to make an essentialist argument based on gender and race exceptionalism. What I am interested in is how a subalternized group can assume its essentialized representations and use them strategically against those who have ascribed them. I am examining the ways in which Islamic feminists, like black Atlantic activists, are navigating those spaces between what appear to be essential, mutually exclusive identities. Demonstrating their continuity, they are engaging in what Gilroy called "a provocative and even oppositional act of political insubordination."[16]

I have come to believe that the effectiveness of Islamic feminists' critique is connected with Arab women's multiple representations as "victims" of transnational systems. First, and like women elsewhere, they are victims of gender relations which benefit men. Second, and like their male counterparts, they are struggling with the problems and challenges left behind by colonial rule. The European colonizers may have left Arab soil, but they also left behind a burden of colonial legacies that link different Arab nations vis-à-vis a global system that may or may not include them in its purview. Women are peculiarly vulnerable where their men are most threatened. Finally, the growing prominence of Islam in world politics has drawn attention to the ways in which Islamist groups use women as passive cultural emblems. Women's responsibilities and images in the new Islamic systems are symbolically foregrounded and then pragmatically relegated to the political margins. Rejecting this characterization of their experiences as victimization, even as they benefit from the fact that the victim is innocent of charges of domination and exploitation, a growing number of Islamic feminists are becoming politically active as women on behalf of women. They are developing a *multiple critique*, a multilayered discourse that allows them to engage with and criticize the various individuals, institutions, and systems that limit and oppress them while making sure that they are not caught in their own rhetoric.

The term *multiple critique* derives from two others: the Moroccan cultural critic Abdelkebir Khatibi's concept of *double critique* and the African American sociologist Deborah K. King's "multiple consciousness." In *Maghreb Pluriel*, Khatibi describes the ways in which postcolonial subjects have evolved an oppositional discourse that simultaneously targets local and global antagonists.[17] In all of his writings, Khatibi focuses on duality and how it can be dialectically mobilized. By injecting gender into his local/global critiques we can imagine a third critique which moves beyond the binary. This third is not numerical but epistemological, because it opens out onto a multiplicity that resolves the problem of mutual exclusivity—one which includes religious zealots and religious others, foreigners, homophobes, and women with different histories. In her essay "Multiple Jeopardy, Multiple Consciousness: The Context of a Black Feminist Ideology," King describes the "multiple jeopardy" of black women who have become invisible in contemporary American oppositional politics. They are "marginal to both the movements for women's liberation and black liberation irrespective of our victimization under the dual discrimination of racism and sexism."[18] She concludes with the assertion that black women who have been characterized as victims are in fact challenging the various systems that oppress and exclude them. She does not, however, describe how such an oppositional praxis might work.

In view of the similarities between black American women's experience of marginalization, as they fall through the cracks of race and gender, and that of postcolonial Arab Muslim women, I use the insights provided by King's notions of multiple jeopardy and multiple consciousness, itself derived from W. E. B. Du Bois's "double consciousness." There is, however, a major difference between the historical experiences of black women in the United States and Muslim Arab women under colonial rule. Whereas women of African descent brought into the slavery economy of North America were crucially important to its flourishing and have been remembered as such, Muslim Arab women were separated from the spaces occupied by the European colonizers and then systematically excluded from collective memory, except as outsiders to colonial history.

Angela Davis describes the pain of African women's centrality to the entire community, where they were exposed to white men's desires and black men's frustrations. At the heart of both white and black households, they became the bridge between the two, a crucial conduit for information and sometimes resistance. Additionally, they provided "the only labor of the slave community that could not be directly and immediately claimed by the oppressor."[19] To survive, these women became so strong and intimidating that black men came to refer to them in derogatory terms as matriarchs. The label has stuck and, according to Davis, many black women today still feel obliged to control their assertiveness.

In 1985, Beth E. Richie declared that the political agenda has to "begin in our homes, our heads, and mostly our hearts to identify the 'traps' of loyalty. We must demand equality in our communities and in our relationship with black men."[20] This is precisely what Arab Muslim feminists are doing, but for them the task is not as charged because of their very different historical experience. Far from being at the epicenter of their own communities, or that of the colonizers, they were always on the margins. That this should be the case is due to the special circumstances surrounding colonialism in Muslim Arab countries. Unlike slave owners in North America, the European colonizers in the Muslim Arab world found themselves obliged to respect the line that separated the private from the public. To be able to rule the men effectively, they had to leave the women in their segregated spaces. The Europeans interacted with or, better, controlled the Muslim men outside their homes. Women's autobiographies and fiction, as well as court records, describe a place of privacy where the colonizer could not go. There are no stories of European men raping Muslim Arab women. As Lebanese critic Mai Ghossoub writes: "What better symbol of cultural identity than the privacy of women, refuge *par excellence* of traditional values that the old colonialism could not reach and the new capitalism must not touch? The rigidity of the status of women in the family in the Arab world has been an innermost asylum of Arabo-Muslim identity."[21] What is germane to my argument in the story about segregated spaces is not their workings as a domain of male domination, but rather their impenetrability to all outsiders, including, especially, European men.

Muslim women, inasmuch as that label implies a colonial identification that is other than that of Muslim men, are not necessarily locked into the postcolonial dynamic of the global system. Because of their marginality under colonialism, their relationship with global capital and culture is attenuated. They are more likely than men to find ways of inventing a humanist nationalism and of holding on to communal, national, and international belonging that do not entail charges of treachery, complicity, or self-sacrifice.

While women's spaces became the heart of the authentic, ahistorical, uncontaminated Muslim nation, the men were locked into a relationship with the colonizers. This relationship persists and influences men's choices and behaviors. Because of their disparate histories due to the radically different positioning of women in slave and colonial economies, as well as the transnationalism of their religious and political affiliations, Arab Islamic feminists have been able to go beyond multiple consciousness to multiple critique. They are inventing new ways of contesting multiple forms of marginalization and silencing.

Veiled Strategies

The veil is playing a role in these contestations. The veil, however, is many things. It may be a traditional, culturally diverse form of body or face covering, or it may be a modern, fashionable form of dress, or it may be a kind of severe political uniform. Despite the wide variety, the veil is often reduced to a simple symbol. For the outsider, it is the emblem of Muslim women's oppression and marginalization. While this may be accurate in the cases where women did not choose to veil, it is not necessarily true for those who have chosen to mark themselves out religiously. For many of these women, the veil can be empowering.

How can this be, when stories of Muslim women's victimization are on the increase. In reactionary Muslim countries like Algeria, Sudan, and Afghanistan, women are told, and, beyond them, the world is told that they must not be seen. An extreme example is the case of women living under the rule of the Taliban in Afghanistan. They are reportedly evicted from the streets, schools and offices, except in dire necessity, and only then when they wear the *burqa*, an all-encompassing cloth that hides the women's heads and bodies. The sinister consequences of this edict came out in a July 20, 1998 National Public Radio program which reported the death of a girl too poor to afford the veil that would allow her to walk through the streets to her doctor.

The increasing visibility of veiled women in Muslim societies, as indeed elsewhere, is playing an important role in the political sphere. At a symbolic level, women wearing the veil highlight the specific ethos of the community in which they live and function: these are pious people who disapprove of public displays of sexuality, particularly when connected with women. Muslim women's public prominence is not only symbolic, it is actual. The more

Muslim women are policed, the more visible they become. It is often the women themselves—some of whom may be feminists—who make the religio-political decision when they adopt the veil. Unlike the traditional covering, the political veil marks a woman as religiously observant.

In her study of the lives of lower-middle-class women in Cairo who have been veiling since the 1970s, Arlene Macleod opens up a new way to understand the contradictions involved in the assumption of the veil in a modernizing society. Without in any way minimizing the religious importance of the decision to veil, she points out the socioeconomic constraints that come into play in this decision. She explains that these Cairene women must work if they and their families wish to retain their precarious lower-middle-class status. In the growing conservatism of their environment, working women must beware of the accusation of moral looseness when away from their homes. Wearing the veil assures everyone that these women will not be harassed in the streets and in the workplace, but also that they have become honorable women.[22]

The veil in this late twentieth century context is riddled with contradictions. It marks the piety of the individual and of the society by reinforcing women's traditional role as cultural custodians, at the same time that it facilitates educational and professional activities. The veil imprisons and liberates. But—and most importantly for the purposes of my argument—the veil is an item of clothing that each woman daily chooses, or is forced to choose, in awareness of the symbolic baggage it carries. As she looks at herself in the mirror in the morning to hide her hair and adjust the cloth, this Muslim woman daily reaffirms the fact that her body marks her out morally and sexually—in other words, as a religious and as a female person. Daily, this veiled woman has a multiple consciousness of herself, as she sees herself, as her community sees her, and as outsider men and women see her.

Critical Networks

Consciousness, however, does not in itself provide protection against ascription and consequent controls on behavior and movement. Arab Islamic feminists are recognizing how their bodies are being used in this struggle over control of public space. They know that they must assume responsibility for naming themselves and assigning their own meanings to their appearance and actions if they are to participate in the construction of a new society based on justice for all. They know also that to succeed they must join forces with others. Coalition building and networking are vital but risky. There are many with whom they may at some point have to work but whose motives they may have reason to suspect, none more than other women, those of their compatriots who are secular—but above all white Western feminists.

The challenge is how to collaborate on behalf of women "without losing the specificity of the concrete struggles of different women."[23] Their concern to remain imbedded in their own cultural, religious, and political realities has made Islamic feminists suspicious of appeals to universal feminist activism, which smack of Western cultural imperialism. Told by generations of men that to fight for women's rights was to line up with Western imperialist women and to betray their culture, they have had to tread very carefully in their relations with women from Europe and the United States. In a context shaped by colonial legacies, women retaining the memory of colonial practices of racialization and subjugation—even if they were not direct targets—may never fully trust the motives of those coming from the erstwhile empire, may doubt the possibilities of finding a common project that will make everyone feel they share a stake in its success. Even if they seem to agree on antipatriarchal goals, how can Algerian and Tunisian women confronting fundamentalism at home trust the French granddaughters of their previous colonizers who insist that they demand their rights and confront their fathers, husbands, brothers, and sons? How can Egyptian and Sudanese women struggling with the problem of female genital mutilation trust American women who demand its abolition, even if they be of African heritage?

It is in withstanding the dictates of systems unfriendly to women, but remaining in these same communities, that Islamic feminists demonstrate most vividly how multiple critique works. They have recognized the importance of networking at all levels, but also the risks that such alliances present, because to be with one group may entail apparent and involuntary opposition to another. At one moment the gender identity of the group may be under fire but the religious identity strong, and then criticism of misogynist behavior may be possible. This would be true, for example, when Islam has become a powerful political protagonist and when resistance to Westernization is strong—this opposition being underwritten by the mobilization of women's bodies to accent the group's rejection of Western values. At another point the religious identity of the group may be vulnerable but the gender identity strong, and it is then that Islamic feminists will join with their men to assert an oppositional religiocultural identity.

Islamic feminists' multiple consciousness allows them to consider the possibilities of alliances others might reject. Some scholars argue that religion gives observant women the tools to construct alliances that secular women may not trust. The Iranian critic Afsaneh Najmabadi suggests that Islamic feminists in Iran are beginning to build bridges of which secular women dare not dream. This is the case because Islam has been construed by secular women as repressive of women's rights and aspirations. These women reject contemporary Islam as a misogynist, extremist religion. This Islam, retort Islamic feminists, is the religion of a very small, if vocal, minority. It is a politics adopted by individuals who have seen no other way of flourishing in the modern world and of saying no to Western hegemony. Some clearly have used the power they have gained from the success of their anti-West position to harm coreligionists. This is not the Islam to which Islamic feminists pay allegiance. The Islam they invoke is the internationally significant political player, but also the individual faith system that eschews violence as it seeks to manage both internal and external conflict. It is only from within this global, political, and religious system that new visions of Islam can be invented.

In her analysis of the Iranian *Zanan*, an Islamic and explicitly feminist journal founded in 1992, Najmabadi describes the writers who engage in scriptural interpretation as "public intellectuals." Reading the Qur'an as women, they aim not merely to produce new legal interpretations for a small group of religious scholars, but rather to "awaken women so that they will proclaim their rights" and thus transform society.[24] By juxtaposing religious texts of all sorts with Western feminist writings, they are confusing the "comforting categories of Islamic and secular [and are making] West and East speak in a new combined tongue in dialogue with rather than as negating of each other." Their radical interpretations are reconfiguring space in such a way that "women of different outlooks can have a common stake."[25]

From within, Islamic feminists are able to recognize the dangers of which the African American feminist Barbara Smith had warned in 1980: political separatism. A single group representing only its own interests will not "topple a system by itself. Forming principled coalitions around specific issues is very important. You don't necessarily have to like or love the people you're in coalition with . . . what *I* feel is radical is trying to make coalitions with people who are different from you."[26] This is what Women Against Fundamentalism (WAF) is doing in Britain today. Mobilized by the 1989 Rushdie Affair, which heightened the sense of communalism in Britain, a group of South Asian, Jewish, Irish, and Iranian women came together as WAF. Despite utterly different histories, they shared an agenda to resist the dangers posed by politicized religious regimes at the communal level, dangers which were tolerated at the national level where the established church has such a privileged position.[27]

Islamic feminists are not afraid to take on the multiple challenges to their right to seek their own well-being, even when they feel they must criticize their men, and they know that such criticism risks being labeled cultural betrayal. Taking advantage of the cognitive dissonance in the label "Islamic feminist" they can ally themselves with the "good" Islamic community and against patriarchal distortions of the values and norms of the founding Muslim nation. These women are playing back to the men the strategies they themselves have long used in their anticolonial struggles: make the master accountable for the ethical discourse that his actions contradict. To be able to do so, some women are studying the same texts that men used to counter the secular West. When Western governments tout human rights and universal justice, Muslim men may respond by pointing to the 1981 Universal Islamic Declaration of Human Rights, or by showing these Western moral arbiters how they consistently violate their own prescriptions. When Western powers are held at bay, Islamic feminists can demonstrate how these self-righteous authorities have done exactly the same—they have vaunted the social justice inherent in Islam, especially in connection with justice for women. Islamic feminists are declaring that, yes, Islam is the ideal just society, but that social justice entails equality, dignity, and respect for all, including women.

Conclusion

In a 1991 essay, the Caribbean-British cultural critic Stuart Hall wrote that the

> most profound cultural revolution in this part of the twentieth century has come about as a consequence of the margins coming into representation— in art, in painting, in film, in music, in literature, in the modern arts everywhere, in politics, and in social life generally . . . Paradoxically, marginality has become a powerful space . . . New subjects, new genders, new ethnicities, new regions, and new communities—all hitherto excluded as decentered or subaltern—have emerged and have acquired through struggle, sometimes in very marginalized ways, the means to speak for themselves for the first time. And the discourses of power in our society, the discourses of the dominant regimes, have been certainly threatened by this decentered cultural empowerment of the marginal and the local.[28]

Surely Hall did not have Islamic feminists in mind when he wrote the above, yet they fit this description of the new subalterns who are finding their voices for the first time. As they come into representation from the margins, they are threatening the discourses of the dominant regimes.

Their history remains—must remain—subaltern, for it is in this subalternity that the ability to act effectively in the global system lies. This history that does not include them as objects of the colonial civilizing mission, that mentions them at most as resisters and survivors, calls into question the global narrative of the totality of European domination and allows these women to construct a pure, empty past they can fill with the kinds of experiences that allow them to be strong, oppositional, and loyal today.

Situating themselves at the nexus of religion, place, transnationality, and feminist practice, some women have collectively placed at the top of their political agenda women's right to examine the gendered formation of religious and local discourses, but always within a global framework. While challenging and deconstructing traditional interpretations of authoritative texts that have served to construct norms that exclude them as women, they continue to defend their transnational, religious, and national communities against detractors. They are asserting and also balancing multiple overlapping and sometimes contradictory allegiances while recognizing that others may ignore these plural identities and ascribe an entirely different communal belonging that would presume another allegiance. Yet they are less susceptible to surprise ascription because of their multiple consciousness of who they are and how others perceive them.

Multiple critique allows those who position themselves as Islamic feminists to speak effectively to, with, and against several audiences. Holding them in tension with each other, Islamic feminists complicate and undermine accusations of cultural betrayal. They reject silence and show it to be a form of acquiescence, capitulation, and abdication of their right to participate in the political process. Having created themselves as subjects of their own histories, they are relocating the knowledges that used to be produced about them. They are pointing to what fills those spaces left empty by official history. Islamic feminist discourse shows that multiple new centers/nodes are networking in those spaces where globalized culture is stopped in its teleological movement because it is forced to take account of local realities. Those moments of rupture and decentering allow for new configurations of Islam and feminism which *disturb the calculations of power and knowledge.*

When women choose to privilege their Muslim identity above others, they are transforming their particular, often marginalized, viewpoint into a universal by *strategically* labeling themselves utterly other while knowing that they are not. They are demonstrating how cosmopolitan individuals can belong to a number of different communities simultaneously while retaining the rights due them in all spheres, including the right to criticize these same communities. They do so as individual members of various groups, as citizens of their nations as well as of the world, and always as women.

In a world no longer divided by ideologies but rather by vague notions of civilizations in collision, conspiracy, and connections, it may be necessary to situate oneself transnationally in order to affirm oneself, to function effectively, and to reach out to others. Islamic identification provides such a transnational sense of belonging. While this identity can become the basis for a global movement of successful, if sometimes violent, contestation against the neoliberal values and aspirations of the United States and its allies, it also allows for the development of an effective strategy of resistance, engagement, and steadfastness that I have called multiple critique.

Notes

1. Mahnaz Afkhami, Greta H. Nemiroff, and Haleh Vazir, *Safe and Secure: Eliminating Violence against Women and Girls in Muslim Societies* (Baltimore, Md.: SIGI, 1998), 7.

2. Karin Ask and Marit Tjomsland, eds., *Women and Islamization: Contemporary Dimensions of Discourse on Gender Relations* (Oxford: Berg, 1998), 7.

3. Wilhelmina Jansen, "Contested Identities: Women and Religion in Algeria and Jordan," in *Women and Islamization*, 86.

4. Paul Gilroy, *The Black Atlantic: Modernity and Double Consciousness* (Cambridge, Mass.: Harvard University Press, 1996), 1.

5. Zaynab al-Ghasali, *Nazarat fi kitab Allah* (Views on the Book of God) (Cairo: Dar al-Shuruq, 1994).

6. Zaynab al-Ghasali, *Ayyam min hayati* (Days from My life) (Cairo: Dar al-Shuruq, 1986). Originally published in 1977.

7. Leila Ahmed, *A Border Passage: From Cairo to America—A Woman's Journey* (New York: Farrar, Straus, and Giroux, 1999), 126.

8. Nazira Zayn al-Din, *Al-sufur wal-hijab* (Unveiling and Veiling) (Damascus: Dar al-Mada, 1998; 1st ed. 1928); *Al-fatat waal-shuyukh* (The Girl and the Shaykhs) (Damascus: Dar al-Mada, 1998; 1st ed. 1929).

9. Zayn al-Din, *Al-sufur wal-hijab*, 15, 32.

10. Dale Eickelman and James Piscatori, eds., *Muslim Travellers: Pilgrimage, Migration, and the Religious Imagination* (Berkeley: University of California Press, 1990), 5.

11. Ibid., xiii.

12. Ibid., xvi.

13. Fathi Triki, *La Strategie de l'identite: Essai* (Paris: Arcanteres, 1998), 18, 47.

14. Ibid., 14.

15. Homi Bhabha, *The Location of Culture* (London: Routledge, 1994), 163.

16. Gilroy, *The Black Atlantic*, 1.

17. Abdelkabir Khatibi, *Maghreb Pluriel* (Paris: Denoel, 1983).

18. Deborah King, "Multiple Jeopardy, Multiple Consciousness: The Context of a Black Feminist Ideology," in *Works of Fire: An Anthology of African-American Feminist Thought*, ed. Beverly Guy-Sheftall (New York: New Press, 1995), 299.

19. Angela Davis, "Reflections on the Black Woman's Role in the Community of Slaves," in *Works of Fire*, 205.

20. Beth E. Richie, "Battered Black Women: A Challenge for the Black Community" in *Works of Fire*, 403.

21. Mai Ghossoub, "Feminism—or the Eternal Masculine—in the Arab World," *New Left Review*, January-February 1987, 4.

22. Arlene Elowe Macleod, *Accommodating Protest: Working Women, the New Veiling, and Change in Cairo* (New York: Columbia University Press, 1991).

23. Clara Connolly and Pragna Patel, "Women Who Walk on Water: Working across 'Race' in Women against Fundamentalism," in *The Politics of Culture in the Shadow of Capital*, ed. Lisa Lowe and David Lloyd (Durham: Duke University Press, 1997), 381.

24. Afsaneh Najmabadi, "Feminism in an Islamic Republic: Years of Hardship, Years of Growth," in *Islam, Gender, and Social Change*, ed. Yvonne Y. Haddad and John L. Esposito (New York: Oxford University Press, 1998), 72, 66, 71.

25. Ibid., 77.

26. Barbara Smith and Beverly Smith, "Across the Kitchen Table: A Sister-to-Sister Dialogue," in *This Bridge Called My Back: Writings by Radical Women of Color*, ed. Cherríe Moraga and Gloria Anzaldúa (New York: Kitchen Table Women of Color Press, 1981), 126.

27. Connolly and Patel, "Women Who Walk on Water," 386.

28. Stuart Hall, "The Local and the Global," in *Dangerous Liaisons: Gender, Nation, and Postcolonial Perspectives*, ed. Anne McClintock, Aamir Mufti, and Ella Shohat (Minneapolis: University of Minnesota Press, 1997), 183.

7

Letting Go of Liberalism

Feminism and the Emancipation of the Jews

LAURA LEVITT

To the Jews as individuals—everything; to the Jews as a group—nothing. They must constitute neither a body politic nor an order; they must be citizens individually.
—Clermont-Tonnerre before the
French National Assembly in 1789

It is as if the very emergence of the colonial is dependent for its representation upon some strategic limitation or prohibition within *the authoritative discourse.*
—Homi Bhabha, "Of Mimicry and Man:
The Ambivalence of Colonial Discourse"

[I]n liberal democratic theory women, the feminine, and the female have been discursively positioned in and as contradiction. Feminism thus exposes, but it is also produced by, the constitutive contradictions of individualism.
—Joan Scott, "Universalism and the History of Feminism"

I offer a close reading of critical documents that spell out the terms of Jewish emancipation in France with an eye to the connections between postcolonial, feminist, and Jewish critiques. In the context of this volume, I hope to demonstrate the fruitfulness of this kind of interdisciplinary practice. I want to encourage other scholars to consider making similar connections in their own work. Only by reimagining these kinds of alliances can we begin to reimagine contemporary struggles for liberation on other terms. Through a close reading of these early texts, I want to shed light on why even those who have remained Other in Western culture—in this case, Jews, women, and Jewish women—nevertheless continue to remain loyal to the liberal states that supposedly emancipated them.[1]

Through the promises of the liberal revolutions of the late eighteenth century, Jews throughout Western Europe and the United States were granted citizenship and offered access to liberal culture. France was the first Western nation to liberate its Jews. In France and elsewhere, emancipation was granted to Jews as individuals. It meant the relinquishing of various forms of Jewish communal authority. Instead, through emancipation, virtually all aspects of collective Jewish life came under the aegis of the liberal state.[2] As a result of this legacy, French Jews embraced the promises of liberalism, positioning themselves as loyal citizens of France.

Offering Jews a new vision of home, liberalism opened up both a conceptual and a political terrain within which Jews could participate in French culture. But the history of Jews, not unlike the history of women in France, makes clear the limitations of this emancipatory project.[3] In fact, the very terms of Jewish emancipation demonstrate the limitations built into liberalism's promise of social equality. Moreover, as cultural critic Homi Bhabha suggests, it is precisely these limitations that most explicitly connect liberalism to colonialism, its historical and ideological counterpart. What links Jews, women, and colonial subjects is liberalism's deceptive promises of liberation with their unexamined limitations. As Napoleon convened the assemblies of Jewish notables, he had already sent troops to quell the uprising in Haiti, France's colonial outpost in the new world. When placed side by side, liberal efforts to emancipate French women, the emancipation of French Jews, and the liberation of Haiti from French rule all share both the universal promises of the revolution as well as a common set of strategic limitations.[4] As I will argue, the initial terms of Jewish emancipation make clear both conceptually and historically that liberalism and colonialism are in fact two sides of the same coin. In both the New and Old World the inclusive vision of the revolution was not so inviting to those the nation continued to other. By seeing these legacies as linked and asking questions about how gender as another form of difference figures in these calculations, I make connections in the present between feminist, postcolonial, and Jewish critiques of liberalism. Only by making these kinds of critical links in the present can we begin to imagine liberation on other grounds. Unfortunately, these kinds of connections are rarely made. Either a text offers a critique of colonialism, or it challenges liberalism in terms of its effects on women, or it offers a critique of the terms of Jewish emancipation. All too rarely are these efforts brought together. This essay challenges these separations. By juxtaposing Homi Bhabha's postcolonial critique with Joan Scott's assessment of French feminism, I reassess the emancipatory promises made to individual Jews through the French Revolution.

The Liberal/Colonial Project

I offer a critique of what I call "the liberal/colonial project" precisely because the pairing of these two discourses has given me some leverage with which to see the larger implications of Jewish and feminist attachments to liberalism.[5] I make links between liberalism and colonialism in order to undo the seeming naturalness of these social arrangements. Following Homi Bhabha, I show that liberalism and colonialism share an ambivalent promise of emancipation and assimilation. In both, power is organized asymmetrically. Some are necessarily excluded. The liberal/colonial project offers both promise and effacement in terms of a kind of cultural mimicry. Like colonialism, liberalism offered formerly subjected peoples a kind of partial emancipation. As Bhabha explains, "By 'partial' I mean both 'incomplete' and 'virtual.' It is as if the very emergence of the 'colonial' [liberal] is dependent for its representation upon some strategic limitation or prohibition *within* the authoritative discourse. The success of colonial appropriation depends on a proliferation of inappropriate objects that ensure its strategic failure, so that mimicry is at once resemblance and menace."[6] In other words, built into both liberalism and colonialism are limitations. As much as these subjects try to become Western or mainstream, they are bound to fail. Asymmetries of power not only remain in place but are essential to the perpetuation of these systems. Lulled by the promises of a place in the dominant culture, they keep trying to fit in. No matter how hard the colonial tries, he or she will remain "a subject . . . that is almost the same, but not quite."[7] This is the bitter irony of mimicry. In order to be effective it must continually produce this kind of slippage or excess.

It is my contention that Jews, like many others in the liberal West, including women, continue to find themselves struggling against "strategic limitations" or "prohibitions." With this in mind, I have found it helpful to understand the dynamics of Jewish assimilation in terms of mimicry. Jews have desired to fit in, to be like everyone else. The problem is that there is an excess expressed in this desire which is aptly captured in the joke that says that Jews are just like everyone else, only more so. This is the kind of difference that Bhabha was talking about. In other words, as hard as Jews try to be like everyone else, the excess of our effort marks us as different.[8]

By juxtaposing the two sides of the liberal/colonial coin—sameness and difference—I want to expose some of the gaps in liberalism's narrative of Jewish emancipation.[9] Although we remain grateful to the liberal revolutions of the late eighteenth century for bringing Jews into the dominant cultures of the West, this is not the entire story. Our acceptance remains partial. Ironically, it has been the fierceness of Jewish loyalty to liberal states like France that has continued to mark Jews as different.

The Emancipation of the Jews

The French Revolution marked the beginning of Jewish emancipation.[10] With the revolution, France was the first nation to grant Jews citizenship and a place within the liberal state. It offered them a new national home. As historian George Mosse explains, the revolution came to solidify national loyalties into an "all embracing principle."[11] The question was, were Jews able to adhere to this principle? To what extent were they Frenchmen like all other Frenchmen? I am interested in what, from the beginning, distinguished Jews from their fellow citizens and how this difference already challenged the revolution's promise of inclusion. By returning to France I try to look at the inception of some of my own deepest commitments to the promises of liberal emancipation.

Like the emerging colonial subject that Bhabha writes about, the emergence of the liberal Jewish subject in France was also dependent for its representation upon certain strategic limitations. In France, this limitation was scripted in terms of fidelity. By blurring the boundaries between nation and family, marriage and citizenship, the question for Jews was one of loyalty. Could Jews be trusted? Did they have dual loyalties? Would or could they ever really become citizens of France like everyone else?

From the beginning Jewish citizenship and cultural acceptance went hand in hand. Liberalism promised both a new cultural and a new civic home. It linked these public and private desires. Citizenship, the pledging of one's loy-

alty to a particular nation-state, became both figuratively and literally a famil-
ial obligation. In France, fidelity not only marked the relationship between
citizens and the state but also defined the proper (state-sanctioned) marital
relationship between a husband and his wife. Marriage became the foundation for the liberal state. By making the nation-state into a kind of home, it
made public and private loyalties into two sides of the same coin. Thus, the
granting of political rights and obligations to Jews came with a series of "private" demands.[12] After the revolution, Jews were required to speak French,
attend French schools, and adhere to French middle-class notions of propriety including notions of taste, decorum, and comportment. They were to do
this even within the private realms of family and religious life as in the state's
control of marriage.

Given the all-encompassing nature of these requirements, there were, necessarily, limitations. Although, as historian Paula Hyman argues, "the majority of French Jews cherished bourgeois values of family, property, and
patriotism with the ferocity of parvenus eager for acceptance,"[13] there were no
guarantees of acceptance. Ironically, Jewish zeal in these matters marked Jews
as different and ensured the failure of their efforts to ever fully assimilate.
Jews remained a distinct group within French society.

In what follows, I flesh out this limitation by looking specifically at the
terms of Jewish political emancipation. I do this first through a brief reading
of *Concerning the Amelioration of the Civil Status of the Jews*, a 1781 tract in
defense of Jewish betterment by Christian Wilhelm Dohm, an enlightened
historian, economist, and Prussian government official,[14] and, second, by
focusing on the 1806 exchange between Napoleon and a gathering of Jewish
notables on the question of Jewish emancipation.[15] Through a careful reading
of this discussion, I point to some of the ambivalences within liberal discourse and its claims to liberation, especially for Jews. I especially want to
examine the role of submission within these negotiations.

More specifically, I look at the critical role of marriage in Napoleon's first
three questions. These questions highlight the role of gender in these negotiations for Jewish emancipation. They also explain how by bringing together
ritual and law, custom and morality, family, and patriae, marriage came to
define the relationship between Jews and liberal states.

The Liberal Solution to the Jewish Problem

The French Revolution brought liberalism's social contract from theory into
practice. In France, it opened up the possibilities of political power to those of
the property-owning class, and this eventually included Jews. By recounting

some of the ideological debates around the "amelioration of the civil status of the Jews" during the 1770s and 1780s,[16] as well as some of the various starts and stops in that process, I will now show the origins of some of the problems that continue to plague Jews within liberal states.

In the period leading up to the French Revolution, there were many questions raised about the status of the Jews in France. Even those who came to the defense of Jews often conceded that there was a "Jewish problem." They argued that exclusionary policies toward Jews led to their degradation and that this "Jewish problem" could be solved by making Jews into productive and loyal subjects or citizens. As Dohm wrote:

> We have found in the oppression and in the restricted occupation of the Jews the true source of their corruption. Then we have discovered also at the same time the means of healing this corruption and of making the Jews better men and useful citizens. With the elimination of the unjust and unpolitical treatment of the Jews will also disappear the consequences of it; and when we cease to limit them to one kind of occupation, then the detrimental influence of that occupation will no longer be so noticeable.[17]

Dohm went on to present a series of concrete suggestions about how France might go about changing these policies. Many of these suggestions became the basis for Jewish emancipation, including the granting of political rights, the opening of various occupations formerly closed to Jews (especially agricultural, public service, and guild positions),[18] the providing of liberal educational opportunities and civil rights to Jews, and the right to worship according to their own faith. In return for these rights and privileges, rabbinic authority was to be ceded and, in its place, Jews were expected to adhere to the authority of the state. The French Revolution's emancipation of the Jews built on these suggestions. In these ways, France became the first Western nation to grant Jews citizenship.[19] As Paula Hyman explains in *From Dreyfus to Vichy: The Remaking of French Jewry, 1906–1939*:

> French Jewry is, in fact, a child of the Revolution. As a result of the revolutionary upheaval in the concept of the nation-state, the 40,000 Jews resident in France in 1789 became the first in the West to achieve full emancipation—that is, acceptance as equal citizens with all the civic and political rights and obligations which citizenship entailed.[20]

> Despite this promise, Jewish liberation did not happen immediately, the debate regarding the emancipation of the Jews was prolonged and acrimonious because of doubts as to the willingness and ability of the Jews to assimilate within French society and fulfill the obligations of citizenship.[21]

Given these tensions, by the time Napoleon came to power there was already a precedent for questioning the efficacy of Jewish emancipation. From the beginning, the question of Jewish loyalty—whether it would be possible for Jews to truly become French citizens—was at issue. The liberal solution was, in the words of Clermont-Tonnerre before the National Assembly in 1789, "To the Jews as individuals—everything; to the Jews as a group—nothing. They must constitute neither a body politic nor an order; they must be citizens individually."[22] This demand echoed liberalism's overarching and indeed revolutionary focus on the presumably undifferentiated individual as the building block of the liberal state. This was also a position that Jews would never quite be able to take. Instead, Jewish entry into liberalism's social contract was partial. It was both incomplete and virtual. Given this, Jews were considered dangerous to the state. For, like colonial subjects outside of Europe, liberal Jewish subjects were dependent for their representation upon a strategic limitation within liberal discourse.[23]

Because Jews resembled but were never quite Frenchmen, they were considered suspect. Fears about Jewish loyalty were present even in the earliest debates leading up to the granting of Jewish emancipation during the revolution.[24] This same trepidation was repeated as a matter of grave and precipitating concern for Napoleon in posing his questions to the Jewish notables. These suspicions about Jewish allegiances were nowhere more apparent than in Napoleon's first three questions about Jews and marriage. By bringing together national and marital fidelity, literally and figuratively, these questions made explicit the overarching nature of liberal emancipation as both a public and private enactment. These questions made clear that marriage was the model for the proper relationship between Jews and the liberal nation state. They also demonstrated the critical role of Jewish women within this emancipatory wager.

Napoleon's Queries: At What Price Jewish Emancipation?

In 1806, Napoleon ordered an Assembly of Jewish Notables and, then, a *Great Sanhedrin*[25] to convene in Paris in order to determine the ongoing viability of Jewish citizenship. The decree read as follows:

> The conduct of many among those of your persuasion have excited complaints, which have found their way to the foot of the throne; these complaints were founded on truth. Nevertheless, His Majesty has been satisfied with stopping the progress of the evil, and he has wished to hear from you on the means of providing a remedy.[26]

Given these problems, Napoleon called upon the Jews to respond. For Napoleon, there were still questions about the alleged inappropriate behavior of some Jews, especially around issues of commerce, for which all Jews were to be called to account. Although these assemblies were ostensibly convened to secure the rights of Jews as individuals within Napoleon's France, ironically the primary task of these assemblies was to have the Jews speak in one collective voice. It was as a group that Napoleon was holding them accountable. Like Dohm and the revolutionary assembly, Napoleon's strategy was also to use citizenship as the means to a solution. Noble Jews were enlisted to help enact this plan.

As the decree continues: "You will, no doubt, prove worthy of so tender, so paternal a conduct, and you will feel all the importance of the trust thus reposed in you."[27] The decree demanded that the Jews assembled pledge the complete loyalty of every individual Jew to the state. "[O]ur most ardent wish is to be able to report to the Emperor that, among individuals of the Jewish persuasion, he can reckon as many faithful subjects, determined to conform in everything to the laws and to the morality which ought to regulate the conduct of all Frenchmen."[28]

In addition to this Jewish notables were asked to answer Napoleon's questions as honestly and openly as possible.

The decree posed twelve specific questions,[29] which read as follows:

1.   Is it lawful for Jews to marry more than one wife?

2.   Is divorce allowed by the Jewish religion? Is divorce valid, although not pronounced by courts of justice and by virtue of the laws in contradiction with the French Code?

3.   Can a Jewess marry a Christian, or a Jew a Christian woman? Or has the law ordered that the Jews should intermarry among themselves?

4.   In the eyes of the Jews are Frenchmen considered as brethren or as strangers?

5.   In either case what conduct does their law prescribe toward Frenchmen not of their religion?

6.   Do the Jews born in France, and treated by the law as French citizens, acknowledge France as their country? Are they bound to defend it? Are they bound to obey the laws, and to follow the directions of the civil code?

7.   What kind of police jurisdiction have the rabbis among the Jews?

8. What judicial power do they exercise among them?

9. Are the forms of the elections of rabbis and their police jurisdiction regulated by the law, or are they only sanctioned by custom?

10. Are there professions from which the Jews are excluded by their law?

11. Does the law forbid the Jews from taking usury from their brethren?

12. Does it forbid or does it allow usury toward strangers?[30]

The Jewish Notables' Response

Given the preoccupations of the decree, the notables' answers to Napoleon's questions were carefully framed within an overarching statement of Jewish loyalty to the emperor. Moreover the declaration was defined in halakhic terms, as Napoleon had requested. The principle of Jewish law invoked was an ancient injunction demanding Jewish obedience to the laws of a prince. Thus, in gratitude to Napoleon, the Assembly of Jewish Notables declared

> that they are fully determined to prove worthy of the favors His Majesty
> intends for them, by scrupulously conforming to his paternal intentions;
> that their religion makes it their duty to consider the law of the prince as
> the supreme law in civil and political matters; that, consequently, should
> their religious code, or its various interpretations, contain civil or political
> commands at variance with those of the French Code, those commands
> would, of course, cease to influence and govern them, since they must,
> above all acknowledge and obey the laws of the prince.[31]

I quote this declaration at length to make clear the deferential stance taken by the Jewish notables. Although this is not surprising given the task before them, there is a deep irony within this position. Despite the overt promise of liberation, the whole interaction between the Jewish notables and Napoleon was framed in terms of paternalistic deference. For his benevolence, Napoleon would be granted complete authority. Emancipation came at the price of subordination. With Napoleon's rise to power, citizenship was literally guaranteed on the basis of loyalty to a prince, a much earlier rabbinic stance toward non-Jewish authority.

According to this rabbinic principle, if there were conflicts between Jewish and princely authority, princely authority would take precedence.[32] Given this, even with liberal emancipation, the structural relationship between Jewish and non-Jewish authority remained constant. With the revolution, the French Code simply took the place of "the law of the prince" only to be reapplied to an emperor with Napoleon's rise to power. Thus, despite the radical nature of much of what Napoleon and, indeed, the revolution had offered French Jews, the mechanism through which rights and privileges were granted did not change. Jews remained at the mercy of those non-Jewish authorities with power over them, grateful for whatever rights and privileges they granted them, however limited.[33]

Part of the Jewish notables' response to Napoleon reads as follows: "That, in consequence of this principle [obedience to the law of the prince], the Jews have, at all times, considered it their duty to obey the laws of the state, and that, since the revolution they, like all Frenchmen, have acknowledged no others."[34] The ancient strategy was given new life with emancipation. Because Napoleon demanded an halakhic response, a legal precedent, the principle of obedience to the law of a prince, with all of its ambiguity, worked perfectly. It gave Napoleon what he wanted. The problem was that if Jews were to remain beholden to Napoleon in precisely the same way in which they had expressed loyalty historically to other princes who had allowed them to live in their lands without political emancipation, to what extent did emancipation really free the Jews?

The Marriage Questions

The notables' response to Napoleon's first three questions, the questions about marriage, are emblematic not only of the emperor's desire for a kind of marriage between the Jews and the state, but of the notables' overarching strategy of deference in response to Napoleon.[35] As I will now demonstrate, the notables' answers to the following three questions clearly signal the ambivalences within France's embrace of Jews.[36]

1. Is it lawful for Jews to marry more than one wife?

2. Is divorce allowed by the Jewish religion? Is divorce valid, although not pronounced by courts of justice and by virtue of the laws in contradiction with the French Code?

3. Can a Jewess marry a Christian, or a Jew a Christian woman? Or has the law ordered that the Jews should intermarry among themselves?

These questions asked Jews to submit not only to French legal authority in the matter of marriage, but also to French middle-class customs and norms in regard to proper heterosexuality. The first question asked literally if Jews were monogamous. The second demanded that the French state have authority over Jewish marriage and divorce proceedings, while the third demanded social integration through marriage.[37] Taken together, these questions challenged the ongoing viability of a separate Jewish community in France. They demanded Jewish assimilation and/or conversion into the dominant culture.

Questions one and two demanded that clear lines of jurisdiction be drawn around the transaction of marriage. In the first instance, the law of the land demanded undivided loyalty. Polygamy was the opposite of such a stance. It overtly challenged the notion of fidelity not only to a spouse but to the state. If Jews had multiple family loyalties, how could they be trusted as faithful citizens of a single nation? Here marriage brings together a vision of long term commitment to both the state and one's family. It brings together both public and private notions of fidelity and belonging.

On another level, this question was about adherence to particular French laws and customs. There was no polygamy in France. Would the Jews, a foreign people known to sometimes allow their men to have more than one wife, follow the laws of France in these most intimate of matters? Here the fear was grounded in both a historical understanding of Jewish communities allowing polygamy as well as evidence of polygamy as an ongoing practice outside of Europe. Was there a legal precedent for supporting Jewish adherence to monogamous French practices?

The notables' answer to this question was yes. They did this by first invoking the custom of European Jews since the eleventh century as law. Since the eleventh century in Europe, Jews had been monogamous. Second, they appealed to colonial assumptions about the backwardness of Eastern practices as a way of acknowledging that there were still Jews who practiced polygamy at that time. Outside of Europe there were, until quite recently, Jewish communities who practiced polygamy. The notables used this acknowledgment of a difference among Jews in order to lay to rest Napoleon's fears about infidelity. By claiming that polygamy was an Eastern practice, they were able to distinguish themselves as Europeans.

Behind this question was, as I have already indicated, a more basic concern about the persistence of Jewish difference in France. Would Jews conform to French social practices? Polygamy marked Jews as Other in a crucial realm: the private sphere upon which civil society was based. Indiscretions in this sphere were particularly dangerous to the stability of the state as a family unit. The notables had to clearly renounce this practice precisely because marriage and family had already become central tropes in defining the nation. As postcolonial critic M. Jacqui Alexander has explained, this renunciation of difference around sexual practices was an important form of social control not only at home in Europe but in the colonies as well. In both instances Others were required to conform to "civilizing" dominant practices.[38] In this way, monogamy reinforced a vision of national loyalty as an all-embracing principle.

Question two demanded loyalty to the law of the land. In this case, the initiation and dissolution of marriage had to be carefully controlled by the state. The question asked who would have jurisdiction over these critical transactions. The second part of this question is especially telling: "Is divorce valid although not pronounced by courts of justice and by virtue of laws in contradiction with those of the French Code?"[39] The clear point of this question was to assure the absolute authority of the French Code in all such matters.

In response to this question, the initial statement of the Jewish notables was quite clear. "Repudiation is allowed by the law of Moses;[40] but is not valid if not previously pronounced by the French Code."[41] This general statement was then followed by a reiteration of the principle of Jewish loyalty and submission to princely authority. More specifically, the notables made reference to oaths taken by French Jews after the revolution. This reminded Napoleon that the Jews of France had already pledged their loyalty to French authority in all such matters. Given this, the notables reassured Napoleon that both initiation and repudiation of marriage rights were to remain under state jurisdiction. "[T]he rabbis could not impart the matrimonial benediction till it appeared to them that the civil contract had been performed before the civil officer, in like manner they cannot pronounce repudiation, until it appears to them that it has already been pronounced by a sentence which gives it validity."[42] In this way the notables' response to this question went on to proclaim that Jewish tradition was at one with the civil code in all such matters for which the rabbis had no authority of their own. Given that civil contracts became critical with the French Revolution and Jewish emancipation, the notables reiterated that formal control of the institution of marriage had already shifted from rabbinic to civil authority.

The liberal marriage contract became Jewish precisely because "it may be justly affirmed that the Jewish religion agrees on this subject with the civil code."[43] Through this statement of accommodation, the notables once again relinquished control over the institution of marriage from Jewish authorities and brought Jewish women under the aegis of the liberal state. By upholding the terms of the liberal marriage contract, they would play a crucial role in Jewish emancipation. Like their Jewish husbands, brothers, and fathers, they also entered into a liberal contractual arrangement that demanded fidelity in the form of subordination.

Question three proved to be the most difficult question of all for the notables to answer. As Robert Chazan and Marc Lee Raphael noted, "The truth would insult French Christians while an accommodation would ignore fifteen hundred years of clear Jewish legislation against intermarriage. The answer, which divided Jewish law into nonexistent categories, was unique in its historical importance as well as its ingenuity."[44] The question of intermarriage made explicit the public/private nature of emancipation for both Jewish men and Jewish women. The question asked not only if Jewish men could marry Christian women but if Jewish women[45] could marry Christian men.

For Napoleon, the question of intermarriage necessarily went both ways. Part of what made this question so troubling for the notables was that it made even more explicit the desire for, as well as the impossibility of, Jewish social integration. In this instance, bringing Jews into French culture was quite literally figured as a family matter. It required bringing Jews into French homes and families. Implicit in this question was both the promise of integration as well as the fear of Jewish difference. It was to be accomplished explicitly through the institution of marriage. By marrying into the dominant culture, one individual at a time, be they male or female, the hope was that Jews would slowly cease to exist as a separate people. They would simply become a part of the French family. This is where the Jewish experience differs most radically from the experience of the colonial subjects whom M. Jacqui Alexander writes about. At issue are constructions of racial differences and their relation to accumulation of wealth. As Alexander explains, in the colonial Caribbean, "[c]onjugal marriage was actively encouraged among slaves but was actively discouraged between white men and colored women because it interrupted the accumulation of private property and wealth by the white father and his 'natural' heirs. According to the planter class, 'free coloreds were acquiring property and wealth by inheriting land from their natural white fathers,' so active measures were put in place to discourage it."[46] Up until the late nineteenth century, Jewish difference was not understood as "racial" in this sense. Given this, it was considered possible for Jews to intermarry into the dominant culture. Jewish women would no longer be Jewish because their identities would be subsumed under their non-Jewish husband's. In the case of Jewish men the lure was ultimately social acceptance through family connections. Either through religious conversion or, at the very least, new family affiliations they would abandon their particularistic ties to a separate Jewish community.

Not surprisingly, the notables' answer to this question was strained. It began by stating unequivocally, "The law does not say that a Jewess cannot marry a Christian, nor a Jew a Christian woman; nor does it state that the Jews can only intermarry among themselves."[47] Following this statement the notables' answer went on to discuss biblically forbidden unions. They argued that these restrictions were only to have applied to Jewish men in relation to peoples who no longer exist: "The prohibition in general applies only to nations in idolatry. The Talmud declares formally that modern nations are not to be considered as such, since they worship, like us, the God of heaven and earth."[48]

This statement was presumably the proof text for the notables' initial assertion that intermarriages were permitted according to Jewish law. Nevertheless, no specific talmudic text is cited. This discussion was then accompanied by a qualification which explained that there were conflicts about this answer among those assembled. They told Napoleon that there was a dispute between the rabbis and lay leaders assembled.[49] Within this answer they explained that the rabbis' position was not unlike that of Catholic clergy in these matters. Like their Catholic counterparts, the rabbis' position was that marriage was a religious ceremony and, as such, in order for them to perform such a ceremony both bride and groom needed to share a single faith.

In contrast to the notables' answer to the previous question, this answer suggested that there were important differences between religious and civil ceremonies despite the Jews' overarching commitment to state authority. In order to temper this claim of difference, however, the position was only made in the name of the rabbis present and not the entire gathering of notables.

Their answer continued by stating that one does not cease to be a Jew by marrying a non-Jew or even by having a civil ceremony. Here again some of the gaps between the practices and the beliefs or, for that matter, between the public statements and the private practices of even those Jews assembled became increasingly apparent. Despite intermarriage, Jews remain Jews. From this answer it became apparent that whether Jewish weddings were in fact ever exclusively civil ceremonies remained a question.

In the case of intermarriage, the rabbis were clearly at odds with the intention of the civil code. These cases called into question the synonymous meaning of Jewish and civil authority. The notables' answer reflects this problem. It made explicit the gap between these two authorities. In cases of intermarriage, Jewish difference continued to make a difference and, ironically, the only way to alleviate the problem was to insist upon even more intermarriage. The more intermarriage, the less need there would be for particularistic authorities altogether. Although this strategy of assimilation through marriage held much promise in the nineteenth century in France, it made explicit ongoing ambivalences within liberal emancipation for Jews. The persistence of Jewish difference, the need for "inter/marriage" and not just "marriage" continued to disrupt any smooth vision of Jewish integration within the liberal state.[50]

Studying this-state-mandated form of assimilation through inter/marriage in France, much less the role of marriage in the Napoleon's other questions, forced me to think again about marriage as a liberal institution. As feminist political theorist Carole Pateman has argued, liberalism's sexual contract simply reinforced male sex rights on other terms.[51] The end of patriarchy did not liberate women. Instead, with the rise of liberal contract theory, a new form of sexual inequity was initiated.[52] Here again parallels between how liberal states like France attempted to homogenize its Jews, and its colonial subjects share all too much in common with what happens to women within the institution of liberal marriage. In all of these instances asymmetrical relationships of power were reinforced and not alleviated.

Toward a Different Future

Despite the liberal democratic ideals of the French Revolution, there were limitations. Like Jews, many others including French colonial subjects and women have stood in an ambivalent position within the authoritative discourse of French liberalism. No matter how hard they have tried to take their place within French culture, they have remained somehow Other. Following contemporary postcolonial and feminist critics, I have focused on the initial terms of Jewish emancipation in order to get at these contradictory dynamics. In so doing, I have come to see that only by letting go of liberalism can any of us begin to envision liberation on other terms.

Notes

1. As I read it, this is why dominant feminism is liberal, why mainstream gay and lesbian organizing is about inclusion, and why the vast majority of Jews remain loyal to the liberal state where they live. For a more detailed account of this dynamic in relation to feminist and gay and lesbian politics, see Janet Jakobsen, *Working Alliances and the Politics of Difference* (Bloomington: Indiana University Press, 1997).

2. On this point see my reading of the questions Napoleon posed to the Jewish notables as a prerequisite to emancipation in Laura Levitt, *Jews and Feminism: The Ambivalent Search for Home* (New York: Routledge, 1997), 51–62. See also Pierre Birnbaum and Ira Katznelson eds., *Paths of Emancipation: Jews, States, and Citizenship* (Princeton, N.J.: Princeton University Press, 1995) and Benjamin Ginsberg, *The Fatal Embrace: Jews and the State* (Chicago: University of Chicago Press, 1993).

3. For more on the issue of women's emancipation in France and the problematics of the legacy of the revolution and its ideals for French women, see Joan Scott, *"Only Paradoxes to Offer": French Feminists and the Rights of "Man," 1789–1944* (Cambridge, Mass.: Harvard University Press, 1996). See also the special issue of *Differences* on

"Universalism" edited by Scott (7:1 [1995]). See especially her introduction "Universalism and the History of Feminism," 1–14.

4. On the brutal and complicated legacy of French colonialism in what became Haiti, see Joan Dayan, *Haiti, History, and the Gods* (Berkeley: University of California Press, 1995).

5. For a fuller feminist critique of these attachments, see Levitt, *Jews and Feminism*, 63–73.

6. Homi Bhabha, "Of Mimicry and Man: The Ambivalence of Colonial Discourse," in *The Location of Culture* (London: Routledge, 1994), 86.

7. Ibid.

8. See for example, Adrienne Rich's account of her father's efforts to fit in, to be an American in "Split at the Root: An Essay on Jewish Identity (1982)," *Blood, Bread, and Poetry: Selected Prose 1979–1985* (New York: W. W. Norton, 1986), 100–23. For an excellent account of these kinds of complicated excesses and the ambivalence of Jewishness, see Linda Nochlin and Tamar Garb, eds., *The Jew in the Text: Modernity and the Construction of Identity* (New York: Thames and Hudson, 1995).

9. Although I have chosen to discuss these gaps here in terms of Jewishness, they are also evident in terms of gender. For a more elaborate discussion of how the experience of Jewish women combines these critiques, see Levitt, *Jews and Feminism*, 63–73. Here I simply want to make clear how the kinds of colonial dynamics Bhabha writes about operate within the liberal West. For a series of nuanced accounts of the problematics of Jewish assimilation in the nineteenth century see Jonathan Frankel and Steven Zipperstein, eds., *Assimilation and Community: The Jews in Nineteenth-Century Europe* (Cambridge: Cambridge University Press, 1992).

10. *Emancipation* in this sense refers specifically to the legal granting of citizenship to Jews, but even this usage is complicated. First, the term itself is used somewhat anachronistically in this context. On this issue, see Jacob Katz, "The Term *Jewish Emancipation*: Its Origin and Historical Impact," in *Studies in Nineteenth-Century Jewish Intellectual History*, ed. Alexander Altmann (Cambridge, Mass.: Harvard University Press, 1964), 1–25. Second, legal, social, and cultural integration were already a part of what it meant to grant Jews citizenship. These processes went hand in hand. Thus, other accounts of this process use terms like Jewish *regeneration, naturalization, amelioration, acculturation, assimilation,* or *betterment*. For more on these imbrications, see Amos Funkenstein, *Perceptions of Jewish History* (Berkeley: University of California Press, 1993), 220–56; Frankel and Zipperstein, *Assimilation and Community*; Jay R. Berkovitz, "The French Revolution and the Jews: Assessing the Cultural Impact," *AJS Review* 20: 1 (1995): 25–86; and Birnbaum and Katznelson, *Paths of Emancipation: Jews, States, and Citizenship*.

11. The French Revolution marked the transformation of the nation from a focus of often divided loyalty to an all-embracing principle. George Mosse, *Nationalism and Sexuality: Middle-Class Morality and Sexual Norms in Modern Europe* (Madison, W.I.: University of Wiconson Press, 1985).

12. For an excellent discussion of some of these issues see Nochlin and Garb, *The Jew in the Text.*

13. Paula Hyman, *From Dreyfus to Vichy: The Remaking of French Jewry, 1906–1939* (New York: Columbia University Press, 1979), 22.

14. Christian Wilhelm Dohm, "Concerning the Amelioration of the Civil Status of the Jews," in *Modern Jewish History: A Source Reader*, ed. Robert Chazan and Marc Lee Raphael (New York: Schocken, 1969), 1–13. All subsequent references to this work will be from this text unless otherwise noted. For more on the innovations of Dohm's approach to the Jewish problem and particularly his move from theology to politics and philosophy see, Katz, "The Term *Jewish Emancipation*," 12–16.

15. The texts I will examine include Napoleon Bonaparte, "Imperial Decree Calling for an Assembly of Jewish Notables (May 30, 1806)"; Count Molé, "Napoleon's Instructions to the Assembly of Jewish Notables (July 29, 1806)"; Abraham Furtado, "Reply on Behalf of the Assembly to Count Molé"; and the Assembly of Jewish Notables' "Answers to Napoleon." Translations of all of these texts are to be found in Paul R. Mendes-Flohr and Jehuda Reinharz, eds., *The Jew in the Modern World: A Documentary History* (New York: Oxford University Press, 1980), 112–20. See also Diogene Tama, "The Emancipation of French Jewry: The Act of the Israelitish Deputies of France and Italy," in Chazan and Raphael, *Modern Jewish History*, 14–31.

16. For more on Jews in France during the period leading up to the French Revolution see Arthur Hertzberg, *The French Enlightenment and the Jews* (New York: Columbia University Press, 1968).

17. Chazan and Raphael, *Modern Jewish History*, 10.

18. For more on these efforts see documents included in Mendes-Flohr and Reinharz, *The Jew in the Modern World*, 103–39.

19. A 1787 essay contest in France asking, "Are there means of making the Jews happier and more successful in France?" came up with a similar strategy. In his winning essay, Adolphe Thie'ry, like Dohm, argued that, "We can make of the Jews what we want them to become, for their faults and vices derive from our institutions." Hyman, *From Dreyfus to Vichy*, 4.

20. Hyman, *From Dreyfus to Vichy*, 3.

21. Ibid., 4.

22. Ibid., 5. For an extended account, see Mendes-Flohr and Reinharz, *The Jew in the Modern World*, 103–5.

23. Bhabha, *The Location of Culture*, 86.

24. See Mendes-Flohr and Reinharz, *The Jew in the Modern World*, 103–11.

25. For a careful account of Napoleon's various encounters with the Jews of France and more specifically the relationship between the Assembly of Notables and the Great Sanhedrin, see Simon Schwarzfuchs, *Napoleon, the Jews and the Sanhedrin* (London: Routledge and Kegan Paul, 1979).

26. Chazan and Raphael, *Modern Jewish History*, 15.

27. Ibid.

28. Ibid., 16.

29. Despite the gains French Jews had made during the revolution, their status remained precarious both socially and politically. See Schwarzfuchs, *Napoleon*, 1–45; and Berkovitz, "The French Revolution," especially 78–86.

30. Chazan and Raphael, *Modern Jewish History*, 16–17.

31. Ibid., 18–19.

32. For an account of the dynamics within the assembly of Jewish notables as not so much class differences but about rabbinic verses enlightenment philosophical authority, see Schwarzfuchs, *Napoleon*, 64–87.

33. This was true in relation to the leaders of the revolution who granted Jews citizenship in 1789; and again in 1806, when Napoleon, the restored monarch, needed to assert his own authority over the Jews of France, whom he could deem worthy of French citizenship. For a more extensive series of classic texts of Jewish emancipation throughout Western Europe, see Mendes-Flohr and Reinharz, *The Jew in the Modern World*, 103–39.

34. Chazan and Raphael, *Modern Jewish History*, 19.

35. These were in fact the first of the questions to be answered and came to model the answers for all of the other questions. Here the important role of the rabbis in framing the answers to these and then all of the other questions became apparent. See Schwarzfuchs, *Napoleon*, 66–71.

36. For a more recent account of this ambivalence in France, see Susan Rubin Suleiman, "The Jew in Sartre's *Réflexions sur la question juive*: Exercise in Historical Reading," in *The Jew in the Text*, 201–18.

37. For more on the issue of "assimilation" in France, see Phyllis Cohen Albert, "Israelite and Jew: How Did Nineteenth-Century French Jews Understand Assimilation?" in Frankel and Zipperstein, *Assimilation and Community*, 88–109.

38. I am indebted to the excellent analysis of this dynamic in the colonial context presented by M. Jacqui Alexander in "Redrafting Morality: The Postcolonial State and the Sexual Offenses Bill of Trinidad and Tobago," in *Third World Women and the Politics of Feminism*, ed. Chandra Talpade Mohanty, Ann Russo, and Lourdes Torres (Bloomington: Indiana University Press, 1991), 133–52. In a lecture at Temple University (April 30, 1992) Homi Bhabha also helped clarify this connection between colonialism and liberalism. On the relationship between Jewish and postcolonial discourse see Jonathan Boyarin, *Storm from Paradise: The Politics of Jewish Memory* (Minneapolis: University of Minnesota Press, 1992). For a more recent deployment of postcolonial theory in context of postzionism see Laurence Silberstein, *The Postzionism Debates: Knowledge and Power in Israeli Culture* (New York: Routledge, 1999), especially chapter 6, "Postzionism, Postmodernism, and Postcolonial Theory: A Radical Postzionist Critique," 165–206.

39. Chazan and Raphael, *Modern Jewish History*, 19.

40. Here the law of Moses seems to refer to rabbinic practices. See Schwarzfuchs, *Napoleon*, 64–87.

41. Chazan and Raphael, *Modern Jewish History*, 19.

42. Ibid., 20.

43. Ibid.

44. Ibid., 14. See also Schwarzfuchs, *Napoleon*, 69–71.

45. The standard translation of these transactions from the French were done in London in 1807 by F. D. Kirwan. This translation is in both the Mendes-Flohr and Reinharz and the Chazan and Raphael collections. M. Diogene Tama, *Transactions of the Parisian Sanhedrin or Acts of the Assembly of Israelitish Deputies of France and Italy*, trans. F. D. Kirwan (London: C. Taylor, 1807). In this translation this reference is to a Jewish woman in the singular, "the Jewess." For an account of various uses of this term and the problematics of its usage, see A. J. Levine "A Jewess, More and/or Less," in *Judaism Since Gender*, ed. Miriam Peskowitz and Laura Levitt (New York, Routledge, 1996). It is striking that in Levine's essay, Jewesses often occupy border positions not unlike this case, where the issue is "intermarriage."

46. See Alexander, "Redrafting Morality," 134.

47. Chazan and Raphael, *Modern Jewish History*, 21.

48. Ibid.

49. Again, on these tensions between rabbis and philosophers among those assembled, see Schwarzfuchs, *Napoleon*, 64–87.

50. This open embrace of Jews and the dream of assimilation was to be superseded in the twentieth century by a much more virulent ideology of racial anti-Semitism which no longer understood this to be possible. For more on these later developments in France, see Hyman, *From Dreyfus to Vichy*.

51. Carole Pateman, *The Sexual Contract* (Stanford, Calif: Stanford University Press, 1988).

52. For more on these issues and their implications for Jewish women see Levitt, *Jews and Feminism*, especially chapters 4, 5, and 6.

8

Body, Representation, and Black Religious Discourse

M. SHAWN COPELAND

Honey, de white man is de ruler of everything as fur as Ah been able tuh find out. Maybe it's some place way off in de ocean where de black man is in power, but we don't know nothin' but what we see. So de white man throw down de load and tell de nigger man tuh pick it up. He pick it up because he have to, but he don't tote it. He hand it to his women-folks. De nigger woman is de mule uh de world so fur as Ah can see.

—Zora Neale Hurston, *Their Eyes Were Watching God*

Introduction

Since the black woman's involuntary arrival in the West, her body has been a site of powerful and painful contention.[1] Almost from the start of the European traffic in African flesh, white traders, and the captains and crews of merchant slave ships judged black female bodies not only as reproductive and productive objects of commercial transaction, but also as opportunities on which to vent sexed aggression and power. Colonization and chattel slavery would require the breaking, taming, breeding, control, and use of black human beings as work animals, as tools in the service of violent expansion, settlement, and domination. Thus, as peculiar objects of colonial desire, that is of property and of release, of production and reproduction, black women were placed, at least physically, at the economic and erotic disposal of European and European-American men (and women).

At the same time, European and European-American representative aesthetics scaled, identified, and labeled the bodies of black women as primitive, lascivious, and repugnant. This evaluation was at once religious and moral. It reflected *both* white Western Christianity's ambivalence toward the body, sex, as well as sexuality, *and* the impact of religion on what Kelly Brown Douglas refers to as the construction and "management of sexual discourse," thus fostering the "domination and demonization" of the different Other.[2]

Finally, even as the passage from Zora Neale Hurston's *Their Eyes Were Watching God* theorizes the compound-complex dynamic of black women's oppression, it must be recognized as cruel theory. For slavery aimed not only to colonize black women's bodies, sex, and sexuality, to undermine her, it sought to subvert and destroy any authentic relationship *between* black women and black men as well as *among* black women themselves. So it was that colonization and slavery, as both ideology and practice, not only sustained patriarchy but also initiated black men into, and rewarded them for, a brutalizing *mimesis*. As Andre Lorde notes, black men were encouraged to view black women as "approved and acceptable targets for Black male rage."[3] At the same time, black women were pitched against one another. Deliberately, Hurston sets the quotation in the mouth of Nanny, Janey's grandmother who loves her with a fierce but misguided love. Rather than helping Janey "to remain self-possessed, to achieve independence," as Sherley Williams suggests, Nanny in fact "shapes her to the demands of the racist and patriarchal culture as an art of survival."[4]

The implications of this compound-complex objectification of black women persist in contemporary social and rhetorical, aesthetic and religious meanings, values, and representation. To critically recognize and contest these meanings, values, and representation is to further anticolonialist, antiracist and antisexist discourses of liberation. Womanist theology presents one way of grappling with and meeting this challenge.[5] As critical faith-based reflection on black human experience, womanist religious discourse seeks to discern the meaning, significance, and role of religion for the differentiated cognitive, moral, cultural, and social praxis of black human beings as persons-in-community. Even as womanist theology is "organically related"[6] to black male liberation theology and to the various differentiated (including African, *mujerista*, Jewish, Asian) critical theologies for the liberation of women, it takes its point of departure from an analysis of the condition and experiences of black women within a social context concretely distorted by the biases or ideologies of white racist supremacy, sexism, heterosexism, cultural imperialism, and economic exploitation. At the same time, womanist theology must come to terms with the biased ways in which black women have been and are perceived in black religious, cultural, and interpersonal contexts. Moreover, as a critical discursive strategy, it must propose an aesthetics capable and worthy of reclaiming black women's bodies, sex and sexuality, minds and culture.

In the following pages, I argue that black women's bodies, sex and sexuality, minds and culture have been colonized by both white and black communities. I interrogate the dialectical relation between black women and black Christianity, and draw out the contributions of womanist critique to black religious discourse. First, this entails an inquiry into slavery's colonizing mythology of white racist supremacy, with its corollary of black inferiority, and its literal impact on black women's bodies, sex, and sexuality; second, it calls for analysis of the ways in which black women remain colonized by representative aesthetics in popular culture, particularly in certain styles of rap music and hip-hop; and third, it suggests ways in which at least one form of religious discourse, the black sermon, can begin to meet the challenge toward a new aesthetic.

Colonization of Black Women's Bodies: Slavery and Its Mythology

The colonization of black women's bodies began in slavery; but only rarely, reluctantly, and often with great discomfit and indirection do we learn the details of their brutalizing sexual assault. White male slaveholders, their adolescent sons, slave traders, and "patterrollers" or slave catchers used black women's bodies with impunity. In 1841, representatives of the British and Foreign Anti-Slavery Society conducted an interview with Madison Jefferson, a fugitive who had been held in slavery in Virginia. Jefferson confirmed reports that enslaved women who refused to submit to the sexual advances of white slaveholders or overseers were repeatedly whipped "to subdue their virtuous repugnance." Should this tactic fail, frequently the woman would be sold.[7] One former enslaved woman gave this description of the brutal beating her mother received for resisting the sexual advances of an overseer

> who use to tie mother up in the barn wid a rope aroun' her arms up over her head, while she stood on a block. Soon as dey got her tied, dis block was moved an' her feet dangled, you know, couldn't tech de flo'. Dis ole man, now would start beatin' her nekked 'til the blood run down her back to her heels.[8]

When British actress Fanny Kemble reproached an enslaved woman for sexual relations with a slaveholder, the woman retorted, "When he make me follow him into de bush, what use me tell him no? He have strength to make me."[9] And Mary Peters gave this account of her mother's ordeal.

> My mother's mistress had three boys—one twenty-one, one nineteen, and one seventeen. One day, Old Mistress had gone away to spend the day. Mother always worked in the house. . . . While she was alone, the boys came in and threw her down on the floor and tied her down so she couldn't struggle, and one after the other used her as long as they wanted, for the whole afternoon.[10]

In a speech to an antislavery audience in Brooklyn, another fugitive, introduced as Lewis Clarke and fleeing Kentucky bondage, stated that "a slave woman ain't allowed to respect herself, if she would."[11] And a former enslaved woman repeated her mother's sad musing on the situation of black women in chattel slavery:

> My mama said that a nigger 'oman couldn't help herself, fo' she had to do what de marster say. Ef he come to de field whar de women workin' an' tell gal to come on, she had to go. He would take one down in de woods an' use her all de time he wanted to, den send her on back to work. Times nigger 'omen had chillun for de marster an' his sons and some times it was fo' de ovah seer.[12]

These accounts expose but a fraction of the torment and abuse black women suffered in their bodies, in their sex, precisely because they were at once objects of property and of twisted desire. But as Deborah Gray White and Kelly Brown Douglas insist, these sexual assaults were rooted in ideologies and attitudes derived both from the earliest encounters between Europeans and Africans and the "ideas that Southern white men had about women in general."[13] [White traders, explorers, and missionaries justified the enslavement and abuse of Africans, through fabricating an "obscene mythology" which absolutized superficial differences in pigmentation of skin color, culture, and religious orientation. In this mythology black skin rendered black men and women synonymous with animality and bestiality, ignorance and stupidity, depravity, and immorality.[14]] Black women were thought to be promiscuous and, therefore, incapable of chastity or modesty. The scant and ragged clothing allotted to them, manual labor which required that skirts be pinned up around hips or waist, the naked exposure and sometimes indecent handling of black women's bodies on the auction block contributed to these ideas. This spurious mythology gave white men the rationale and the license, even a false sense of obligation, to exercise full and willful power over blacks in any and all situations. For the black woman, this meant that the dynamics of oppression were compounded due to her race and her sex.

Gray White makes an important connection between the way in which planter's economic interests intersected with black women's reproductive capability. In the accumulation of wealth, the planter class depended upon ready labor; this was achieved most easily through the reproduction of laborers. John Smith, a former enslaved man, maintained that his master started out with just two women, but eventually owned three plantations with approximately three hundred slaves.[15] Hannah Jones, a former enslaved woman, remembered two planters, Ben Oil and John Cross who "just raised niggers . . . [who] had nigger farms."[16] And Gray White in her research discovered that

> [m]ajor periodicals carried articles detailing optimal conditions under which bonded women were known to reproduce, and the merits of a particular "breeder" were often the topic of parlor or dinner table conversations. The fact that something so personal and private became a matter of public discussion prompted one ex-slave to declare that "women wasn't nothing but cattle."[17]

The enslaved black woman's body was held, at once, in contempt and in contemptuous value. On the one hand, the black woman was thought to be "sly," "sensual," and "shameless";[18] but these characteristics were valued in relation to a libidinous economics: after all, such a woman made a good brood sow. On the other hand, those same characteristics only reinforced negative stereotypes about the black woman's lasciviousness and immorality. Then again, since even economically valuable slaves could be killed at whim, neither the black woman's body nor her life commanded authentic respect. Rather, the black woman was reduced to body parts—parts which allowed white men pleasure, however unsettling; parts which afforded white men economic gain; parts which literally nursed the heirs to white racist supremacy. Yet, black women clung to what dignity and humanity they created: recognizing the distorted and repugnant nature of their sexual circumstance, resisting when they could, enduring when they were unable.

Rap Culture's Popular Representation of Black Women

Slavery aimed to dissociate black women from their humanity, to objectify them and subordinate them to a classical European aesthetic scale, to a pornographic gaze. Even "some whippings of female slaves were sexually suggestive." We cannot dismiss, Gray White observes, the "sexual overtones" in the whipping of a thirteen-year-old Georgia slave girl who "was put on all fours sometimes her head down and sometimes up, and beaten until froth ran from her mouth."[19] The disturbing character of this pitiable image is heightened when we recall the cartoon on the cover of Snoop Doggy Dogg's *Doggy Style*: a naked black female on all fours, her head in a doghouse, her naked buttocks with a dog's tail offered to the viewer. Positioned at "the nexus of America's sex and race mythology," once again, the black woman finds it "most difficult" to escape the disfiguring representation of her body, her sex and sexuality.[20]

For African-American youth and young adults, especially males, rap music has become, as Tricia Rose puts it, a crucial "cultural vehicle for open social reflection on poverty, fear of adulthood, the desire for absent fathers, frustrations about black male sexism, female sexual desires, daily rituals of life as an unemployed teen hustler, safe sex, raw anger, violence, and childhood memories."[21] Rap music and hip-hop culture, she says, provide a dynamic innovative intellectual, political, and spiritual form of resistance to the "cultural fractures produced by postindustrial oppression."[22]

At the same time, rap music and hip-hop culture provide a primary way of interpreting the world, of "negotiat[ing] the experiences of marginalization, brutally truncated opportunity, and oppression within the cultural imperatives of African-American history, identity, and community."[23] Rap music and hip-hop have had a large role in shaping representations of black women, their bodies, sex, and sexuality. And as bell hooks contends, "representations of black female bodies in contemporary popular culture rarely subvert or critique images of black female sexuality which were part of the cultural apparatus of 19th century racism and which still shape perceptions today."[24]

Too often representations of black women, especially in gangsta rap, continue to disrespect and disfigure black women's bodies, sex, and sexuality. The photographs on the covers of 2 Live Crew's *As Nasty as They Wanna Be* and *Shake a Lil' Somethin'* display black women wearing thong-bikinis, standing with their legs wide apart, their buttocks displayed to the camera, the rappers lying between their legs. And D.R.S. (Dirty Rotten Scoundrels) raps about the torture and dismemberment of women as a sexual act. Such instances disclose an imagination in bondage, diluting and defiling the real mysterious joy of passion and erotic power. These women are not presented to us as whole human beings, but as body parts, objectified and displayed for sale: the transcendent being reduced to spectacle.

Rap's rampant sexist and violent lyrics reflect both the sexism and misogyny that pervade the wider white U.S. culture, and the male attempt to establish heterosexual masculine identity by abusing and dominating women. Yet, as bell hooks so correctly observes,

> When young black males labor in the plantations of misogyny and sexism to produce gangsta rap, white supremacist capitalist patriarchy approves the violence and materially rewards them. Far from being an expression of their "manhood," it is an expression of their own subjugation and humiliation by more powerful, less visible forces of patriarchal gangsterism. They give voice to the brutal, raw anger and rage against women that it is taboo for "civilized" adult men to speak. . . . The tragedy for young black males is that they are so easily duped by a vision of manhood that can only lead to their destruction.[25]

At the same time, we cannot overlook the real collusion of black women in these displays. In her study of rap hip-hop culture, Tricia Rose writes that the women who participate in rap videos, who allow themselves to be photographed for the purpose of marketing hip-hop culture, are called "video ho's or skeezers." Their motivation for such cooperation and "participation in this video meat market is closely related to the rock/sports/film star groupie phenomenon, in which fans, especially female, get momentary star aura by associating closely or having sex with rich and famous figures." How great must be the desire, how profound must be the need of these young women for attention, for care, for affirmation. How poignant, how piteous that their complicity in their own debasement is understood or misunderstood as a means toward a career in the entertainment business or a way out of economically fragile circumstances.[26]

The media and the film industry bathe violence and misogyny in surreal and romantic light. Violence is excessive, gratuitous, made strangely compelling, roughly erotic, determining and redetermining "thresholds" of pleasure, pressure, and pain.[27] Far too often, black women are the objects of this violence. Black films like *She's Gotta Have It, School Daze,* and *Boyz N the Hood* either eroticized black women or depicted them as emasculating and overbearing; they do "violence and mayhem to body and soul."[28] Weighing in on Spike Lee's *School Daze*, bell hooks praises its attempt to contest both the "sexual iconography of the traditional black pornographic imagination [in which] the protruding butt is seen as an indication of a heightened sexuality [and the] racist assumptions that suggest it is an ugly sign of inferiority."[29] hooks singles out for comment the all-black party scene in which a swim-suited group is dancing—doing "the butt."

> The black "butts" on display are unruly and outrageous. They are not the still bodies of the female slave made to appear as mannequin. They are not a silenced body. Displayed as playful cultural nationalist resistance, they challenge assumptions that the black body, its skin color and shape, is a mark of shame.[30]

Given its power to inform the viewer's gaze, to disrupt and contest notions of black bodies, female bodies specifically, hooks judges this scene as "the most transgressive and provocative moment in *School Daze*." But she contends that this opportunity to reinforce recognition and delight in the black body "was undercut by the overall sexual humiliation and abuse of black females in the film."[31]

Brown Douglas comments, "If films made by black men manifest trouble between black men and women, so too do those based on texts written by black women."[32] Films such as *Waiting to Exhale*, based on Terry Macmillan's novel, or *The Color Purple*, based on Alice Walker's novel, have been charged with negatively representing black men. Brown Douglas writes, "Black male responses to these movies are foreboding, as they suggest that many Black men are unwilling to hear the stories of Black women. . . . to recognize and appreciate the complexity of Black women's experiences."[33] Moreover, she concludes, "The critical response to various Black female movies also signals the insidious sexism present within the Black community."[34]

Whether intentionally or not, Hollywood "in black and in white" desensitizes, manipulates, and manages our response to the body, to sex and sexuality—to seduction and rape, to betrayal and violation, to torture and killing. Whether intentionally or not, print and visual media, films, MTV, and video games transmit gross and distorted images of the body that penetrate our subconscious. Unnoticed and unreflected upon, these images suffuse our thoughts, speech, bodily reactions to others, judgments, and ordinary practices of everyday interaction.[35] Thus, misogyny and violence have become common, ordinary, expected, accepted, perhaps normative. For even as misogyny and violence sustain our aggression, they undermine our efforts to respond and critique that aggression, to engage in and be engaged by open and nonviolent personal and social transformation, humane and holistic relationships. Misogyny and violence have deformed our imagination. They leave us discouraged, dispirited, and numb; wounded culturally and socially, psychically and physically, morally and religiously.

Black Religious Discourse: Preaching a New Aesthetic

Thus far I have shown how slavery's colonizing mythology of white racist supremacy, with its corollary of black inferiority, had a literal impact on black women's bodies, sex, and sexuality. By focusing critically on rap music and hip-hop, I have pointed out some of the ways in which black women's bodies, sex, and sexuality remain colonized and displayed by representative aesthetics in certain expressions of popular culture. Rap, hip-hop, violence, and misogyny meet, as Tricia Rose so aptly puts it, at the "crossroads of lack and desire."[36] In the social matrix on which rap comments, and often so prophetically, human life has lost preeminent value, and the body, sex, and sexuality have been dispossessed of erotic, joyful, holy possibility.

I hope, in this last section, to suggest how a womanist critique might contribute to rethinking the black sermon as a vehicle through which to address the construction of sexist and racist representation of black women. This, of course, will not be a simple task. Black women have an ambivalent relationship with churches. On the one hand, black Christian churches have been places of spiritual, psychological, and social refuge from the burdens in black women's lives. On the other hand, those same churches in "their patriarchally and androcentrically biased liturgy and leadership have been primary agents" of the colonization of black women's bodies and minds.[37] Contemporary Christian churches, and black Christian churches in particular, must affirm the sacredness and transcendent quality of black human life, of the black woman's human life and the sacredness of the black human body, of the black woman's body, sex, and sexuality, specifically. The sermon can serve as one mediation of this affirmation in its retrieval of a notion of the human person as a dynamic moral agent, rather than a passive consuming being who is the reductive product of advertising and marketed change. The sermon's effectiveness will depend both upon excising religious attitudes and theological positions that foster sexist representations of black women and upon cultivating a new aesthetic which can heal distortions of the imagination and contest the reign of violence, nihilism, and despair.[38]

The religiocultural world from which the black sermon emerged was forged in the fusion of fragmented elements and beliefs drawn from several

West African cosmologies. Although the enslaved peoples fitted Christianity to their own situation, that fusion laid the ground on which that adaptation took place.[39] The most essential characteristics of an African-American (Christian) worldview include: (1) creative and tensive holding of the sacred and secular, without separation or dilution; (2) profound respect for all human life and interpersonal relationships; (3) individual identity formation from and in relation to community, along with regard for the wisdom of elders; (4) empathetic, symbolic, diunital, and associative understanding; (5) unity of being and doing; (6) commitment to freedom and liberation due to centuries of oppression and communal and personal anxiety; (7) ambiguous toleration and transcendence of a notion of limited reward in the context of slavery and stigmatized social history; (8) indirection and discretion in speech and behavior; and (9) affirmation of styling: intentional or unintentional improvisation in language, gestural, or symbolic mannerisms to favorably effect the receipt of a message.[40]

As perhaps *the* chief exemplar of an African-American (Christian) worldview, the black sermon is also the key to understanding and projecting this worldview. The sermon is a rhetorical space in which preacher and people "articulate the self, challenge the dominant culture's ordering of reality, and contest its authoritative discourse," as Dolan Hubbard writes. In that space, the preacher recovers the community's voice, binds the present to the past, while striving against dehumanization, social dislocation, value disorientation, and psychic breakdown, to imagine and "project a benevolent cosmology and teleology" in which black women and men apprehend and know themselves as subjects of their own history and destiny, as a people of God's own making.[41] For those who respond to its beauty, truth, and power, the sermon signifies and effects a healing shift in religious, cultural, social, psychological imagination. It is a powerful and dangerous tool in decolonizing the mind.

One of the ways that the preacher does this is by *drawing out* the centuries-old history of Africans in the Americas and by *drawing on* what literary critic Stephen Henderson terms "mascon" images and symbols. With the word *mascon*, Henderson denotes words that mediate a "massive concentration of Black experiential energy which powerfully affects the meaning of Black speech, Black song, and Black poetry." Henderson contends that "certain words and constructions seem to carry an inordinate charge of emotional and psychological weight, so that whenever they are used they set all kinds of bells ringing, all kinds of synapses snapping, on all kinds of levels."[42] These words and images are mined from what Henderson calls "the soul-field," the dense set of "personal, social, institutional, historical, religious, and mythical meanings that affect everything we say or do as black people sharing a common heritage."[43]

Henderson offers some examples of mascon words (not code words, but "innocent enough") words and phrases like "rock" and "roll," "slip, slide, and ride." Some illustrations of their use: "Roll, Jordan, Roll," "Rock! Oh, Rock in This Weary Land," "It takes a Rockin' Chair to Rock," "Rock and Roll," "Rollin' with my Baby," "I'm Rollin' through an Unfriendly World," "Let the Good Times Roll." These phrases imply and mediate the creative tensive union of sacred and secular; they pray and play; they suggest and signify joy and pleasure in the body and sexuality; they evoke associative, diunital understanding.

Through improvisational word construction, symbols and images, music and song, mascons configure and mediate meaning, constitute and effect community, generate appreciative awe. Deceptively simple while never simplistic, common while never clichéd, mascons possess magnitude.[44] For generations, African-American people have used mascons (1) to remember and to pass on their unspeakable suffering under slavery, their thirst for life, their unyielding spirit, and their relationship with the Divine; (2) to bind the people to each other and to themselves, although this may never be fully realized in the here and now; (3) to liberate themselves, if only for a brief time, from the material power of the capitalist dispensation; and (4) to transcend societal and personal limitation. The use of mascons in the black sermon is all but required.

Womanist ethicist Katie Cannon maintains that while most African-American churchgoers are capable of grasping and judging the aesthetic landscape of the black sermon, we find it difficult to identify, analyze, and articulate its patterns of misogyny, androcentricity, and patriarchy.[45] Theologian Garth Baker-Fletcher concurs. "How," he asks, "can Black churches really mount a sustained critique of woman-degrading rhetoric when so many preachers and churches devalue women on a regular basis."[46] If the sermon is to heal distortion and to nourish imagination, then the preacher is morally obliged to grasp and plumb the experiences of the whole congregation, to "satisfy the *whole* congregation's spiritual hunger." Cannon proposes a womanist critique of homiletics that will "identif[y] the frame of sexist-racist social contradictions housed in sacred rhetoric that gives women a low image of ourselves."[47] This critique involves asking and answering these questions: "how is meaning constructed, whose interests are served, and what kind of worlds are envisioned in Black sacred rhetoric?"[48] This critique, then, calls the preacher and the church to jettison that *aesthetics of submission* through which the central images, symbols, metaphors, narrative interpretations, traditions, and rituals of Christian practice, explicitly and implicitly, coach tame women to surrender to patriarchal and kyriarchal prerogatives and privilege.

If the sermon is to heal and to nourish imagination toward decolonization of mind and living, then its message must be rooted in exegetical and theological content that projects a reality worthy of black Christianity. Given the failure of the churches to take women seriously and given society's proclivity to reduce black women to body parts and to tolerate sexual and physical violence against women, the preacher's theological attitude toward personhood, toward the humanity of women, is of paramount concern.

For centuries religion and theology have used women as a "special symbol of evil."[49] The contemporary residue of this usage, coupled with cultural disregard for human life, quite literally has had fatal consequences for black women. The identification of women with nature, bodiliness, and emotion, and the identification of men with culture, spirit, and reason abets the subordination of women to men in nearly all spheres of human activity. Long-standing theological debates about the constitution and origin of female being (body and soul) have left black women wounded and suspicious of their authentic humanity. And, although we recognize that the soul is without gender, we still doubt women's *full participation* in the *imago dei*. The notion of woman as a self-transcending, autonomous human subject, a moral agent capable of forming and acting in accord with her responsibly formed conscience, remains, for not a few men and women, still disquieting. Contemporary Christianity, and in particular black Christianity, must contest the imagination's downward spiral into the lewd and pornographic—wordplay that warps black women's bodies, photographs that simulate steamy violent sex, sadomasochism, and addiction. At the same time, however, Cannon insists that black Christianity purge itself of "biblically based sermons [as well as representations and messages] that portray female subjects as bleeding, crippled, disempowered, objectified, purified, or mad." These representations trivialize and distort the humanity of women, for inevitably young black girls and women internalize these malformations. These representations undermine the "historical contributions of African American women's leadership and participation in the church" and in society.[50] These representations deface the divine image in the person of women.

We are in a position, now, to suggest how the sermon might recover and heal distortion in communal and personal imagination, how the sermon might begin to subvert the sexist/racist, pornographic imagination. *First*, as Cannon says, since the primary "purpose of preaching is to call the worshipping congregation to *an ultimate response to God*," the preacher stands between God and the people—"with one ear to the ground hearing the cries and longings of the people and the other ear at the mouth of God."[51] The sermon is the vehicle by which the preacher defines, interprets, and instructs the congregation in what it means to live a just and holy life, what it means to be God's own people in history. Thus, the people are called to grasp, incarnate, and proclaim the liberating character and deed of God. In the sermon, preacher and congregation dramatically, rhythmically, and existentially reenact the history of the mighty acts of God. Through "a rhetorical methodology of definition, elaboration, exemplification, and justification," the sermon reestablishes "a line of continuity inside the mind," Cannon writes.[52] The psychic and aesthetic aspects of imagination are engaged and energized, cleansed and refreshed, reanimated and redirected.

Second, the sermon structures a symbolic universe in which, in response to the sound of the preacher's voice, an aggregate of isolated individuals emerges as a community. The preacher "encodes the corporate community with a culturally regenerating vision as preacher and community assert their rights to genuine existence."[53] This vision must project a prophetic critique against all that threatens to maim and destroy black life, black women's lives specifically, against all that presents itself as misogyny and androcentricity. And it must grapple with social dislocation and cultural disorientation, equipping women and men for dignity in life and creative social praxis aimed at communal and personal transformation.

The community as community evaluates and judges this vision, even at the affective height of its delivery. "African-American congregations are not driven to uncontrollable frenzy [even] at times of seeming emotional abandon . . . [a]nd do not suspend judgment."[54] In the sermon, the preacher charts a series of imaginal constructions and intelligible conceptions that convey the community's ideal meanings and values. If those ideals are transgressed or exploited, disapproval is expressed, and the direction of the sermon will shift.

Third, the sermon heals and frees the congregation and each of its members from dread, from psychic breakdown, from nihilism. Hortense Spillers writes that the passional movement of the sermon as oral poetry aims for "a complete expression of a gamut of emotions whose central form is the narrative and whose end is cathartic release . . . binding once again the isolated members of a community."[55] The sermon gives back to the community its own history, its cultural memory, its creative potential, its *soul.* The sermon pours out a healing balm and binds up psychic and spiritual wounds of a community oppressed and violated by structural violence, of women degraded and debased, of men maimed and assaulted by face-to-face acts of violence. As the community becomes its "authentic self," each member finds her and his own "self" and discovers personal history and potential nourished, and alienated and disordered affective patterns remade. Each member experiences a sense of release, of being at home, of being *at-one-with* the other members of the community. The sermon reestablishes the principles of truth, trust, justice, and integrity as the norms by which the black community and its members evaluate and reorient themselves. The sermon clears a path for the intervention, the irruption of the Spirit in former lives of disorder and disgrace.

Fourth, the sermon is a challenge to the members of the community to question, to analyze, and to transform their social and historical situation, and, to do so *as* and *in community*. The sermon proposes practical solutions to the social dislocations of joblessness, homelessness, hunger, and poverty, and thus "invites the congregation to make a decision for or against emancipatory praxis."[56] The community and its members in response act out their self-determination and self-actuation in responsibly life-valuing ways. The day care-centers, job training programs, housing plans, and social ministries of African-American churches are efforts to realize the symbolic vision of a human, whole, and holy life in the concrete. To the cultural, social, moral, and psychic alienations that give impetus to irrationality, chaos, and evil, the sermon evokes an *aesthetics of redemption* that orders a vision of another and different city.

Fifth, sexual abuse of black women and children, battering, and psychological assault are deeply disturbing; they are sins as well as crimes. Inasmuch as preacher and people believe and act and move as if the authority of the sermon comes directly from God, then the sermon must be a self-critical practice. It must continually measure the vision it projects and the message it proclaims against "God's Agapic love."[57] Indeed, the blood of raped, battered, abused, and murdered (black) women (and children) summons the church to its own *kenosis*. If the church is to be a credible, purified, authentic witness, and servant of the message of that love, then it must effect in its own life and structures what it preaches.

Sixth, the church must develop creative ways and means "to establish a nonintimidating environment for engaging in sexual discourse."[58] The preacher must search out and cultivate a vocabulary for preaching that accords the body, sex, and sexuality a respect and esteem coincident with their origin, functions, and end. At the same time the preacher must find ways to educate the congregation on its worth. Brown Douglas suggests that church-based discussions of black novels might serve to provoke critical reflection on the "realities of black sexuality, including male/female relationships, self-esteem, and sexual intimacy." Such discussions would assist black women and men in "recognizing the interconnections between black sexuality and white racism, as well as how distortions of black sexuality have impacted black intimacy and relationships."[59]

Seventh, the sermon is to be "disruptive," therefore "transformative," discourse.[60] In other words, the sermon is not only to push the congregation from its comfort zone, but toward critical social action. Brown Douglas calls upon black churches to develop a "sexual discourse of resistance" which demands a change in the way "black church community, especially its leaders, has conducted itself in terms of women and gay and lesbian persons."[61] The sermon provides a crucial vehicle for critique of behaviors that demean and degrade the body, sex, and sexuality, as well as for affirmation and encouragement of behaviors that indicate conversion or change, that promote healthy appreciation of the body, sex, and sexuality.

Conclusion

The black sermon can serve as an instrument in the recovery and healing of distorted and wounded imagination which is the ground of representation. At the same time, religion and theology, language and art all too easily can be insinuated in the legitimation of misogyny and sexism. Thus, the sermon achieves an aesthetic function only insofar as preacher and congregation participate in the retrieval of those meanings and values that affirm the body, sex, and sexuality as good and beautiful. The ability of transformed black religious discourse to shape and to project new representations of aesthetic consciousness demonstrates just how imagination constitutes the ground not only of our historical transformation, but of a critical hope. Finally, black women have become signs and signifiers; they stand, as Gray White says, "at the crossroads of two of the most well-developed ideologies in America, that regarding women and that regarding the Negro."[62] The sermon can provoke a new *representative aesthetic* that intentionally, attentively, intelligently, rationally, responsibly, and lovingly purges and recovers mascons; that brings forth and tests fresh images, symbols, metaphors, and narratives; that supports black women and men in planning and building a nondominative, antiviolent, nonsexist, truly human and Christian future.

Notes

1. Leela Ghandi, *Postcolonial Theory: A Critical Introduction* (New York: Columbia University Press, 1998), 83.

2. Kelly Brown Douglas, *Sexuality and the Black Church: A Womanist Perspective* (Maryknoll, N.Y.: Orbis Books, 1999), 22.

3. Audre Lorde, "Sexism: An American Disease in Blackface," in *Sister Outsider* (Trumansburg, N.Y.: Crossing Press, 1984), 65.

4. Sherley Anne Williams, introduction, to Zora Neale Hurston, *Their Eyes Were Watching God* (Urbana: University of Illinois Press, 1991; 1st ed. 1937), xxv.

5. Alice Walker coined the term *womanist* from the African American folk expression *womanish*; for the extended definition of the term, see her *In Search of Our Mothers' Gardens, Womanist Prose by Alice Walker* (New York: Harcourt Brace Jovanovich, 1983), xi.

6. Delores S. Williams, *Sisters in the Wilderness: The Challenge of Womanist God-Talk* (Maryknoll, N.Y.: Orbis Books, 1993), xiv.

7. John W. Blassingame, ed., *Slave Testimony: Two Centuries of Letters, Speeches, Interviews, and Autobiographies* (Baton Rouge: Louisiana State University Press, 1989, 1st ed. 1977), 221.

8. Dorothy Sterling, ed., *We Are Your Sisters: Black Women in the Nineteenth Century* (New York: W. W. Norton, 1984), 25.

9. Ibid., 24.

10. James Mellon, ed., *Bullwhip Days: The Slaves Remember, An Oral History* (New York: Avon Books, 1988), 297.

11. Blassingame, ed., *Slave Testimony*, 156.

12. Sterling, ed., *We Are Your Sisters*, 25.

13. Deborah Gray White, *Ar'n't I a Woman? Female Slaves in the Plantation South* (New York: W. W. Norton, 1985), 29.

14. Brown Douglas, *Sexuality and the Black Church*, 32.

15. Mellon, ed., *Bullwhip Days*, 148.

16. Ibid.

17. Gray White, *Ar'n't I a Woman?*, 31.

18. Frederick Law Olmstead, *Cotton Kingdom*, 63, quoted in Gray White, *Ar'n't I a Woman?*, 33.

19. Ibid., 33.

20. Ibid., 28.

21 Tricia Rose, *Black Noise: Rap Music and Black Culture in Contemporary America*

(Hanover, N.H.: Wesleyan University Press, 1994), 18. For some other theological discussions of hip-hop culture and rap see Michael Eric Dyson, *Between God and Gangsta Rap: Bearing Witness to Black Culture* (New York: Oxford University Press, 1996), and Garth Kasimu Baker-Fletcher, *Xodus: An African American Male Journey* (Minneapolis: Fortress Press, 1996), especially 131–94.

22. Rose, *Black Noise*, 21

23. Ibid., 40, 21.

24. bell hooks, *Black Looks: Race and Representation* (Boston: South End Press, 1992), 62.

25. bell hooks, *Outlaw Culture: Resisting Representations* (New York: Routledge, 1994), 122–23.

26. Rose, *Black Noise*, 169.

27. Felipe E. MacGregor and Marcial Rubio Correa, "Rejoinder to the Theory of Structural Violence," in *The Culture of Violence*, ed. Kumar Rupesinghe and Marcial Rubio Correa (New York: United Nations University Press, 1994), 54.

28. Emilie M. Townes, "Washed in the Grace of God," in *Violence against Women and Children: A Christian Theological Sourcebook*, ed. Carol J. Adams and Marie M. Fortune (New York: Continuum Books, 1995), 69.

29. hooks, *Black Looks*, 63.

30. Ibid.

31. Ibid., 64.

32. Brown Douglas, *Sexuality and the Black Church*, 79.

33. Ibid.

34. Ibid.

35. Iris Marion Young, *Justice and the Politics of Difference* (Princeton, N.J.: Princeton University Press, 1990), 148; see also, David Theo Goldberg, *Racist Culture: Philosophy and the Politics of Meaning* (Oxford: Blackwell, 1993).

36. Rose, *Black Noise*, 21.

37. Williams, *Sisters in the Wilderness*, xii.

38. For some studies of black preaching see Charles V. Hamilton, *The Black Preacher in America* (New York: William Morrow, 1972); Gerald L. Davis, *I Got the Word in Me and I Can Sing It, You Know: A Study of the Performed African American Sermon* (Philadelphia: University of Pennsylvania, 1985); Henry H. Mitchell, *Black Preaching: The Recovery of a Powerful Art* (Nashville: Abingdon Press, 1990); James Henry Harris, "Preaching Liberation: The Afro-American Sermon and the Quest for Social Change," *Journal of Religious Thought* 46 (winter–spring 1989–1990): 72–89.

39. In *The Black Church in the African American Experience* (Durham, N.C.: Duke University Press, 1990), C. Eric Lincoln and Lawrence H. Mamiya argue that the health,

vibrancy, and potent sway of the historic black churches were uncontested for more than two hundred years. However, the forces of modernity—secularization with its accompanying processes of class/social stratification and differentiation, increasing tolerance for social and cultural pluralism in the larger United States society and, I believe, the end, more or less, of *de jure* and *de facto* segregation, have tended "to diminish the cultural unity provided by the black sacred cosmos" (383).

40. For some discussions of Africanisms or the retentions of personal, religious, cultural, social West African traditions, patterns, and practices see Molefi Kete Asante, *The Afrocentric Idea* (Philadelphia: Temple University Press, 1987), especially 34–39; Molefi Kete Asante and Kariamu Welsh Asante, eds., *African Culture: The Rhythms of Unity* (Trenton, N.J.: African Third World Press, 1990); Joseph E. Holloway, ed., *Africanisms in American Culture* (Bloomington: Indiana University Press, 1990); Marimba Ani, *Yurugu: An African-Centered Critique of European Cultural Thought and Behavior* (Trenton, N.J.: African Third World Press, 1994); and Vernon Dixon and Badi Foster, *Beyond Black or White* (Boston: Little, Brown, 1971).

41. Dolan Hubbard, *The Sermon and the African American Literary Imagination* (Columbia: University of Missouri Press, 1994), 5.

42. Stephen Henderson, *Understanding the New Black Poetry: Black Speech & Black Music as Poetic References* (New York: William Morrow, 1973), 44.

43. Ibid., 41.

44. Clarence Joseph Rivers, *The Spirit in Worship* (Cincinnati: Stimuli, 1978), 199.

45. Katie Geneva Cannon, *Katie's Canon: Womanism and the Soul of the Black Community* (New York: Continuum, 1995), 113.

46. Baker-Fletcher, *Xodus: An African American Male Journey*, 327–28.

47. Cannon, *Katie's Canon*, 114.

48. Ibid., 121.

49. Margaret A. Farley, "Sources of Sexual Inequality in the History of Christian Thought," *Journal of Religion* 56: 2 (April 1976): 37.

50. Cannon, *Katie's Canon*, 114.

51. Ibid., 116.

52. Ibid., 117, 119.

53. Hubbard, *The Sermon and the African American Literary Imagination*, 11.

54. Davis, *I Got the Word in Me*, 94.

55. Hortense Spillers, "Fabrics of History: Essays on the Black Sermon," 4, quoted in Hubbard, *The Sermon and the African American Literary Imagination*, 7.

56. Cannon, *Katie's Canon*, 118.

57. Baker-Fletcher, *Xodus: An African American Male Journey*, 190.

58. Brown Douglas, *Sexuality and the Black Church*, 135.

59. Ibid.

60. Ibid., 139.

61. Ibid.

62. Gray White, *Ar'n't I a Woman?*, 27.

Selected Bibliography

Afkhami, Mahnaz, Greta H. Nemiroff, and Haleh Vazir. *Safe and Secure: Eliminating Violence against Women and Girls in Muslim Societies.* Baltimore, Md.: SIGI, 1998.

Ahmed, Leila. *A Border Passage: From Cairo to America—A Woman's Journey.* New York: Farrar, Straus and Giroux, 1999.

———. "Western Ethnocentrism and Perceptions of the Harem." *Feminist Studies* 8 (fall 1982): 521–34.

———. *Women and Gender in Islam: Historical Roots of a Modern Debate.* New Haven, Conn.: Yale University Press, 1992.

al-Ghazali, Zaynab. *Ayyam min hayati* (Days from My life). Cairo: Dar al-Shuruq, 1986.

———. *Nazarat fi kitab Allah* (Views on the Book of God). Cairo: Dar al-Shuruq, 1994.

Alcoff, Linda. "Cultural Feminism versus Post-Structuralism: The Identity Crisis in Feminist Theory." *Signs* 13 (1988): 405–36.

Allen, Paula Gunn. *Off the Reservation: Reflections on Boundary-Busting, Border-Crossing, Loose Canons.* Boston: Beacon Press, 1998.

———, and Patricia Clark Smith. *As Long as the Rivers Flow: The Stories of Nine Native Americans.* New York: Scholastic Press, 1996.

Alloula, Malek. *The Colonial Harem.* Minneapolis: University of Minnesota Press, 1986.

Amadiume, Ifi. *Male Daughters, Female Husbands: Gender and Sex in an African Society.* London: Zed Books, 1987.

Anderson, Benedict R. *Imagined Communities: Reflections on the Origin and Spread of Nationalism.* New York: Verso Books, 1983.

Apess, William. *On Our Own Ground: The Complete Writings of William Apess, A Pequot.* Edited by Barry O'Connell. Amherst: University of Massachusetts Press, 1992.

Asad, Talal, ed. *Anthropology and the Colonial Encounter.* London: Ithaca Press, 1973.

Ashcroft, Bill, Gareth Griffiths, and Helen Tiffin. *The Empire Writes Back: Theory and Practice in Post-colonial Literatures.* London: Routledge, 1989.

_____. *Key Concepts in Post-Colonial Studies.* London: Routledge, 1998.

Bahri, Deepika, and Mary Vasudeva, eds. *Between the Lines: South Asians and Postcoloniality.* Philadelphia: Temple University Press, 1996.

Bal, Mieke, *Double Exposures: The Subject of Cultural Analysis.* New York: Routledge, 1996.

Basil, David. *Modern Africa: A Social and Political History.* London: Longman, 1989.

Basu, Srmati. *She Comes to Take Her Rights: Indian Women, Property, and Propriety.* Albany: State University of New York Press, 1999.

Bilimoria, Purushottama. *Sabdapramana: A Doctrine in Mimamsa-Nyaya Philosophy.* Dordrecht: Kluwer Academic, 1988.

Bhabha, Homi. *The Location of Culture.* London: Routledge, 1994.

Blake, C. Fred. "Foot-binding in Neo-Confucian China and the Appropriation of Female Labor." *Signs* 19 (1994): 676–712.

Blaut, James. M. *The Colonizer's Model of the World: Geographical Diffusionism and Eurocentric History.* New York: Guilford Press, 1993.

Bloom, Harold. *The Anxiety of Influence.* New York: Oxford University Press, 1973.

Boehmer, Elleke. *Colonial and Postcolonial Literature: Migrant Metaphors.* Oxford: Oxford University Press, 1995.

Boyarin, Jonathan. *Storm from Paradise: The Politics of Jewish Memory.* Minneapolis: University of Minnesota Press, 1992.

Braidotti, Rosi. *Nomadic Subjects: Embodiment and Sexual Difference in Contemporary Feminist Theory.* New York: Columbia University Press, 1994.

_____. *Patterns of Dissonance.* Translated by Elizabeth Guild. New York: Routledge, 1991.

Brontë, Charlotte. *Jane Eyre.* Second Norton critical edition. Edited by Richard J. Dunn. New York: W. W. Norton, 1987.

Brown Douglas, Kelly. *Sexuality and the Black Church: A Womanist Perspective.* Maryknoll, N.Y.: Orbis, 1999.

Butler, Judith. *Bodies That Matter: On the Discursive Limits of "Sex."* New York: Routledge, 1993.

Cannon, Katie Geneva. *Katie's Canon: Womanism and the Soul of the Black Community.* New York: Continuum, 1995.

Ceci, Lynn. "Native Wampum as a Peripheral Resource in the Seventeenth-Century World-System." In *The Pequots in Southern New England: The Fall and Rise of an American Indian Nation,* edited by Laurence M. Hauptman and James D. Wherry. Norman: University of Oklahoma Press, 1990.

Chambers, Iain, and Lidia Curti, eds. *The Post-Colonial Question: Common Skies, Divided Horizons.* New York: Routledge, 1996.

Chatterjee, Partha. "Colonialism, Nationalism, and Colonized Women: The Contest in India." *American Ethnologist* 16: 4 (1989): 622–33.

―――. "The Nationalist Resolution of the Women's Question." In *Recasting Women: Essays in Colonial History,* edited by Kumkum Sangari and Sudesh Vaid. New Brunswick, N.J.: Rutgers University Press, 1990.

Chazan, Robert, and Marc Lee Raphael, eds. *Modern Jewish History: A Source Reader.* New York: Schocken, 1969.

Chidester, David. *Savage Systems: Colonialism and Comparative Religion in Southern Africa.* Charlottesville: University Press of Virginia, 1996.

Chow, Rey. *Ethics after Idealism: Theory—Culture—Ethnicity—Reading.* Bloomington: Indiana University Press, 1998.

―――. *Woman and Chinese Modernity: The Politics of Reading between West and East.* Minneapolis: University of Minnesota Press, 1991.

Clarke, J. J. *Jung and Eastern Thought: A Dialogue with the East.* London: Routledge, 1994.

―――. *Oriental Enlightenment: The Encounter between Asian and Western Thought.* London: Routledge, 1997.

Clifford, James. *The Predicament of Culture: Twentieth Century Ethnography, Literature, and Art.* Cambridge, Mass.: Harvard University Press, 1988.

―――. *Routes: Travel and Translation in the Late Twentieth Century.* Cambridge, Mass.: Harvard University Press, 1997.

Columbus, Christopher. *The Four Voyages of Christopher Columbus.* Edited and translated by J. M. Cohen. New York: Penguin Books, 1969.

Daly, Mary. *Beyond God the Father: Toward a Philosophy of Women's Liberation.* Boston: Beacon Press, 1973.

―――. *The Church and the Second Sex.* Boston: Beacon Press, 1968.

―――. *Gyn/Ecology: The Metaethics of Radical Feminism.* Boston: Beacon Press, 1978.

―――. *Pure Lust: Elemental Feminist Philosophy.* Boston: Beacon Press, 1984.

Dayan, Joan. *Haiti, History, and the Gods.* Berkeley: University of California Press, 1995.

De Rougemont, Denis. *The Idea of Europe.* Translated by Norbert Guterman. New York: MacMillan, 1966.

Debo, Angie. *The Road to Disappearance.* Norman: University of Oklahoma Press, 1941.

Derrida, Jacques. *Dissemination.* Translated by Barbara Johnson. Chicago: University of Chicago Press, 1981.

_____, and Christie V. McDonald. "Choreographics." *Diacritics* 12: 2 (1982): 66–77.

Di Leonardo, Micaela, ed. *Gender at the Crossroads of Knowledge: Anthropology in the Postmodern Era.* Berkeley: University of California Press, 1991.

Dirlik, Arif. "The Postcolonial Aura: Third World Criticism in the Age of Global Capitalism." *Critical Inquiry* 20: 2 (1994): 328–56.

Donaldson, Laura E. *Decolonizing Feminisms: Race, Gender, and Empire-Building.* Chapel Hill: University of North Carolina Press, 1992.

_____. "On Medicine Women and White Shame-ans: New Age Native Americanism and Commodity Fetishism as Pop Culture Feminism." *Signs* 24 (1999): 677–96.

_____, ed. "Postcolonialism and Scriptural Reading." *Semeia* 75 (1996).

Dube, Musa W. "Consuming a Colonial Cultural Bomb: Translating Badimo into Demons in the Setswana Bible." *Journal for the Study of the New Testament* 73 (1999): 33–59.

_____. "Readings of *Semoya*: Batswana Women's Interpretations of Matt. 15: 21–28." *Semeia* 73 (1996): 111–29.

_____. *Postcolonial Feminist Interpretation of the Bible.* St. Louis, Mo.: Chalice Press, 2000.

Edmunds, R. David. "American History, Tecumseh, and the Shawnee Prophet." In *Major Problems in American Indian History: Documents and Essays,* edited by Albert L. Hurtado and Peter Iverson. Lexington, Mass.: D.C. Heath and Company, 1994.

Eickelman, Dale, and James Piscatori, eds. *Muslim Travellers: Pilgrimage, Migration, and the Religious Imagination.* Berkeley: University of California Press, 1990.

Ellison, Grace. *An Englishwoman in a Turkish Harem.* London: Methuen, 1915.

Emberley, Julia V. *Thresholds of Difference: Feminist Critique, Native Women's Writings, Postcolonial Theory.* Toronto: University of Toronto Press, 1993.

Erdrich, Louise. *The Antelope Wife.* New York: HarperFlamingo, 1998.

Fabian, Johannes. "Remembering the Other: Knowledge and Recognition in the Exploration of Central Africa." *Critical Inquiry* 26 (1999): 49–69.

_____. *Time and the Other: How Anthropology Makes Its Object.* New York: Columbia University Press, 1983.

Fanon, Frantz. *A Dying Colonialism.* Translated by Haakon Chevalier. New York: Grove Weidenfeld, 1965.

Foucault, Michel. *Discipline and Punish: The Birth of the Prison.* Translated by Alan Sheridan. Harmondsworth: Penguin, 1977.

_____. *The History of Sexuality,* vol. 1, *An Introduction.* Translated by Robert Hurley. New York: Vintage, 1990.

_____. *Language, Counter-Memory, Practice: Selected Essays and Interviews.* Edited by Donald Bouchard. Oxford: Blackwell, 1977.

Frankel, Jonathan, and Steven Zippenstein, eds. *Assimilation and Community: The Jews in Nineteenth-century Europe.* Cambridge: Cambridge University Press, 1992.

Friedman, Susan Stanford. *Mappings: Feminism and the Cultural Geographies of Encounter.* Princeton, N.J.: Princeton University Press, 1998.

Gandhi, Leela. *Postcolonial Theory: A Critical Introduction.* New York: Columbia University Press, 1998.

Ghossoub, Mai. "Feminism—or the Eternal Masculine—in the Arab World." *New Left Review,* January–February 1987, 3–18.

Gilbert, Sandra M., and Susan Gubar. *The Madwoman in the Attic: The Woman Writer and the Nineteenth-Century Literary Imagination.* New Haven, Conn.: Yale University Press, 1979.

Gilmartin, Christina K., et al., eds. *Engendering China: Women, Culture, and the State.* Cambridge, Mass.: Harvard University Press, 1994.

Gilroy, Paul. *The Black Atlantic: Modernity and Double Consciousness.* Cambridge, Mass.: Harvard University Press, 1996.

Goldberg, David Theo. *Racist Culture: Philosophy and the Politics of Meaning.* Oxford: Blackwell, 1993.

Goldenberg, Naomi R. *Returning Words to Flesh: Feminism, Psychoanalysis, and the Resurrection of the Body.* Boston: Beacon Press, 1990.

Green, Rayna. *Women in American Indian Society.* Edited by Frank W. Porter III. New York: Chelsea House, 1992.

Gross, Rita M. *Buddhism after Patriarchy: A Feminist History, Analysis, and Reconstruction of Buddhism.* Albany: State University of New York Press, 1993.

_____. "Buddhism after Patriarchy." In *After Patriarchy: Feminist Transformations of the World Religions,* edited by Paula M. Cooey, William R. Eakin, and Jay B. McDaniel. Maryknoll, N.Y.: Orbis Books, 1991.

_____. *Feminism and Religion: An Introduction.* Boston: Beacon Press, 1996.

_____. "A Rose by Any Other Name . . .: A Response to Katherine K. Young." *Journal of the American Academy of Religion* 67 (1999): 185–94.

Grosz, Elizabeth. *Volatile Bodies: Toward a Corporeal Feminism.* Bloomington: Indiana University Press, 1994.

Guy-Sheftall, Beverly, ed. *Words of Fire: An Anthology of African-American Feminist Thought.* New York: New Press, 1995.

Hall, Stuart. *Critical Dialogues in Cultural Studies.* Edited by David Morley and Kuan-hsing Chen. London: Routledge, 1996.

Henderson, Stephen. *Understanding the New Black Poetry: Black Speech and Black Music as Poetic References.* New York: William Morrow, 1973.

hooks, bell. *Black Looks: Race and Representation.* Boston: South End Press, 1992.

_____. *Outlaw Culture: Resisting Representations.* New York: Routledge, 1994.

Hopkins, Dwight N., and Sheila Greeve Davaney, eds. *Religious Reflection and Cultural Analysis.* New York: Routledge, 1996.

Hubbard, Dolan. *The Sermon and the African American Literary Imagination.* Columbia: University of Missouri Press, 1994.

Huggan, Graham. "Decolonizing the Map: Post-Colonialism, Post-Structuralism and the Cartographic Connection." In *Past the Last Post: Theorizing Post-Colonialism and Post-Modernism,* edited by Ian Adam and Helen Tiffin. Calgary: University of Calgary Press, 1990.

Hurston, Zora Neale. *Their Eyes Were Watching God.* Urbana: University of Illinois Press, 1978; 1st ed. 1937.

Hyman, Paula. *From Dreyfus to Vichy: The Remaking of French Jewry, 1906–1939.* New York: Columbia University Press, 1979.

Irigaray, Luce. *Speculum of the Other Women.* Translated by Gillian Gill. Ithaca: Cornell University Press, 1985.

Jacobs, Jane M. "Earth Honoring: Western Desires and Indigenous Knowledges." In *Writing Women and Space: Colonial and Postcolonial Geographies,* edited by Allison Blunt and Gillian Rose. New York: Guilford Press, 1994.

Jakobsen, Janet. *Working Alliances and the Politics of Difference.* Bloomington: Indiana University Press, 1997.

JanMohamed, Abdul R., and David Lloyd, eds. *The Nature and Context of Minority Discourse.* New York: Oxford University Press, 1990.

Jenson, Lionel M. *Manufacturing Confucianism: Chinese Tradition and Universal Civilization.* Durham, N.C.: Duke University Press, 1997.

Jung, C. G. *Jung on the East.* Edited by J. J. Clark. London: Routledge, 1995.

Kalu, Anthonia C. "Those Left in the Rain: African Literary Theory and the Re-invention of the African Woman." *African Studies Review* 37: 2 (1994): 77–95.

Keddi Nikkie, and Lois Beck. *Women in the Muslim World.* Cambridge, Mass.: Harvard University Press, 1978.

Keller, Catherine. *Apocalyse Now and Then: A Feminist Guide to the End of the World.* Boston: Beacon Press, 1996.

_____. "The Breast, the Apocalypse, and the Colonial Journey." *Journal of Feminist Studies in Religion* 10: 1 (spring 1994): 53–72.

———. "Seeking and Sucking: On Relation and Essence in Feminist Theology." In *Horizons in Feminist Theology: Identity, Tradition, and Norms*, edited by Rebecca S. Chopp and Sheila Greeve Davaney. Minneapolis: Fortress Press, 1997.

Khatibi, Abdelkabir. *Maghreb Pluriel.* Paris: Denoel, 1983.

Kilpatrick, Alan. *The Night Has a Naked Soul: Witchcraft and Sorcery among the Western Cherokee.* Syracuse, N.Y.: Syracuse University Press, 1997.

King, Richard. *Orientalism and Religion: Postcolonial Theory, India, and "The Mythic East."* London: Routledge, 1999.

Kirby, Vicki. "Corporeal Habits: Addressing Essentialism Differently." *Hypatia* 6: 3 (fall 1991): 4–24.

Kitagawa, Joseph M. "The History of Religions in America." In *The History of Religions: Essays in Methodology*, edited by Mircea Eliade and Joseph M. Kitagawa. Chicago: University of Chicago Press, 1959.

Kolodny, Annette. *The Land before Her: Fantasy and Experience of the American Frontiers, 1630–1860.* Chapel Hill: University of North Carolina Press, 1984.

Kristeva, Julia. *About Chinese Women.* Translated by Anita Barrows. New York: Urizen Books, 1977.

Kwok Pui-lan. *Chinese Women and Christianity, 1860–1927.* Atlanta, Ga: Scholars Press, 1992.

_____. "Jesus/The Native: Biblical Studies from as Postcolonial Perspective." In *Teaching the Bible: The Discourses and Politics of Biblical Pedagogy.* Edited by Fernando F. Segovia and Mary Ann Tolbert. Maryknoll, N.Y.: Orbis Books, 1998.

_____. "The Sources and Resources of Feminist Theologies: A Post-Colonial Perspective." *Yearbook of the European Society of Women in Theological Research* (1997): 1–16.

Laclau, Ernesto. "Universalism, Particularism, and the Question of Identity." *October* 61 (summer 1992): 83–90.

LaRiviere, Richard. "Protestants, Orientalists, and Brahmanas: Reconstructing Indian Social History." *1994 Gonda Lecture.* Netherlands: Royal Academy of Arts and Sciences, 1994.

Lerner, Gerder. *The Creation of Patriarchy.* New York: Oxford University Press, 1986.

Leslie, Julia. *The Perfect Wife: The Orthodox Hindu Woman According to the Stridharmapaddhati of Tryambakayajvan.* New York: Oxford University Press, 1989.

Levitt, Laura. *Jews and Feminism: The Ambivalent Search for Home.* New York: Routledge, 1997.

Lewis, Nantawan Boonprasat, and Marie M. Fortune, eds. *Remembering Conquest: Feminist/Womanist Perspectives on Religion, Colonization, and Sexual Violence.* New York: Haworth Pastoral Press, 1999.

Lloyd, David. "Race under Representation." *Oxford Literary Review* 13: 1–2 (1991): 62–94.

Long, Elizabeth. "Reading as Collective Action." In *Ethnography of Reading*, edited by Jonathan Boyarin. Berkeley: University of California Press, 1993.

Loomba, Ania. *Colonialism/Postcolonialism*. New York: Routledge, 1998.

Lopez, Donald S. Jr., ed. *Curators of the Buddha: The Study of Buddhism under Colonialism*. Chicago: University of Chicago Press, 1995.

_____. *Prisoners of Shangri-La: Tibetan Buddhism and the West*. Chicago: University of Chicago Press, 1998.

Lorde, Audre. *Sister Outsider: Essays and Speeches*. Trumansburg, N.Y.: Crossing Press, 1984.

Lowe, Lisa, and David Lloyd, eds. *The Politics of Culture in the Shadow of Capital*. Durham, N.C.: Duke University Press, 1997.

Macleod, Arlene Elowe. *Accommodating Protest: Working Women, the New Veiling, and Change in Cairo*. New York: Columbia University Press, 1991.

Mani, Lata. *Contentious Traditions: The Debate on Sati in Colonial India*. Berkeley: University of California Press, 1998.

Manyarrows, Victoria Lena. "Confronting and Surpassing the Legacy of Columbus: A Native Woman's View." In *With-Out Discovery: A Native Response to Columbus*, edited by Ray Gonzalez. Seattle: Broken Moon Press, 1992.

Martin, Joel W. *Sacred Revolt: The Muskogees' Struggle for a New World*. Boston: Beacon Press, 1991.

Masuzawa, Tomoko. *In Search of Dreamtime: The Quest for the Origin of Religion*. Chicago: University of Chicago Press, 1993.

Maw, Martin. *Visions of India: Fulfillment Theology, the Aryan Race Theory, and the Work of the British Protestant Missionaries in Victorian India*. Frankfurt and Main: Verlag Peter Lang, 1990.

Mazrui, Ali A. *Cultural Forces in World Politics*. London: James Currey, 1990.

McClintock, Anne. *Imperial Leather: Race, Gender and Sexuality in the Colonial Contest*. New York: Routledge, 1995.

_____, Aamir Mufti, and Ella Shobat, eds. *Dangerous Liaisons: Gender, Nation, and Postcolonial Perspectives*. Minneapolis: University of Minnesota Press, 1997.

Mendes-Flohr, Paul R., and Jehuda Reinharz, eds. *The Jew in the Modern World: A Documentary History*. New York: Oxford University Press, 1980.

Mgadla, Patrick. "Missionary Wives, Women, and Education: The Development of Literacy among Batswana, 1840–1937." *Pula: Botswana Journal of African Studies* 11: 1 (1997): 70–81.

Mignolo, Walter D. *The Darker Side of the Renaissance: Literacy, Territoriality, and Colonization*. Ann Arbor: University of Michigan Press, 1995.

Minces, Juliet. *The House of Obedience.* London: Zed Books, 1980.

Mohanty, Chandra Talpade, Ann Russo, and Lourdes Torres, eds. *Third World Women and the Politics of Feminism.* Bloomington: Indiana University Press, 1991.

Moore, Robert L., and Daniel J. Meckel, eds. *Jung and Christianity in Dialogue: Faith, Feminism, and Hermeneutics.* New York: Paulist, 1990.

Moraga, Cherríe, and Gloria Anzaldúa, eds. *This Bridge Called My Back: Writings by Radical Women of Color.* New York: Kitchen Table Women of Color Press, 1981.

Morgan, Robin, ed. *Sisterhood Is Global: The International Women's Anthology.* New York: Doubleday, 1984.

Mudimbe, V. Y. *The Idea of Africa.* Indianapolis: Indiana University Press, 1994.

_____. *The Invention of Africa: Gnosis, Philosophy and the Order of Knowledge.* London: James Currey, 1988.

Müller, Max. *Comparative Mythology.* New York: Arno Press, 1977.

Naggar, Carole. "The Unveiled Algerian Women, 1960." *Aperture* (summer 1990): 2–11.

Narayan, Uma. *Dislocating Cultures: Identities, Traditions, and Third World Feminism.* New York: Routledge, 1997.

Nochlin, Linda, and Tamar Garb, eds. *The Jew in the Text: Modernity and the Construction of Identity.* New York: Thames and Hudson, 1995.

Noll, Richard. *The Jung Cult: Origins of a Charismatic Movement.* Princeton, N.J.: Princeton University Press, 1994.

Parry, Benita. "Problems in Current Theories of Colonial Discourse." *Oxford Literary Review* 9: 1–2 (1987): 27–58.

Pateman, Carole. *The Sexual Contract.* Stanford, Calif.: Stanford University Press, 1988.

Patton, Laurie L., ed. *Jewels of Authority: Women and Textual Tradition in Hindu India.* New York: Oxford University Press, 2001.

Pawde, Kumud, "The Story of My 'Sanskrit.'" In *Subject to Change: Teaching Literature in the 90s,* edited by Susie Thar. Hederabad: Orient Longman, 1998.

Perdue, Theda. *Cherokee Women: Gender and Culture Change, 1700–1835.* Lincoln: University of Nebraska Press, 1998.

Peskowitz, Miriam, and Laura Levitt, eds. *Judaism Since Gender.* New York: Routledge, 1996.

Poliakov, Léon. *The Aryan Myth: A History of Racist and Nationalist Ideas in Europe.* Translated by Edmund Howard. New York: Meridian, 1971.

Pollock, Sheldon. "India in the Vernacular Millennium: Literary Culture and Polity, 1000–1500." *Daedalus* 127: 3 (summer 1998): 41–74.

_____. "Deep Orientalism? Notes on Sanskrit and Power beyond the Raj." In *Orientalism and the Postcolonial Predicament,* edited by Carol A. Breckenridge and Peter Van Der Veer. Philadelphia: University of Pennsylvania Press, 1993.

Pratt, Mary Louise. *Imperial Eyes: Travel Writing and Transculturation.* London: Routledge, 1992.

Prior, Michael. *The Bible and Colonialism: A Moral Critique.* Sheffield, U.K.: Sheffield Academic Press, 1997.

Probert, Belinda, and Bruce W. Wilson, eds. *Pink Collar Blues: Work, Gender and Technology.* Carlton, Victoria: Melbourne University Press, 1993.

Rabasa, José. *Inventing A-M-E-R-I-C-A: Spanish Historiography and the Formation of Eurocentrism.* Norman: University of Oklahoma Press, 1993.

Radhakrishnan, R. "Nationalism, Gender and the Narrative of Identity." In *Nationalisms and Sexualities,* edited by Andrew Parker et al. New York: Routledge, 1992.

Rose, Tricia. *Black Noise: Rap Music and Black Culture in Contemporary America.* Middletown, CT: Wesleyan University Press, 1994.

Rowlandson, Mary. "A True History of the Captivity and Restoration of Mrs. Mary Rowlandson." In *Colonial American Travel Narratives,* edited by Wendy Martin. New York: Penguin Books, 1994.

Ryan, Simon. "Inscribing the Emptiness: Cartography, Exploration and the Construction of Australia." In *De-Scribing Empire: Post-Colonialism and Textuality,* edited by Chris Tiffin and Alan Lawson. London: Routledge, 1994.

Said, Edward W. *Culture and Imperialism.* New York: Viking, 1993.

_____. *Orientalism.* New York: Vintage, 1978.

Sale, Kirkpatrick. *The Conquest of Paradise: Christopher Columbus and the Columbian Legacy.* New York: Alfred A. Knopf, 1990.

Sankar, Tanika, and Urvashi Butalia, eds. *Women and the Hindu Right.* Delhi: Kali for Women, 1995.

Schwarzfuchs, Simon. *Napoleon, the Jews and the Sanhedrin.* London: Routledge and Kegan Paul, 1979.

Scott, Joan. "Multiculturalism and the Politics of Identity." *October* 61 (summer 1992): 12–19.

_____. *"Only Paradoxes to Offer": French Feminists and the Rights of "Man," 1789–1944.* Cambridge, Mass.: Harvard University Press, 1996.

_____. "Universalism and the History of Feminism," *Differences* 7: 1 (1995): 1–14.

Shoemaker, Nancy. "The Rise or Fall of Iroquois Women." *Journal of Women's History* 2: 3 (winter 1991): 39–57.

Silverman, Kaja. "Fragments of a Fashionable Discourse." In *Studies in Entertainment: Critical Approaches to Mass Culture,* edited by Tania Modleski. Bloomington: Indiana University Press, 1986.

Silverstein, Laurence. *The Postzionism Debates: Knowledge and Power in Israeli Culture.* New York: Routledge, 1999.

Smith, Linda Tuhiwai. *Decolonizing Methodologies: Research and Indigenous Peoples.* London: Zed Books, 1999.

Spivak, Gayatri Chakravorty. "Can the Subaltern Speak?" In *Marxism and the Interpretation of Culture*, edited by Cary Nelson and Lawrence Grossberg. Urbana: University of Illinois Press, 1988.

_____. *A Critique of Postcolonial Reason: Toward a History of the Vanishing Present.* Cambridge, Mass.: Harvard University Press, 1999.

_____. "French Feminism Revisited: Ethics and Politics." In *Feminists Theorize the Political*, edited by Judith Butler and Joan Scott. New York: Routledge, 1992.

_____. "Imperialism and Sexual Difference." *Oxford Literary Review* 8: 1–2 (1986): 225–40.

_____. "Introduction," Mahasweta Devi, *Breast Stories*, translated by Gayatri Chakravorty Spivak. Calcutta: Seagull Press, 1998.

_____. *Outside in the Teaching Machine.* New York: Routledge, 1993.

_____. *The Post-Colonial Critic: Interviews, Strategies, Dialogues.* Edited by Sarah Harasym. London: Routledge, 1990.

_____. "Subaltern Studies: Deconstructing Historiography." In *The Spivak Reader: Selected Works of Gayatri Chakravorty Spivak*, edited by Donna Landry and Gerald MacLean. New York: Routledge, 1996.

_____. "Three Women's Texts and a Critique of Imperialism." In *"Race," Writing, and Difference*, edited by Henry Louis Gates, Jr. Chicago: University of Chicago Press, 1986.

Stannard, David E. *American Holocaust: The Conquest of the New World.* New York: Oxford University Press, 1992.

Stoler, Ann Laura. *Race and the Education of Desire: Foucault's History of Sexuality and the Colonial Order of Things.* Durham, N.C.: Duke University Press, 1995.

Strong, John A. "Algonquian Women as Sunksquaws and Caretakers of the Soil: The Documentary Evidence in the Seventeenth Century Records." In *Native American Women in Literature and Culture*, edited by Susan Castillo and Victor M. P. Da Rosa. Porto, Portugal: Fernando Pessoa University Press, 1997.

Sugirtharajah, R. S. *Asian Biblical Hermeneutics and Postcolonialism: Contesting the Interpretations.* Maryknoll, N.Y.: Orbis Books, 1998.

_____, ed. *The Postcolonial Bible.* Sheffield, U.K.: Sheffield Academic Press, 1998.

Suleri, Sara. *Meatless Days.* Chicago: University of Chicago Press, 1989.

Thomas, Nicholas. *Colonialism's Culture: Anthropology, Travel, and Government.* Princeton, N.J.: Princeton University Press, 1994.

Tiffin, Helen. "Introduction." In *Past the Last Post: Theorizing Post-Colonialism and Post-Modernism*, edited by Ian Adam and Helen Tiffin. Calgary: University of Calgary Press, 1990.

Timberlake, Lieutenant Henry. *Memoirs: 1756-1765.* Edited by Samuel Cole Williams. Marietta, Ga.: Continental Book Company, 1948.

Triki, Fathi. *La Strategie de l'identite. Essai.* Paris: Arcanteres, 1998.

Trinh, Minh-ha T. *Woman—Native—Other: Writing Postcoloniality and Feminism.* Bloomington: Indiana University Press, 1989.

Viswanathan, Gauri. *Outside the Fold: Conversion, Modernity, and Belief.* Princeton, N.J.: Princeton University Press, 1998.

Vizenor, Gerald Robert. *Manifest Manners: Postindian Warriors of Survivance.* Hanover, N.H.: University Press of New England, 1994.

Wach, Joachim. *The Comparative Study of Religions.* New York: Columbia University Press, 1958.

Waldseemüller, Martin. *The Cosmographia Introductio in Facsimile*, United States Catholic Historical Society, Vol. 4. Edited by Charles George Herbermann, translated by Joseph Fischer and Franz Von Wieser. New York: United States Catholic Historical Society, 1907.

Walker, Alice. *In Search of Our Mothers' Gardens, Womanist Prose by Alice Walker.* New York: Harcourt Brace Jovanovich, 1983.

Warrior, Robert Allen. "A Native American Perspective: Canaanites, Cowboys, and Indians." In *Voices from the Margin: Interpreting the Bible in the Third World,* edited by R. S. Sugirtharajah. Maryknoll, N.Y.: Orbis Books, 1991.

Wehr, Demaris S. *Jung and Feminism: Liberating Archetypes.* Boston: Beacon Press, 1987.

Wezler, Albrecht. "Towards a Reconstruction of Indian Cultural History: Observations and Reflections on 18th and 19th Century Indology." *Studien zur Indologie and Iranistik* 18 (1993): 305–29.

White, Deborah Gray. *Ar'n't I a Woman? Female Slaves in the Plantation South.* New York: W. W. Norton, 1985.

Williams, Delores S. *Sisters in the Wilderness: The Challenge of Womanist God-Talk.* Maryknoll, N.Y.: Orbis Books, 1993.

Williams, Patrick, and Laura Chrisman, eds. *Colonial Discourse and Postcolonial Theory: A Reader.* New York: Columbia University Press, 1994.

Williams, Sherley Anne. "Introduction," Zora Neale Hurston, *Their Eyes Were Watching God.* Urbana: University of Illinois Press, 1991.

Wilson, Bryan R. *Magic and the Millennium: A Sociological Study of the Religious Movements of Protest among Tribal and Third World Peoples.* New York: Harper and Row, 1973.

Woodsmall, Ruth Francis. *Women in the Changing Islamic System.* Delhi: Bimla Publishing House, 1983; 1st ed. 1936.

Yeğenoğlu, Meyda. *Colonial Fantasies: Towards a Feminist Reading of Orientalism.* Cambridge: Cambridge University Press, 1998.

Young, Iris Marion. *Justice and the Politics of Difference*. Princeton, N.J.: Princeton University Press, 1990.

Young, Katherine K. "Having Your Cake and Eating It Too." *Journal of the American Academy of Religion* 67 (1999): 167–84.

Zayn al-Din, Nazira. *Al-fatat waal-shuyukh* (The Girl and the Shaykhs). Dasmacus: Dar al-Mada, 1998.

———. *Al-sufur wal-hijab* (Unveiling and Veiling). Damascus: Dar al-Mada, 1998.

Zweig, Stefan. *Amerigo: A Comedy of Errors in History*. Translated by Andrew St. James. New York: Viking Press, 1942.

Contributors

Miriam Cooke is professor of Arabic studies at Duke University. Her research has focused on the intersection of war and gender in the post-colonial Arab world and is now turning to an examination of the role of religion in Arab feminist discourse. Her publications include *War's Other Voices: Women Writers on the Lebanese Civil War, Women and the War Story,* and *Women Claim Islam: Creating Islamic Feminism through Literature.* She has coedited several anthologies of Arab feminist writings.

M. Shawn Copeland is associate professor of systematic theology at Marquette University, and adjunct associate professor of systematic theology at the Institute for Black Catholic Studies, Xavier University of Louisiana, in New Orleans. Professor Copeland is the author of more than sixty articles, reviews, and commentaries in professional journals and books on such topics as suffering, identity, and difference; and the common human good, social analysis, and freedom.

Laura E. Donaldson is of Scotch-Irish and Cherokee descent, and an associate professor of English at Cornell Unversity. She teaches American Indian literatures with a particular focus on American Indian women's writing as well as postcolonial literatures. Her published works include *Decolonizing Feminisms: Race, Gender, and Empire-Building.* She edited a special issue of *Semeia: A Journal of Experimental Biblical Criti-*

cism titled "Postcolonialism and Scriptural Reading" and has published many articles in journals such as *Diacritics, American Indian Quarterly, Signs,* and *Cultural Critique.* Her most recent work focuses on developing the contact zone as a paradigm of Native reading and writing.

Musa W. Dube is a senior lecturer of New Testament in the department of theology and religious studies at the University of Botswana. She has contributed several essays in *Semia* and the *Journal for the Study of the New Testament.* She is the author of *Postcolonial Feminist Interpretation of the Bible* and coedited the *Semeia* volume "Reading With African Overtures."

Kwok Pui-lan is William F. Cole Professor of Christian Theology and Spirituality at Episcopal Divinity School, Cambridge, Massachusetts. She has published extensively in Asian feminist theology, biblical hermeneutics, and postcolonial criticism. Her recent books include *Discovering the Bible in the Non-Biblical World* and *Introducing Asian Feminist Theology.* She is coeditor of the *Journal of Feminist Studies in Religion* and is working on postcolonial interpretations of Christology.

Laura Levitt is director of Jewish studies at Temple University, where she teaches in the religion department and the women's studies program. She is the author of *Jews and Feminism: The Ambivalent Search for Home* and with Miriam Peskowitz coedited *Judaism Since Gender.* She is currently working on a book about American Jews and family photography.

Laurie L. Patton's interests are in interpretation of early Indian ritual and narrative, twentieth-century Vedic interpretation, comparative mythology, and literary theory in the study of religion. She is the chair of the department of religion at Emory University and author of *Myth as Argument: The Brhaddevata as Canonical Commentary.* She has edited *Authority, Anxiety, and Canon: Essays in Vedic Interpretation* and *Jewels of Authority: Women and Textual Tradition in Hindu India* and coedited *Myth and Method.* She is completing a second book on the use of poetry in Vedic ritual and coediting another volume on the debates about Indo-Aryan origins.

Meyda Yeğenoğlu is associate professor in the department of sociology at the Middle East Technical University, Ankara. She has also taught in North America and published in Turkish and English on Orientalism, and cultural and women's studies. She is the author of *Colonial Fantasies: Towards a Feminist Reading of Orientalism* and coeditor of "Orientalism and Cultural Differences," a special issue of the journal *Inscriptions.* She is currently completing a book on globalization and migrancy.

Index